Upriver

Upriver

The Turbulent Life and Times
of an Amazonian People

Michael F. Brown

Harvard University Press

Cambridge, Massachusetts & London, England

2014

Library of Congress Cataloging-in-Publication Data
Brown, Michael F. (Michael Fobes), 1950–
Upriver : the turbulent life and times of an Amazonian people /
Michael F. Brown.
pages cm
Includes bibliographical references and index.
ISBN 978-0-674-36807-1 (alk. paper)
1. Indians of South America—Peru—Amazonas—Social
conditions.   2. Indians of South America—Peru—Amazonas—
Social life and customs.   3. Indians of South America—Peru—
Amazonas—Folklore.   4. Amazonas (Peru)—Social conditions.
5. Amazonas (Peru)—Social life and customs.   I. Title.
F3429.1.A3B76 2014
306.0985'46—dc23   2014004981

Contents

A Note to Readers

Spelling of words in the Awajún (Aguaruna) language follows the orthography developed by missionary linguists from SIL International and now used by thousands of literate Awajún. In general, pronunciation is consistent with Spanish. The letter *j*, for example, is pronounced like the English *h*; Awajún, therefore, is pronounced like "Awahoon." The letter *e*, however, represents a midcentral vowel closer to the *u* in the English "put" than to the Spanish *e*; the Awajún *g* approximates the *ng* of the English "ring." For the convenience of readers, I have included stress accents in most Awajún personal names even though the Awajún use them only when required by Spanish writing conventions. Unless otherwise noted, all translations of Awajún and Spanish texts are mine.

Most Peruvians follow the Iberian practice of using both their father's and mother's surnames in formal settings. To avoid confusing English-speaking readers, I normally use only the first (patrilineal) surname in the main text.

Following standard practice in anthropology, a handful of personal names have been changed to protect individuals whose stories might cause embarrassment or expose them to harm.

Upriver

Introduction

On a bitterly cold winter day in 1995, I received a telephone call from a stranger. Her name was Sandra Miller, she said, and she was calling from New Hampshire. She told me that her twenty-six-year-old son, Patchen Miller, had recently been murdered by men who were almost certainly Aguaruna, a people native to the mountainous rainforest region just east of the Andes in northern Peru. She had found my name in the card catalog of her local college library, whose holdings included a book about the Aguaruna that I had written a decade earlier. She hoped that I could help her make sense of the killing. As a practicing Quaker, she insisted, she bore no grudge against the Aguaruna. She simply wanted to understand who they were and why some of them had killed her son.

I knew nothing of the circumstances of the murder other than what Sandra Miller told me. News reports of the attack were only beginning to circulate, and the information they conveyed was sketchy. I fear that I offered little that could have set her mind to rest. Under the circumstances, perhaps no one could.

Later I was able to speak to Patchen Miller's traveling companion, Josh Silver, who had been brought up in a town close to my home in western Massachusetts. Josh explained that he and Patchen, inspired by books about adventure travel in Peru, had decided to raft down the Río Marañón to Iquitos, Peru's major Amazon port city. On the third night of the river journey, they tied up at an island not far from an Aguaruna village. A young man rowed out to the raft and spent time chatting with them in Spanish. Later they were visited briefly by two men who were less friendly. At about nine-thirty that night, they heard a noise in the forest near the raft. Patchen went to investigate and was hit by a blast from a shotgun. The force of the buckshot spun him into the Marañón. Josh was wounded in the leg by a second blast but managed to swim away and hide in dense vegetation on the riverbank. After a night of moving cautiously toward what he hoped would be safety, Josh was rescued by a boatman, also Aguaruna. This man led him to a military post, from which he was rushed to a regional hospital. Josh eventually recovered; Patchen's body was never found.

The motive for the crime and the identity of the perpetrators have not been revealed, although it is likely that the Aguaruna themselves know the killers' identities. Their goal may have been robbery. It might have had something to do with the border war brewing immediately to the north, along the contested frontier with Ecuador. Deeper conspiracies may have been in play, involving indigenous leaders determined to demonstrate their control over outsiders' access to their communities. The two unlucky travelers were pawns in a larger game—or so some Aguaruna intimate today. In the end, all one could say was that an appealing, idealistic young American, someone who hoped to devote his life to progressive causes, fell victim to members of the kind of society he was determined to defend.[1]

This was not just any indigenous society. It was the Aguaruna, who today prefer to be called Awajún, their own self-designation. In what the historian John Hemming calls the Amazon's "tree of rivers," the Awajún can be counted among those who occupy the highest branches, where the heat and moisture of the rainforest collide with the eastern slopes of the Andes. They are upriver people. The trails in their country are steep and mud-slick, the rivers pitiless and mercurial. It is hardly surprising that this place gave rise to men and women renowned for their physical sturdiness, self-confidence, and pugnacity. These qualities have served them well, and their rapidly growing population now exceeds 50,000. Because of their numbers and their reputation for combativeness, the Awajún have come to represent tribal Amazonia for many Peruvians: proud, uncompromising exemplars of life on civilization's unruly edge.[2]

As long as there have been hierarchical societies governed by powerful leaders and formal institutions, thinkers have commented on the life of those living just beyond civilization's reach. Their view of such people has been an unstable mix of disdain and envy. The uncivilized are said to live in a state of near anarchy, with too few chiefs and laws, too many gods and wives. Alternatively, they are seen as virtuous innocents unburdened by the tyranny of property or a ruling elite. In Western social thought, Thomas Hobbes and Jean-Jacques Rousseau hold squatters' rights on the extremes of this spectrum. Countless other thinkers have pondered the contrast between the civilized and the not, either directly or by implication: Montaigne, Spencer, Durkheim, Marx, Weber, Simmel, Boas, Benedict, Lévi-Strauss—the list is long and distinguished. There is no more foundational question in the social sciences.

There may be no more tiresome one, either. A case in point is the endless fussing over what we should call civilization's counterpoint. Today "primitive" is allowed on the catwalk only when dressed in scare quotes. "Preindustrial" or "preliterate" define societies in terms of qualities that they lack or haven't yet acquired. "Simple societies" gets us partway there, but anthropologists are quick to complain that many attributes of such societies are far from simple. Jared Diamond has settled on "traditional societies," an expression so vague that its chief virtue is inoffensiveness.[3]

The most serviceable label for an age hypersensitive to linguistic slight is "tribal," which at least denotes a particular scale and set of social arrangements. Its clarity is blurred by the notion of "tribe," a term that has fallen from favor because of its imprecision. But if we specify that tribal societies are primarily defined by small-scale, family-based relationships and shallow social hierarchies, then the word does useful work.

The philosophical contest between civilizations and tribal societies persists because it serves many ends. Critics of civilization use the intimacy of tribal life as a foil for civilization's grasping ambition, its suffocating hierarchies, and its hivelike specialization. Civilization's boosters, in contrast, portray tribal societies as fated to drift aimlessly while the rest of humanity moves toward mastery of the natural world and more refined ways of organizing social life.

These debates show few signs of slackening. Tribal peoples continue to be put forward as role models of "living lightly on the land" and practitioners of a spirituality that stands allied with nature rather than being committed to its domination. Environmental activists routinely deploy images of the Kayapó, the San, the Cree, and other indigenous peoples as icons of sustainability. This provokes would-be debunkers to claim that these same peoples are guilty of overhunting and other environmental sins.

One version of this contest uses the alleged shortcoming of tribal societies as a platform for attacks on relativism and multiculturalism. The Australian anthropologist Roger Sandall alleges that "culture cultists"—his unflattering term for defenders of tribal lifeways—"forget that modern civilization . . . allows changes of government without bloodshed, civil rights, economic benefits, religious toleration, and political and artistic freedom."[4] A more nuanced assessment is offered by Robin Fox, whose book *The Tribal Imagination* considers the persistence of tribal values and modes of thought in the modern world. For Fox, this is because tribal structures are the "default system of human nature." He is coy about whether he believes this default system to be encoded in our genes or perpetuated by more indirect means. Perhaps it is enough to say that a pattern of social life that has served our species through more than 90 percent of its history is not easily supplanted by the demands of civilization.[5]

Fox recognizes that the tribal and the civilized are as much ideal types as locatable societies. Key elements of the tribal include an inclination to treat existing practices and social arrangements as divinely ordained and to value loyalty to kin over the whisper of individual conscience. Civilizations—or, at any rate, modern civilizations—have moved from *Gemeinschaft* to *Gesellschaft*, from kinship to more utilitarian forms of association. They tend to foster habits of mind that question existing practices in the interest of achieving greater understanding or technical virtuosity. The founding thinkers of modernity, according to the sociologist Anthony Giddens, were convinced that "the claims of reason were due to overcome the dogmas of tradition." Yet these are no more than tendencies or predilections. No tribal society is completely closed in its outlook, nor are civilizations always intellectually open and self-critical. The psychological burdens of civilization prove intolerable to many. Hence the lure of more primal forms of solidarity, especially in difficult times. We don't have to look far to find members of complex industrial societies who are willing to abandon principles of universal citizenship in favor of identities based on shared tradition, imagined racial similarity, or a common language. They are equally inclined to spurn the findings of science in favor of more comforting doctrines based on received truth.[6]

Fascination with tribal societies persists not just because their lifeways lend themselves to tendentious arguments or gratify someone's sense of cultural superiority. Contrast and comparison are fundamental to human understanding. Social norms are notoriously inclined to naturalize themselves. We become aware of the arbitrariness of deep-seated practices and beliefs only when forced to confront other societies whose customs differ from our own. Any exploration of other social worlds, whether informal or systematic, relies on this simple truth.

Late in 1976 I began a journey into the tribal world that lasted roughly two years, encompassing a single twenty-one-month period of research followed by several shorter visits in the 1980s. It was a conventional apprenticeship in cultural anthropology: immersion in an alien society with the goal of collecting enough information to complete a degree. By the standards of the time, my stay in the field was about average and my location only of middling remoteness. The circumstances might appear precarious from the perspective of an era marked by frictionless communication, yet I don't recall feeling that way most of the time. Months passed without access to a telephone. Mail, of the old-fashioned, handwritten variety, was slow and unreliable. Personal computers and the Internet existed only in the minds of technovisionaries. Left to my own devices, I improvised.

The Awajún were the focus of my attention. For reasons to be explained shortly, I knew almost nothing about them when I was allowed to settle in one of their villages in the valley of the Alto Río Mayo in Peru's Department of San Martín. Landing there was a lucky break. Because the Alto Mayo was distant from Peru's contested border with Ecuador, the region lacked the military posts that often sparked conflicts between indigenous and nonindigenous Peruvians. Villagers in the Alto Mayo had received few visits from missionaries, prospectors, or scientists, and they expressed no overt hostility toward me. If anything, they were curious about foreigners, whose role in the changes taking place around them they were eager to comprehend.

Awajún life was poorly documented then. The main reasons for this were their legendary belligerence and, for much of the modern era, the highly dispersed nature of their settlements. These consisted of large households located in isolated, defensible places, sometimes fortified by log palisades. A visitor lived entirely at the sufferance of his host, hardly an ideal situation for someone committed to spending the months or years required to learn a difficult language. The indefatigable Finnish anthropologist Rafael Karsten, who visited several Awajún households on the Río Apaga in 1929, was able to stay with them only a few days because his frightened boatmen convinced him that they would bolt if he did not return to safer territory immediately.[7]

Beginning in the 1950s, these loosely organized neighborhoods began to coalesce into more compact villages. Many had elementary schools whose bilingual curriculum was the fruit of decades of work by American missionary-linguists and the indigenous teachers they trained. Christianity, especially its evangelical Protestant strain, had become familiar to most Awajún and embraced fervently by some. New highways and the quickening pace of jungle colonization forced the Awajún to defend their lands and the forests essential to their way of life. Yet aside from having added certain manufactured goods—trade cloth, steel tools, firearms and ammunition—to their material culture, they still maintained a largely independent economy based on farming, hunting, and the collection of wild forest foods well into the 1980s. In common with all tribal societies that survived into the latter half of the twentieth century, the Awajún had been drawn into the orbit of a nation-state and were struggling to accommodate themselves to it or, when necessary, learning how to resist its meddling.

It is to these irascible, independent-minded, energetic people that I attached myself in late 1976. When my first long stint of fieldwork concluded in October 1978, I returned to my university, completed my doctoral degree, and joined the faculty of a liberal arts college in New England. I continued to make summer research trips to the Alto Mayo in the 1980s. During two brief sojourns I served as consultant to a World Bank–funded development project that helped to transform the Alto Mayo into a major agricultural production zone, a process that by the 1990s had allowed some Awajún to achieve levels of prosperity rarely seen among indigenous South Americans. My advisory role consisted largely of ensuring that Peru complied with policies designed to protect Awajún land rights and access to project services.

Development work nudged me into the fractious arena of Awajún politics. As a short-term consultant, I had little direct influence on policy decisions. But to the Awajún I had become a player, which meant that I instantly acquired critics. The ensuing squabbles were neither surprising nor consequential. They did, however, dull the sense of wonder that animated so much of my early experience. By the late 1980s, a decade after my first visit to the Alto Mayo, I felt depleted of fresh insights into Awajún life. Meanwhile, Peru's intensifying political violence made further visits unacceptably risky for me and anyone who might offer me shelter. By the time the guerrilla wars of the Shining Path and the Tupac Amaru Revolutionary Movement had dwindled to insignificance, the thread of my Awajún research had been broken.

The Awajún were never far from my mind, however. Another anthropologist, Shane Greene, began fieldwork in the Alto Mayo in 1998, and he occasionally passed along news of happenings there. During a trip to Lima in 2002, I met several Awajún university students at a public event. Their infectious energy and commitment to an indigenous identity were inspiring. I also interviewed a feisty Awajún leader whose organization was then embroiled in a high-profile conflict over the search by American scientists for new drugs based on indigenous medicines.[8]

Several years later, while digitizing photographs and handwritten field notes, I was forced to reacquaint myself with events that had taken place during my first sustained period of residence with the Awajún. This was not the gauzy exercise in middle-age nostalgia that it might seem. I was disappointed by the callowness of some of my observations about people whose depth of experience exceeded my own. Having by then endured a share of life's vicissitudes—serious illness, the joys and anxieties of family life, and the pain of losing loved ones to disease or misadventure—I could understand more viscerally what it meant to live one misstep away from hunger, crippling injury, or death.

More important, I found myself drawn in by stories of generosity, cruelty, resourcefulness, and intercultural misunderstanding about which I had never written. I had long regarded these observations as outtakes from research focused on what social scientists rather grandly call cognition: how the Awajún organized their thinking about everyday activities such as gardening and hunting, as well as their efforts to influence the world through the application of practical knowledge and magic. It was Awajún life as seen from an altitude of 30,000 feet. Looking at the same notes decades later and with fresh eyes, I found a story closer to the ground and more fundamentally human. My conversation with Patchen Miller's grieving mother led me to the recovery of an Awajún pentimento, images and patterns lying beneath the surface of ones with which I had lived for decades.

My curiosity about the Awajún aroused anew, I visited several Alto Mayo communities in 2012 to take stock of their current situation. I also interviewed university-educated Awajún and prominent Awajún political figures to gain a sense of their aspirations in a period when Peru grapples with the growing militancy of indigenous citizens, who find themselves excluded from the fruits of their country's booming economy.

What emerged from this return to earlier interests—a kind of homecoming, although, like many homecomings, an unsettling one—was a vision of how one tribal population struggled to order social life in the absence of formal institutions, including secure leadership and well-defined customary law. Equally important were the efforts of a formerly sovereign people to respond to the new realities of the nation-state, including its relentless promotion of a market economy and its vision of indigenous citizens as childlike primitives fated to join the lowest ranks of the rural working class. The Awajún remain convinced that their destiny is separate, that their pride, ambition, and assertiveness set them apart from others. The evidence suggests that their optimism may be warranted, in part because they have proven adept at seizing powerful elements of civilization—literacy, formal education, and a questioning attitude, among others—and using them to advance their own interests.

I revisit the Awajún with several goals in mind. The first is to offer an accessible account of Amazonian life that shuns both Hobbesian and Rousseauian stereotypes. This is harder than it sounds. Accounts that present tribal peoples as saintly victims invite accusations that the author is peddling advocacy clothed in the trappings of academic rigor. Given the precarious circumstances of most indigenous groups, however, some anthropologists judge it unethical to report disturbing practices that might give governments a pretext for denying indigenous peoples their civil and political rights (as if governments needed such a pretext).

These conflicting currents converged in a widely publicized dispute about the research of Napoleon Chagnon, an anthropologist who for four decades studied the Yanomami, a people whose territory straddles the border between Venezuela and Brazil. In the late 1970s Chagnon became one of the best-known anthropologists in America thanks to an ethnography whose first edition was entitled *Yanomamö: The Fierce People*. Chagnon's book, along with a series of related documentary films, made the Yanomami famous. They became known especially for their spectacular club fights, one step in a graduated series of aggressive displays that occasionally included homicidal raids on other villages.

By the 1980s, some anthropologists had begun to question the ethics of Chagnon's research methods and his representation of Yanomami culture. These complaints, mostly limited to professional circles, became a matter of broad public discussion in 2000 after the publication of a journalist's account that accused Chagnon of exaggerating Yanomami violence to advance a theory that linked interpersonal aggression to reproductive success. More disturbing still was the claim that Chagnon and a distinguished geneticist, James V. Neel, knowingly vaccinated hundreds of Yanomami with an early version of the measles vaccine that might have induced transmissible cases of the disease, thereby exacerbating an epidemic that produced many fatalities. Upon investigation, the latter allegation proved completely false. Lesser complaints—for instance, that Chagnon had failed to meet prevailing standards of informed consent when collecting Yanomami blood samples—remain credible to some anthropologists. Others disagree. A particularly thorny question is whether Chagnon's books and films somehow injured the Yanomami by presenting them as a violent people. Should he have emphasized this aspect of their society to the extent that he did, especially when advocates for indigenous peoples were mobilizing support to defend the Yanomami from invading gold miners and other threats to their survival? Evidence of direct harm is thin, but the critical firestorm rages on. Chagnon's fame and his embrace of sociobiology, a form of Darwinian thought that many anthropologists regard as scientifically unsound, make him an especially attractive target for critics.[9]

Chagnon is not the only anthropologist who has written about raiding and other disturbing practices in Amazonia. Scholars have documented the execution of accused child sorcerers among the Asháninka of eastern Peru, high levels of violence among the Waorani of Ecuador, narratives of homicidal big men among the Ecuadorian Shuar, and ritual consumption of dead relatives among the Wari' of Brazil. To my knowledge, none has evoked significant criticism. This is due to the delicateness of touch that they bring to their controversial subject matter and their efforts to contextualize such practices within a larger social whole.[10]

Circumstances sometimes require that an anthropologist remain silent about things witnessed in the field. Members of a study population may feel strongly that certain religious understandings are nobody's business but their own. They might voice risky political opinions. They may have been promised anonymity in exchange for sensitive personal information. Ethical protocols require that fieldworkers consider the possible impact of their books and articles on the people about whom they write. Against this must be weighed the ethical implications of distorting the truth, even when this is effected through strategic silence. In this book events are described as I witnessed them out of a conviction that presenting the Awajún as complex people, with admirable qualities and troubling ones as well, is the best way to honor their robust self-confidence.

Although the Awajún offer a window on the dynamics of tribal life, they cannot be considered typical. Many Amazonian peoples display far less aggression in their attitudes toward outsiders and one another. They have worked out clever ways to settle conflicts peacefully and strike a balance between individual ambition and group unity. Why some societies are more prone to violence than others is a question that continues to puzzle social scientists. The public, and even some scholars, love simple answers to this riddle: "Their warlike tendencies were a response to colonialism." "They fought to gain access to sources of protein, which are scarce in the tropics." "Sorcery killings were a product of social suffering brought about by dispossession and environmental destruction." "Raiding expressed a Darwinian imperative: killers had higher status and more wives, which increased their reproductive success." Anyone seeking monocausal explanations for the Awajún's pugnacity will not find them in this book. The ultimate causes of violence interest me less than do its effects: how the Awajún manage aggression—sometimes successfully, sometimes not—and how they are now reshaping their martial tradition to counter the multiple threats that confront them. It is these distinctive expressions of ambition and assertiveness that set the Awajún apart from other peoples in the region.

Upriver is also a reflection on craft. We typically think of craftsmanship as the expression of skill in some practical domain rather than a quality found in the work of the mind. Yet ethnography involves craftsmanship precisely because it demands what the sociologist Richard Sennett refers to as an "intimate connection between hand and head." Ethnographers have no choice but to use their bodies as well as their minds as they document the lives of others. Socially isolated, often far from home, voluntarily thrusting themselves into awkward circumstances at the boundaries of their competence, ethnographers have embraced a demanding vocation that depends on systematic observation in search of rational explanations for human behavior. By focusing on craft, I call attention to the standards of thoroughness and impartiality to which I and other ethnographers aspire and the challenge of meeting those standards in a recalcitrant world.[11]

To give the reader a better sense of the process of ethnographic discovery, Part One of this book emphasizes the ambiguity and confusion of my initial experiences as well as the gradual, cumulative understanding that emerged after months living with my Awajún hosts. This what-I-knew-when-I-knew-it framework shifts in Part Two to a more comparative and analytical one that brings the Awajún's trajectory up to the present day.

There are aspects of another people's collective experience that require a lifetime to understand fully. Most young scholars are reluctant to speak frankly about the limits of their knowledge. They want their competence to be noted and ratified by others. I was one of those young scholars once. I wrote about what I understood and for the most part avoided discussion of everything else. The first crack in that wall came when confronting the Awajún predilection for suicide, a shockingly common feature of their everyday life that has now been documented independently by others. My training and temperament did not equip me to comprehend it. I avoided the subject for years even though its significance was inescapable. When I finally tried to make sense of it, the results met accepted standards of professional rigor but remained unconvincing to me on an emotional level. The same can be said about intense fear of sorcery, a primal anxiety that motivates violent thoughts and acts in Awajún society to this day.

With the passing years I have come to appreciate what Bill Vitek, a philosopher, and Wes Jackson, a prominent advocate of sustainable agriculture, call the "virtues of ignorance." Vitek and Jackson focus attention on what we don't know about the complexities of the environment on which we all depend for survival. They want scientists to "operate as though the twentieth century will be the last century in which we believe that knowledge is adequate to run the world." Ultimately, they call for humility rather than arrogance. In much the same way, the untroubled self-confidence of the anthropologists of the early twentieth century seems increasingly tone-deaf from the perspective of those of us who work in the twenty-first. For anthropologists to admit that many of our hard-won insights are provisional and incomplete is not to reject empirical methods or surrender to personal idiosyncrasy. It is only to acknowledge that we are engaged in a difficult enterprise that will always leave room for differing outlooks and vexing uncertainties. Voltaire put it best: "Doubt is not a very agreeable status, but certainty is a ridiculous one."[12]

Upriver offers a portrait of a resourceful people fighting to sustain their place in a world largely indifferent to their fate. It also conveys affection for an intellectual tradition, arising from the ferment of the Enlightenment, that asks practitioners to see past their own habits of mind in search of the internal logics of other societies. Like all ambitions, even the most noble, this quest is vulnerable to smugness, self-delusion, and error. Despite imperfections, it remains an indispensable tool for understanding human life on a fractious planet.

PART ONE

1976–1978

Anthropology—a professional commitment
to understanding different others—is always
a reckless enterprise; and exposing how it is
actually done, more reckless still.

—Inga Clendinnen,
"The Power to Frustrate
Good Intentions"

1

Andean Prelude

Morning fog blanketed the trail rising out of Molinopampa, a village on the eastern flanks of the Andes in northern Peru. Both sides of the rutted path were lined with cloud forest vegetation: towering ferns and gnarled, moss-covered trees from which bromeliads swayed like silvery apparitions. In the distance, it was possible to make out rolling bogs stippled with low hummocks of grass. Molinopampa's plank-sided houses gradually faded into the mist below.

I toiled up the track at the rear of a packtrain led by two Andean women, Sonia and Carmen, plus a boy brought along as their helper. They had reluctantly allowed me to accompany them to a remote village called Quinjalca, to which they were returning after working in Lima for several years. Sonia and Carmen knew the trail; I didn't.

Just after dawn I'd been introduced to them by the owner of the shabby *pensión* where I had passed the night. "The *ingeniero* wants to find people who still speak Quechua," he explained. Sonia and Carmen were loading two horses and a mule with

focused attention. They carefully divided the cargo into portions of similar weight for balance, then lashed it to pack frames
with plaited wool cords. They were wary. The unspoken issue
was fear of *pishtacos,* ghoulish hunters of human body fat. Andean people believed that pishtacos resembled tall, fair-haired,
bearded, blue-eyed *gringos,* a decent match for me. High-country
trails were a pishtaco's hunting ground. In the end, local rules of
courtesy to fellow travelers prevailed, and I was allowed to fall
into step behind them as they left the village.

The ascent was hot work. When we stopped to rest, Sonia
and Carmen kindly shared provisions, but their reticence remained firmly in place. A raw wind cooled us, then drove us back
into motion. Another hour of climbing brought us to a plain,
called a *puna* in these parts. The trail wove between marshy
areas of reeds and bunchgrasses where cattle browsed and
wallowed. Mud sucked at our feet and slowed the horses. They
became balky and threw their loads, which had to be retied.
After another short rise, the trail dropped into a narrow valley.
Clinging to the nearest of its steep sides was Quinjalca, a scatter
of crumbling adobe houses roofed with barrel tiles. Not long
after midday my companions left me in front of the police post
on the patch of bog that served as the village plaza.

In those days foreign travelers were obliged to register with
Peru's paramilitary police force, the Guardia Civíl, when staying overnight in the towns and villages of the interior. The GC
office in Quinjalca had the look of a punishment post, and so it
proved to be. The mournful sergeant and his two men each eventually admitted to some blunder or lapse of discipline elsewhere
that had gotten him assigned to this remote village, so far from
running water, electric lights, or an unattached woman who might
be receptive to male attention. The sergeant offered me a place
to bunk down for the night, which solved the problem of how
he would keep an eye on a mysterious visitor.

A gaggle of village boys, all dressed in identical brown home-spun ponchos, pointed me to the village school. The teachers insisted that Quechua-speakers had mostly died off and that tra-ditional Andean customs were in decline. Families were aban-doning played-out fields for dreams of prosperity in the rainforest frontier to the east. They said that Olleros, a still more remote village across the valley, was the place to find old-timers who spoke Quechua. Having been told some version of this story every day for the past two weeks, I was doubtful.

That night I buried myself under thick blankets provided by my hosts. The sergeant slept elsewhere, and I shared quar-ters with his two men, like me bachelors in their twenties. We swapped stories to pass the time. In Quinjalca, the biggest crime problem was cattle rustling. Several months before, a local farmer had found a deserted hut well stocked with food—a rus-tler's hideout. One of the cops spent a miserable night there, shivering in his poncho, service revolver in hand, without fire or lantern. No rustler appeared. The next night it was his partner's turn. A suspect eventually arrived but managed to flee into the dark after being hailed. The storyteller laughed bitterly about this wasted sleuthing, then sought my advice about the best medicine for curbing a man's sex drive.

Breakfast was taken in the house of a woman who cooked for visiting state employees. By midmorning I was descending from Quinjalca to the Río Imaza, which farther north becomes a for-midable river that empties into the Alto Marañón and then the Amazon. The recent rains had given the river enough power to make fording it impossible on foot, forcing a half-hour detour to the valley's only bridge. Ascending the valley's other side, I reached Olleros at noon. After the near silence of Quinjalca, it was startling to hear conversation and laughter. The commo-tion came from the house of the village mayor, who was serving lunch to a group of eight or nine adults. After listening to my story, he invited me to eat. Lunch consisted of roasted guinea pig, astringent tubers called *oca,* boiled large-kernel corn called *mote,* and cooked cabbage.

While the dishes were cleared, the mayor excused himself to attend to business. A table was brought outside. Someone produced a battered typewriter. A young man, the mayor's nephew, laboriously typed a bill of sale for land that the mayor's wife was purchasing from her widowed sister. The widow was moving to her son's new farm in the Alto Río Mayo, jungle land that he had recently cleared. After spirited discussion about landmarks for the property's boundaries—paths, stone walls, rows of trees, prominent boulders—the document was complete. Buyer and seller, both illiterate, sealed the transfer with fingerprints. Then someone yanked the stopper from a liter of *aguardiente,* a liquor made from sugar cane.

Drinking aguardiente in prodigious quantities was an essential element of Andean ceremonies then. It may still be, although the spread of evangelical Christianity in Peru has thrown the tradition's future into doubt. The adulterated aguardiente consumed in places such as Olleros was only a step removed from paint thinner and had a less appealing bouquet. Its effect on a drinker's judgment was rarely salutary.

As the shot glass was passed around, I asked whether people in the village still spoke Quechua. "Hardly anyone," the mayor said. "Just a few old people. The younger ones are moving east to the jungle."

The party took a maudlin turn. The two sisters began to weep, the sadness of their imminent separation sharpened by the alcohol. Dark clouds piled up at one end of the valley and spilled toward us. Soon it was pouring. A return to Quinjalca that day began to look doubtful, as did my ability to stand upright. Not to worry, the mayor said, there would be somewhere for me to sleep. The mayor's nephew, a man named Leonidas,

The mayor of Olleros (second from left) oversees preparation of a deed transfer, 1976. The aguardiente had not yet begun to flow.
Photograph courtesy of Michael F. Brown.

suggested that I visit him in Atumplaya, his new home on the Amazon frontier. "There are lots of real Indians, Aguarunas, who live nearby," he said. "You'll find all the natives you want near my farm."

The mood soured as the rain hammered down. The mayor became inquisitive, then belligerent. He demanded my identity documents and insisted that the photograph in my passport showed someone else. I was carrying falsified papers, he said. I was a spy, an agent of the CIA. Another nephew, a young man named Roger, pulled me away. "You can stay at my family's house, mister," he said. The mayor's face twitched as he pondered whether to throw a punch, if he could only stop swaying and get his bloodshot eyes to focus. No one but the mayor wanted a brawl. Roger led me away as fog closed in around us.

We stumbled down the hill to his grandmother's kitchen, where a fire cast trembling light on soot-blackened walls. Guinea pigs scrabbled under a couple of benches. Roger's grandmother, an elderly woman covered by countless layers of wool clothing, prepared us soup, roasted maize, and herbal tea. As I ate the piece of dried meat that she gave me, I noticed that the others were doing without. I felt both gratitude for her kindness and shame for being singled out this way.

Roger led me to a storage room with a thatched roof. In the darkness it was possible to make out a bed in the corner, a saddle and tools on the walls. Plaited garlic strands hung from the ceiling. Roger piled the bed high with blankets and said goodnight. Too wired on alcohol to sleep, I stood for an hour outside the storage shed, watching the fog roll past and listening to the soft percussion of rainwater dripping from the thatch. Waking once or twice during the long night, I experienced momentary disorientation because of the room's absolute darkness.

In the morning Roger's grandmother served breakfast. Again I was given meat, as well as a fried egg, while the others spooned down what appeared to be maize gruel. My hosts gossiped about the mayor, who had beaten his wife after our departure. "He does that a lot," Roger explained. The brothers discussed whether to join a communal work party, called a *minga,* that was to begin shortly at the other end of the village. Flute and drum music announced that work was about to commence. They left to join their neighbors. The event would end with the serving of more cane alcohol. I thanked Roger's grandmother and gave her a hundred *soles,* which seemed to please her.

My worn boots proved useless on the return to Quinjalca. I tumbled several times in the greasy mud, cursing. Near the bridge over the Imaza two fierce-looking dogs made for me with teeth bared, but they backed off when I grabbed a handful of stones. In a description of this area dating to the 1890s, the archaeologist Adolph Bandelier reported that these valleys were "perhaps the most broken and accidented country" he had ever seen. "Traveling there is almost an uninterrupted clambering up and down, and the valleys are so narrow that they might more appropriately be called gorges."[1]

By midmorning I was back at the police post in Quinjalca watching another wave of rain sluice off the roof tiles. The next day, after retracing the trail to Molinopampa, I made my way to Chachapoyas, the region's largest town. In 1945 the English botanist Christopher Sandeman said of Chachapoyas that "in spite of a large plaza, a cathedral of minor pretensions, a library, and some ten thousand inhabitants, the place is little more than an overgrown Indian village with open drains running down the middle of the cobbled streets and small, jerry-built adobe houses, vulnerable to even minor earthquakes, which are frequent here." In the rainy season Chachapoyas was as sad as Molinopampa, only on a larger scale.[2]

The fruitless journey to Olleros was an attempt to salvage research that was foundering. I faced the prospect of returning to my university in the American Midwest as one of those wraiths about whom faculty and other graduate students spoke in funereal tones: the promising doctoral student whose project turned to dust.

My original plan, for which a private foundation had awarded me a modest research grant, had been to study the use of medicinal plants by the Lamistas, a native people whose widespread population was centered in the Upper Amazonian town of Lamas. I had come to know Lamas two years earlier while working in the central Andes with a team of archaeologists. We were based in the highest of the high country on the shore of Lake Junín, Peru's second-largest lake. Our sleeping quarters were located at 14,300 feet above sea level. Even for fit young adults, the main challenge of each day was finding enough oxygen to sustain life. Altitude and bad food played havoc with digestion, regularly giving rise to a condition known as the "purple burps," a noxious gastric detonation that made its victims unpopular in the small, windowless rooms where we bunked. The locals were outwardly friendly, but the appearance of graffiti promising "death to agents of the CIA" on the walls outside our lab showed that some harbored more complicated feelings.

During the field season I visited another research team working in Lamas. Like the area around Lake Junín, the terrain was mountainous, but a subtropical climate gave it a completely different feel. The lush vegetation was exhilarating. The locals seemed more relaxed and open than the Andean villagers I had encountered. The tropics worked their spell.

Lamas was a curious place that blended the Andean with the Amazonian. Richard Spruce, the great botanical explorer of the Amazon, spent time there in 1855. He described it as "a town of 6000 inhabitants, near the top of a conical hill, that reminded me of similarly situated towns and villages in Valencia."[3] In the 1970s, as in Spruce's time, the town was ruled by a mestizo elite whose houses surrounded the inevitable plaza and Catholic church, as well as a town hall, schools, and small shops, all pastel-colored and made of adobe or cinder block. Away from the center were discrete neighborhoods—urban villages, really—occupied by Lamistas.

Lamista men were not especially distinctive-looking, although they were more likely than mestizos to be seen walking barefoot and carrying enormous bales of cotton or bags of coffee beans on their backs, their hands braced on cotton tumplines stretched taut by the weight of their burdens. Lamista women were unmistakable, however. All but the youngest girls wore embroidered white or blue cotton blouses and full, pleated

Lamista woman, 1976.
Photograph courtesy of Michael F. Brown.

black skirts from which they hung brightly colored scarves at rakish angles. Necklaces of heavy gold-plated beads, metallic hair clips, and multicolored hair ribbons formed a brilliant ensemble. Religious holidays brought forth even more flamboyant color.

Despite the relative accessibility of Lamas and the size of the Lamista population, then greater than fifteen thousand, little was known about them. They were nominally Catholic, but their social separateness was marked by worship of a patron saint different from that of the town's mestizos. Lamista men enjoyed fame in the region for their tenacity as *cargadores* who could move enormous loads through the cruelest terrain. They were also respected for their knowledge of healing plants and sorcery. In the colonial period, the arrow poison made by Lamistas was so coveted that merchants used it as a form of currency.

Their neighborhoods were said to be organized around extended families that feuded among themselves.[4]

Lamistas spoke a regional dialect of Quechua, a language usually associated with descendants of the Incas. For reasons still not completely understood, some rainforest peoples abandoned Amazonian languages in favor of Quechua, and it is now spoken by indigenous Amazonian groups in Peru, Ecuador, and Colombia. It seemed likely that the Lamistas descended from demoralized rainforest tribes, thinned by European arms and epidemics, who had been gathered together in missionary enclaves to exploit their labor and promote Christianization.[5]

An inescapable feature of the town was mestizo domination of Lamista economic life. Mestizo buyers of Lamista coffee, cotton, and maize routinely paid Indians less than market rates. By extending credit to Lamistas for the purchase of basic goods, *patróns* lured them into a web of debt passed from generation to generation. The predatory nature of the relationship was softened slightly by the custom of asking patróns to serve as godfathers to Lamista children, but this also bound the Lamistas more tightly to a system designed to exploit their labor.

For all that, few patróns appeared wealthy by American standards or even by those of middle-class Lima. Lamas was a poor province, its economy subject to unpredictable fluctuations in the price of cotton and coffee. The handful of patróns with social pretensions—usually requiring the purchase of a house in Lima from which wives and children could enjoy life in the capital—were, after a few drinks, likely to lament the vast sums they owed to merchants and bankers a step above them in the financial food chain.

I occasionally glimpsed how relations between mestizos and Lamistas had been in the past, when Indians had been expected to step off sidewalks to let their betters pass. Merchants continued to defraud illiterate Indians with impunity. They also had a way of talking to foreign visitors about Lamista character when Lamistas themselves were present. Such rudeness brought to mind the declaration of a Franciscan historian, Antonine Tibesar, that for missionaries Peru's rainforest Indians were as simple as children.[6]

This colonial mentality was in decline in the early 1970s. The leftist military junta that had taken control of Peru in a 1968 coup was moving rightward, but not before it had enacted laws giving the nation's indigenous peoples a greater degree of control over their economic and political fortunes. More significant still was the construction of a road, the Carretera Marginal de la Selva (Marginal Jungle Highway), which would eventually connect Lamas and other nearby towns to the Pacific coast.

In October 1976 I returned to Lamas with the expectation that it would serve as home base for my field research. I began studying the language with a few Lamista men and making steadily longer trips into the countryside. I talked to schoolteachers and other government employees about Lamista life. Sustained contact with Lamistas themselves, however, proved elusive. Their neighborhoods on the town's edge were mostly vacant during the week as families shuttled to agricultural fields located hours away by foot. More challenging than physical separation were the social barriers between the Lamista and mestizo worlds. In town, Lamistas appeared reticent and uneasy. Mestizos, in turn, rarely missed an opportunity to express disbelief that anyone would come from so far away to study Lamista culture, which they saw as colorful but ultimately worthless.

Memorable things happened during those weeks. In a village several hours' walk from Lamas, I attended an event called a *velada,* at which people danced through the night to the music of flutes and drums. I harvested coffee berries with a man named Antonio Salas and his wife. (Don Antonio saved my

Lamista revelers near the village of Pamashto, Department of San
Martín, 1976.
Photograph courtesy of Michael F. Brown.

hand, and possibly my life, by gently pulling me back from a
coffee bush just as I reached for a berry positioned inches away
from a sleeping palm viper, locally known as *loro machaco,* that
was nearly invisible against the deep green of the plant's leaves.)
From Don Antonio and other men, I collected stories of epic
battles between shamans and the sorcerers who tried to con-
found them. I inventoried an array of "purges," rainforest plants
said to cleanse body and mind.

As time passed, however, I became disheartened. Lamistas
proved frustratingly elusive. Most were civil enough, and a few
were genuinely helpful. But the accumulated injuries of centuries of exploitation had hardened into a shell of reserve that was

difficult to crack. A more mulish or self-confident person might have stayed on and found ways to gain the trust of enough Lamistas to move the project forward. Instead, I listened to my gut, my growing sense that Lamas wasn't the right place for me. The stress of studying a community sharply divided by inequality and suspicion was a consideration. Another was the difficulty of gaining ready access to Lamista daily life. I had already witnessed their annual saint's day feast, a colorful public spectacle rich in interpretive possibilities. But I was just as interested in the everyday intimacies of village life, the business of getting along in a small-scale, face-to-face society.

Thus began the quest for another research site. Initially I focused on remote Quechua-speaking communities in a neighboring province to draw on my basic training in the language, a change of location that would have shifted my focus from the Amazon to the Andes. This search ultimately led to the drunken encounter in Olleros.

My situation was sufficiently desperate that I decided to follow up on the invitation of Leonidas, one of the partiers in Olleros, to visit the Indians living near his frontier settlement, who he said were Aguarunas. Reluctant to embark on another punishing trip over the unfinished segment of the Marginal Highway, which had involved walking for miles through deep mud, I decided to take a bus to the Peruvian coast and then fly by commercial airline to Rioja, the town nearest Leonidas's farm. This journey proved no less eventful than its predecessor. The bus taking me and forty others to the coastal city of Chiclayo broke down en route, leaving passengers to their own devices halfway to nowhere. I completed the overnight trip wrapped in a wool poncho atop an open truck loaded with sacks of green coffee beans. For once, there was no rain. As the truck lumbered over the Andes, unfamiliar Southern Hemisphere constellations wheeled overhead. In Chiclayo I threw financial caution to the wind and checked into a hotel with a couple of stars to its name and reliable hot water. Two days later I was on a prop plane bound for Rioja. The earnest American missionary seated next to me on the flight promised to keep me in his prayers.

Rioja was the epicenter of rainforest colonization in the region. From the Marginal Highway, colonists moving down from the highlands of Amazonas and Cajamarca cut trails and bulldozed rough tracks in a dendritic settlement pattern blocked only by the Andes to the west and the Río Mayo to the east. The new settlers were different from the region's longtime residents. The latter, affectionately called *charapas,* the local name for a species of Amazonian turtle, were nearly indistinguishable from indigenous people in some ways. They moved on the river or through the forest with an ease based on profound intimacy. Their Spanish was spiced with hundreds of words borrowed from the region's native languages. Their worldview encompassed magic, sorcery, and such quasi-mythical animals as the *chicharra machacuy,* a cicada whose lethal sting can be survived, it was said, only if the victim has immediate intercourse with a member of the opposite sex willing to provide emergency therapy.[7]

Highland colonists were easily distinguished from charapas by their wool clothing and awkwardness in the forest. Growing numbers of them arrived after converting to austere evangelical sects focused on the end times, an obsession that led to frequent queries about whether a recent American moon landing signaled the coming of the last days. They also brought a tradition of violent conflicts over land, something rare among charapas.

After a long wait, a truck transported me to the road that led to Leonidas's village, Atumplaya. The corrugated dirt track passed through a settlement called Tahuantinsuyu, then to another new village called San Fernando, whose only public buildings were a tiny shop and a Seventh-day Adventist chapel with a hand-lettered sign that read "Your King is coming. Prepare yourself." I reached the Río Mayo at dusk. A dugout canoe served as the local ferry. The boatman punted the narrow, unstable craft by standing in the bow with a long bamboo pole, pushing the end into the river bottom, and walking it to the stern as the canoe slipped forward. With only six or seven inches of freeboard, there was little room for error. He poled the canoe upstream, then cut sharply across the current, using the pole as a paddle. The canoe put in gracefully at my feet.

Atumplaya was a collection of shacks on the opposite bank of the river. After the abundant rain, the village paths stood ankle deep in mud. Feral-looking pigs rooted noisily in the soil. The air was thick with the smell of decomposition and human waste. The first villager I encountered repeatedly asked whether I found Atumplaya attractive. I lied and said yes. He pointed to a tiny shop fashioned of scrap wood, whose owners could provide lodging and food. The following morning, after a fitful night listening to rats dart around the beds and up the walls, I went in search of Leonidas. He was astonished to see me again but agreed to guide me to an Awajún village called Huascayacu. We walked for several hours, first through areas of muck and standing water, then into drier gallery forest. Leonidas was a man of few words, but he knew the way.

We eventually came upon a dozen men clearing the trail with machetes. They were laughing boisterously, obviously enjoying themselves. Leonidas identified them as Aguarunas and said that he knew one or two who spoke a little Spanish. They offered us bowls of *masato*, a beer made from fermented manioc tubers. Although the men were dressed like other rural people, their blackened teeth and straight-cut bangs marked them as indigenous, as did their slightly Asiatic facial features. Two women, there to serve the beer, wore simple shifts made of

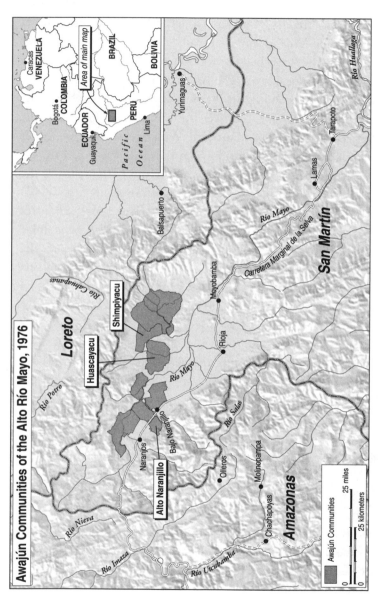

Map copyright © 2014 by Michael F. Brown.

manufactured cotton cloth. I was immediately struck by the difference between these people and the Lamistas. They were ebullient and good-humored. They showed no deference to me or to Leonidas, only a lively curiosity.

Huascayacu consisted of a simple school building and a half dozen impressively large houses ranged around a field with wooden soccer goals at either end. The houses were sided with vertical wood slats and thatched with palm leaves. There were no pigs in evidence, and the village was immaculate. Children, including a few naked boys, came out of the schoolhouse to stare. Leonidas took me to the house of the teacher, the only villager who was truly bilingual. He introduced himself as Tomás. Trained in bilingual education by American missionary linguists, Tomás had served as the village's teacher for several years. His teaching job did not officially include proselytizing, but he said that his introduction of evangelical Christianity to the people of Huascayacu had convinced them to turn away from traditional beliefs.

As the sun touched the treetops to the west, we went to the house of Eladio, the community *ápu* or headman, to drink more beer. Two women used gourd strainers to fill pottery bowls that were refilled after each man drank. The taste was pleasantly tart and faintly alcoholic. Adult men and teenage boys lounged on benches around a homemade kerosene lamp. With Tomás acting as interpreter, the men began a friendly interrogation. What was my name? How old was I? What were the names of my father, mother, siblings? Why wasn't I married? What kinds of animals lived in my country? What had I done to make my beard grow? Tomás insisted that the Aguaruna admired beards. Several pulled at their own sparse facial hair and laughed. When talking about the United States and its people, they used the word *gringo,* which in Aguaruna sounded like *kirínku* or *irínku.*

I asked Eladio for permission to return to Huascayacu in a few weeks to study how the Awajún lived and worked and thought. Exactly how I described my goals is lost to me after so many years. I dimly recall saying that I would write about the people of Huascayacu so that my people, the kirínku, could better understand them. After discussing this with the other men present, Eladio said that I could stay in a small house that the community had built for visitors. Tomás agreed that he and his wife would provide meals in exchange for a small board fee. My notes from the encounter record no hesitation on their part or mine. No matter that I would be grappling with an entirely new language and a culture about which my ignorance was complete. It was settled as simply as that.

This tale of false starts and awkward transitions may make cultural anthropology sound too slapdash to be a proper science. An unavoidable reality of ethnographic work is that it entails uncertainties rarely encountered in other approaches to the study of human social life. Psychologists and sociologists who use experimental methods or analyze demographic data can control the terms of their research nearly as well as chemists. But anyone committed to studying human beings in vivo rather than in vitro is subject to the winds of fate. Borders close; wars are declared; visas are denied for unknown reasons; populations relocate; new social movements change a community's attitude toward outsiders from one day to the next. A database doesn't know whether the person questioning it is male or female; human interviewees do. Ethnographers have little choice but to remain adaptable, responding creatively to conditions as they present themselves.

Then there is the matter of whether fieldworkers succeed in finding common ground with the people who are the focus of their research. Most books written by anthropologists intimate, if they don't say so directly, that the author was fond of the people he or she studied and that this affection was reciprocated. As a graduate student I was shocked by a passage in Weston La Barre's study of the Aymara people of Bolivia, published in 1948. Speaking of the Aymara's dogs, he says, "Like their owners, they detest white people and attack all strangers indiscriminately." In a later work he describes the Aymara as "truculent, hostile, silent, suspicious, treacherous, and vindictive." Whether La Barre's assessment is defensible is less interesting than is his willingness to violate the narrative conventions of his trade. Such bluntness in print shocks even more than Bronislaw Malinowski's famously unkind words for the Trobriand Islanders he studied, which were recorded in a private diary published only after his death.[8]

That temperament and luck play an important role in ethnography doesn't imply that it lacks rigor. Although the work of Margaret Mead, particularly her study of Samoa, has come under attack since the 1980s, the fieldwork that she conducted in 1938 in Papua New Guinea's Sepik region with her husband, Gregory Bateson, still stands as a model of thoroughness and subtlety. The level of discipline required to prepare 2,500 pages of notes and develop 10,000 photographs during a six-month research period under challenging field conditions beggars the imagination. Surveying the results of this feverish work, one wonders when Mead and Bateson found time to sleep.[9]

Discussing such ambitions in a seminar room in Berkeley or Oxford or Paris is one thing. Actually launching the research—alone, insecure, awkwardly poised between social realities—is another. Ethnography has adventurous moments, especially in comparison to the bookish life of graduate students, but my months in Lamas had taught me that the main test would be psychological. Every hour of adventure is offset by hundreds of hours of tedium. Dogged persistence, coupled with fear of failure, may be the only thing that gets one out of bed in the morning. An adage usually attributed to Woody Allen applies to ethnography as well as filmmaking: "Eighty percent of success is just showing up." Now, after years of training and months of stumbling through wretched backwoods villages in the Andean *montaña,* it was my turn to show up.

2

Armadillo for Breakfast

Two weeks later I returned to Huascayacu with a mestizo named Julio, hired to help carry my gear. Julio moved effortlessly over the muddy trail even though he was carrying a machete and shotgun in addition to a heavy bag. We arrived before noon and were welcomed by Tomás. After a meal at Tomás's house, Julio solemnly collected his pay and slipped back into the forest in the direction of Atumplaya.

On that uncommonly sunny day, Huascayacu was a vision of civic order. Women returned from their fields straining against heavy baskets of manioc supported by tumplines that crossed their foreheads. Their husbands were hunting, taking advantage of dry weather. Hens scratched in the dirt. Swallow-tailed kites cruised high overhead. A score of children milled about in front of the one-room school, waiting for Tomás to begin the afternoon class. Although rainforest crowded the village's perimeter, its sounds were mostly limited to the biting glissando of the screaming piha, a bird whose call would have rattled window glass had there been any.

I was quartered in a palm-thatched house roughly ten feet by twenty, divided into two rooms. The floor was packed dirt. Palm-wood staves, each standing about a half inch from the next, served as walls. Strips of light passed through them and pinwheeled across the floor as the day wore on. For furniture, there were palm-wood benches and a table in the sitting room, a sleeping platform in the bedroom. Sheets of flattened bamboo lent the bed a springy feel that proved surprisingly comfortable. The door consisted of a half dozen stout cylinders of dried bamboo, held loosely by wooden crosspieces, that had to be pushed apart by visitors. The distinctive sound of the hollow bamboo tubes knocking together as people came and went from nearby houses soon became part of the auditory backdrop, as did the barking of Tomás's pack of gaunt hunting dogs. At night, I was soon to discover, other sounds dominated: the close-in rustle of mice, rats, and immense cockroaches as they carried on a noisy struggle to survive in the palm leaves of the roof. The vampire bats that patrolled for blood meals outside my mosquito net were, in contrast, eerily silent.

Organizing my clothing and equipment in the house took a half hour. Now what? You can study anthropology for years, talking constantly about "the field," without ever being told what you're supposed to do when you get there. Of course you expect to learn the language, ask people how they're related to one another, document their rituals, and, provided that the climate hasn't yet clotted your camera lenses with fungus or cooked the emulsion on your photographic film, take plenty of pictures. How one does this in the absence of a shared language remains a mystery.

It didn't help that the late 1970s marked the apogee of French structuralism, a recondite theory focused on the logical operations of the human mind. At my university, several prominent members of the faculty renounced their former materialist approach to anthropology and embraced structuralism with an enthusiasm that approached religious fervor. This hyperintellectual turn made it especially awkward to ask questions on the order of "What the devil am I supposed to do with myself in the months before I can ask a grammatically correct question?"

The answer was not obvious. Of the villagers, only Tomás was truly bilingual. A handful of men and one woman had a limited command of Spanish. They could talk about the weather, food, and how much things cost. When students from Tomás's school, including a few little boys dressed in nothing but T-shirts, stopped by to peer through the wall slats, I tried to engage them in Spanish or with the few words of Awajún that Tomás had taught me. Mostly there was mutual staring and, on their part, conversations that I imagined were about me and my meager array of stuff. During the day, however, when children were in school and most adults had vacated their houses to hunt or work in their gardens, it was hard to find something useful to do. The voracious biting flies that infested Huascayacu were a constant torment. A vortex of self-pity danced at the edge of my waking hours. The temptation to succumb was powerful.

A different challenge lay in the nature of Awajún society. In common with nearly all indigenous peoples, the Awajún organized their social world around family ties, which give everyone a place in the social order. Where kinship ties didn't exist, they had to be invented. Nonkinship created a moral vacuum. I knew I would be expected to adopt these conventions, addressing everyone by kinship terms that they would reciprocate. Yet beneath this veneer of familiarity, I would still be an enigmatic visitor adrift from any visible family ties, fated to live in a penumbra of moral ambiguity.

A few things worked in my favor. One was the humdrum reality of village life. The resident alien was a diversion, a social science experiment, and, I soon discovered, an inmate in a petting zoo. During afternoon social calls men and boys showed little hesitation about rubbing the hair on my arms or pulling my beard. Submitting to such frank curiosity was sometimes tiresome but preferable to staring at an empty notebook.

Americans aroused suspicion throughout the Andes, but the Awajún thought differently. Every household owned a copy of *Yamajam Chicham Apu Jisukristu pachisa etsegbau,* an Awajún translation of the New Testament, published in 1973 by the Wycliffe Bible Translators. This was the fruit of decades of work by American evangelical linguists living in Awajún villages to the north of the Alto Mayo. Although people in Huascayacu remained uncertain about the Christian message, they were impressed that citizens of a powerful foreign nation showed more interest in them than did most Peruvians. Some of my hosts briefly imagined that I was an evangelical pastor. This notion was put to rest by my willingness to drink manioc beer, the staple beverage that Protestant missionaries exhorted them to abandon.

At the time, reliable information about the Awajún was scarce. It was known that they were a numerous people whose population then exceeded 25,000. Most lived in communities located some distance to the northeast of the Alto Río Mayo, along the Alto Río Marañón and several of its tributaries. They were the southernmost members of a loose network of societies that Spanish colonial officials and missionaries called the "great Jívaro nation." Their ancestors dominated the area between the Andes and the Amazon rainforest on both sides of the frontier that today separates Peru from Ecuador. Recent evidence suggests that proto-Jivaroan culture had a significant Andean presence, although these populations seem to have been transformed or dispersed by the dual impact of Inca expansion and Spanish conquest.[1]

Surviving Jivaroan peoples thought of themselves as distinct from one another even as they shared closely related languages, a preference for dispersed settlements organized around a prominent male leader, and recognition of the power of shamans to heal or kill. The traditional dress of Jivaroan men was a single piece of cotton that covered them from waist to knee, like a kilt or short sarong. On festive occasions they donned toucan feather headdresses, necklaces of iridescent beetle wings, and bandoliers of beads and bird bones. Jivaroan women, usually described as less flamboyant than their husbands, favored plain homespun dresses tied at one shoulder. For colonial officials, the most important trait of Jivaroans, aside from determined resistance to outside authority, was their practice of turning the heads of murdered enemies into fist-sized, smoke-blackened war trophies called *tsántsa* as part of a ritual to harness the enemy's spiritual power. Every North American and European museum of natural history wanted tsántsa for its collection. A single item of material culture was instrumental in turning the Jívaro into icons of primitivism for the West.

The fall of the Inca Empire in 1533 and subsequent incursions by Spanish settlers and missionaries unleashed changes whose repercussions continued for centuries. The northern corner of Awajún territory contained gold deposits that attracted settlers until the early 1600s. Although colonists were subject to royal laws defining how indigenous populations could be treated, circumstances favored what the anthropologist Anne-Christine Taylor calls a "piratical life-style" that included de facto enslavement of Indians. A major native uprising in Logroño led to a dramatic decline in colonization efforts. The Jesuits tried a different approach, establishing a network of missions that encompassed an enormous area stretching from Borja, on the Alto Río Marañón, to a point east of present-day Iquitos. Among the tens of thousands of Indians brought into the Jesuit mission system, often unwillingly, were doubtless some Awajún, although mission records generally tend to portray Jivaroans as a nearly hopeless case for priests whose energies were already taxed to the limit. As was true elsewhere in the New World, clustering indigenous peoples in densely settled "reductions" made them more vulnerable to the epidemics that regularly swept through the region. The Jesuit system was stretched too thin to be fully integrated, and it proved incapable of protecting missions from Portuguese slavers in its eastern extreme. The network largely collapsed when the Jesuit order was expelled from Peru in 1768.[2]

The earliest known reference to the Awajún dates to the mid-1700s, in a Jesuit account that mentions "Ahuarunes, natives of the Río Santiago." The origin of the name Aguaruna remains the subject of speculation to this day. The most obvious etymological theory—that it represents a combination of the Spanish word for "water" and the Quechua word for "people"—has few adherents among experts, but alternative etymologies are no less contested.[3]

Specific information about the Awajún remains scarce until the last two decades of the nineteenth century. There are intriguing glimpses here and there. One is found in the diary of the naturalist Alexander von Humboldt, who in 1802 traveled on the Ríos Chinchipe and Marañón. He describes an encounter with "Jíbaros"—most likely Awajún—who were "the happiest savage Indians I have seen." He continues: "They have lively faces that advertise the great vivacity of their character. . . . How different the free, savage man is from those of the missions, slaves of opinion and priestly oppression! What vivacity, what curiosity, what good memories, what drive to want to learn the Spanish language and to make himself understood in his own!" His opinion was echoed nearly seventy years later by the American naturalist James Orton. Orton refers to the Jívaro

Awajún family, Río Apaga, 1929.
From Rafael Karsten, *The Head-Hunters of Western Amazonas,* 1935. Image VKK
721:219, National Board of Antiquities, Finland.

as the " 'Red Indians' *par excellence* . . . the most numerous and
the most spirited of the oriental tribes. They are brave and re-
sentful, yet hospitable and industrious."[4]

Descriptions of the Awajún—referred to by such terms as
Antipa, Ahuaruna, Ahuarone, or Aguaruna—became more numerous when the Amazonian rubber boom (roughly 1880–
1912) increased the number of travelers and government officials
moving along the Río Marañón and its tributaries. Courtenay
De Kalb, an American mining engineer who wrote occasional
articles for *Harper's Magazine* and the *New York Times,* describes his first encounter with an Awajún couple in 1891:

> But at Barranca and westward, I met a tribe called Ahuarunas,
> which departs in many characteristics from those around them.

The first whom I saw were the chieftain and his wife. He was tall and heavy, and had a pleasant face, with well-chiseled features, the forehead high, the nose long and perfectly straight. His hair, in addition to hanging down his back, had been made into two little braids which hung like horns from his temples. His only garment was a brown striped waist-cloth. In manner he was as simple and naïve as a child. His wife, who followed along behind, stopping when he stopped, advancing when he moved, like a faithful dog, was a mere girl, of slight form and delicate features, with a small chin, and an almost Grecian nose. Her arms and hands were of an absolutely perfect mould. Later in my journey I met others of the Ahuarunas, and these exceptional characteristics seemed to be a persistent quality of the tribe.[5]

Traveling in the same region only a few years after De Kalb, the American engineer and explorer Fritz Up de Graff portrayed the Awajún in a less favorable light: "Contrary to what is generally supposed, these untamed sons of the forest are a compendium of all that is cunning, knavish, and diabolical." Up de Graff's distaste for the Awajún was matched by that of a Passionist priest, Silvio de San Bernardo, who in 1922 characterized them as devoted to "laziness, drunkenness, polygamy, hatred of other peoples [and] aversion to the white man," qualities that the priest judged to be "powerful obstacles that make civilizing them morally impossible by human means."[6]

De Kalb and Up de Graff explored Awajún country during a period considered the most violent in the Amazon's modern history, at least until the rise of the cocaine industry in the 1980s. Downriver from the Awajún, rubber barons based in Iquitos and Manaus bankrolled armies of barefoot mercenaries to defend tapping territories and prevent heavily indebted mestizo and indigenous workers from fleeing. The Alto Marañón, a river less endowed with rubber-producing species than areas to the east and south, attracted minor-league but equally vicious patróns—men such as Amadeo Burga, Miguel Hurtado, and Fabriciano Yajamanco. Some Awajún worked as part-time tappers; others served as occasional oarsmen. They were drawn into the orbit of patróns by a desire for steel tools, firearms, trade cloth, and sometimes aguardiente. Nevertheless, there is little evidence that they were as deeply involved in the rubber trade as the Bora and Witoto, indigenous groups enslaved by rubber barons farther east.[7]

Accounts portray the Alto Marañón of this period as an intractably violent place, with parties of Awajún men, armed with steel-tipped lances and later muzzle-loading guns and Winchester rifles, cruising the rivers or patrolling the trails in search of Wampis (Huambisa), Shawi (Chayahuita), and mestizo settlers to kill. Some of the attacks were proxy conflicts instigated by local patróns vying for influence. Among the most notorious was the coordinated mass killing at several rubber stations, including Huabico, by large parties of Awajún in 1904, which some accounts imply had its origin in a long-simmering rivalry between two patróns. The precise number of fatalities in the 1904 attack is hard to piece together, although it appears to have been at least twenty, including women and children. Among these were two visiting missionaries, Father Bernardo Calle and Brother Miguel Villajolí, who may have been unlucky bystanders rather than intended targets. Another large-scale Awajún assault in 1914 led to the immediate abandonment of the Marruecos rubber station. "Uprising of Aguaruna Indians," clamors the headline of an account of the attack published in a Lima newspaper. "They mete out a horrible death to fifty people." Later accounts suggest that long-standing hostility between local Awajún and Wampis leaders may have been exploited by the manager of the Marruecos rubber post.[8]

Awajún belligerence cannot be attributed solely to the rubber boom. José María Guallart (1915–2002), a Spanish Jesuit who worked among the Awajún for nearly fifty years, collected documents and oral histories that shed light on attacks reaching back as far as the 1830s. The administrative chaos unleashed by Peru's struggle for independence in the early nineteenth century created a power vacuum in the Alto Marañón that the Awajún were happy to fill. They wiped out mestizo settlements in Puyaya, Copallín, Borja, Santa Teresa, and Barranca, among others, and mounted serious attacks as far west as Bagua Chica. Guallart insists that most of these assaults were provoked by mestizo abuses, although the scale of the response often exceeded that of the alleged provocation.

Other Catholic missionaries and, beginning in the 1920s, their Protestant counterparts offer accounts of relentless conflicts involving the Awajún. Reporting on a visit to the nominally Christianized Shawi people in 1926, the Passionist priest Martín Corera describes the Indians as having abandoned their mission village out of "fear of an uprising of the infidel Ahuarunas because these savages, who are close by, were wont to hurl themselves unexpectedly on the Christians, kill them, and then loot and burn their houses." An Awajún raid in Cahuapanas in 1925 resulted in fifteen dead and nineteen people taken captive. A rescue party from Cahuapanas managed to locate and kill five of the attackers, but the rest escaped.[9]

Elsewhere Padre Corera provides a detailed account of a large party of Awajún fighters planning vengeance on Wampis enemies who murdered one of their kinsmen, a man named Nantipa. Corera presents their declaration of intent as it was conveyed to him in broken Spanish: "Aguaruna, going to kill, taking oath to kill. Doing nothing else before killing. Not eating, not doing anything else first; only killing. Likewise, others taking oath, all going to kill."[10]

Awajún family, Río Cenepa, 1946. Two men on the left are holding blowguns.

From Leonard F. Clark, *The Rivers Ran East*, 1953. Used with kind permission of Melinda (Clark) B. Price, David L. Clark, and Gregory G. Clark. Copyright © 1946 by Leonard F. Clark.

Probably the most widely read description of Awajún life is found in a book published in 1953, *The Rivers Ran East,* written by a flamboyant adventurer and former American military officer named Leonard Clark. In 1946 Clark traveled through Awajún country searching for ancient gold deposits, a quest that years later cost him his life in Venezuela. Like Up de Graff before him, Clark's characterization of the Awajún emphasizes their cruelty. Although elements of his account seem over-wrought, his observation that the Awajún were enmeshed in bitter reciprocal warfare with the Wampis is accurate enough.[11]

Conflict was by no means limited to intertribal raiding. The murder of alleged sorcerers also figures prominently in missionary reports. "In September [1947] a young man named Cuyu, a

student in the Protestant school at Yamayacat, died in the house
of Sijapa in Chinimpi," wrote the Jesuit José Martín Cuesta.
"They say that before dying, Cuyu did nothing more than re-
peat that he had been bewitched by a *túnchi* named Ichiás from
Chimutás. Four fellow students were by his side: Shuc, Pate,
Chimbucát, and Pitón. . . . The four students, along with a
group of Awajún from Chinimpi, left with their guns and lances
in search of the sorcerer Ichiás. . . . After spying on him for several days, they surprised him alone and cruelly victimized him
with bullet and lance in late September or early October, days
after my visit to Guayampiác." Countless stories of this kind,
strikingly similar in their plot lines, can be found in the accounts
of missionaries working among the Awajún from the 1940s until the 1970s.[12]

Routine exploitation of the Awajún by patróns and merchants
continued through the 1950s. Immediately after completing his
university degree, the future writer Mario Vargas Llosa accompanied a research team on a trip down the Marañón in 1958.
Merchants, "barefoot and semi-literate . . . savagely punished
any attempt by the Indians to escape from their control," writes
Vargas Llosa. He continues: "When we reached the settlement
of Urakusa, the chieftain, an Aguaruna called Jum, came out to
meet us and it was terrible to see him and hear his story because
here was a man who had been recently tortured for having attempted to create a cooperative. In the lost villages of the Upper
Marañón, I saw and touched the violence that the struggle for
existence in my country could cause."[13]

By the time of Vargas Llosa's visit, the Awajún had begun to
cluster in villages. They were drawn by the gravitational pull of
schools, health posts, and secure land titles. Missionaries played a
part in this shift. The Kansas-based Church of the Nazarene
established a foothold among the Awajún in the early 1920s. This
provided a setting for American evangelical linguists whose

skillful work produced the Awajún translation of the New Testament, as well as bilingual teaching materials for use in schools. They trained a cohort of young Awajún men, most of whom eventually worked as elementary school teachers in Awajún communities. The educational efforts of American evangelicals were complemented by those of the Catholic Church, which intensified missionary activities among the Awajún beginning in the early 1950s.

In 1977 few maps showed Awajún populations reaching as far south as the Alto Río Mayo. This suggested that Awajún families were relatively recent arrivals who had come in search of game or a place of refuge. Elementary schools had been founded only a few years before I settled in Huascayacu. The teachers, all from the Alto Marañón, were inclined to see their Alto Mayo cousins as uncouth rustics. This didn't stop many of them from marrying local women and settling in the region permanently.

Huascayacu's imposing houses, some more than sixty feet long and thirty feet from floor to roof peak, scarcely differed from those visible in grainy photos from the early twentieth century. People still depended on foods they could grow, gather, or hunt. But homespun cloth was now rare. Clothing followed rural Peruvian fashion: men wore trousers and loose shirts, while women favored one-piece dresses of trade cotton. Around cooking fires, ceramic pots competed with aluminum pans and plastic tubs. The ubiquitous steel machetes, axes, and shotguns were all imported. For school, children needed pens and notebooks. None of these things could be acquired without money, which families obtained by selling commercially valuable trees, game meat, and rice that they had recently begun to cultivate as a cash crop.

A few days after my arrival, the villagers began a series of parties to mark the New Year. Before the foundation of the elementary

school, calendars and clocks had meant little to them. It was
sufficient to divide the year into rainy and dry seasons and the
day into periods defined by the sun's movement. But contact
with government agencies and the schedule followed by the village school forced them to reckon time in more precise units.
Thus began an interest in time that bordered on obsession. Tomás
and I owned the only two functional wristwatches in the village. While he was teaching or away, I became the village time-
keeper, constantly answering passersby, eventually including
every ambulatory child, who wished to inquire about the hour.
It soon became clear that my answers meant nothing in themselves, and people left perfectly content when, at nine in the
morning, I replied that it was eleven or three.

Eladio, the Huascayacu headman, promoted the New Year's
celebration with a zeal that reflected this collective fascination
with clocks and calendars. Eladio's leadership role coincided
with his standing as father, elder brother, or father-in-law of
most of Huascayacu's adult male residents. In pursuit of his official duties, Eladio wore a battered blue sport coat that seemed
particularly incongruous with his callused bare feet. His age
was impossible to determine with precision, although he was
probably in his fifties. Like most men in Huascayacu, his hair
was short on the back and sides, with straight bangs in front.
His weather-beaten face was often creased by a sly smile. Eladio
spoke a rough-and-ready Spanish based exclusively on the present participle. His invitation to the party can be rendered literally as, "You coming to the *fiesta* tonight. We drinking lots of
beer." Compared to my command of Awajún, then limited to
the equivalent of "hello," Eladio was as eloquent as Cervantes.

The essential element of any party was manioc beer, the dietary and social pillar of Awajún life. Its preparation was an
unchanging part of a woman's working day. Most afternoons,
women returned from their gardens bearing heavy baskets of

tubers. These were peeled, split into smaller pieces, and boiled in large aluminum pots. The cooked manioc was then tumbled into concave wooden platters. While smashing the tubers with a heavy, clublike pestle, women chewed bits of the mash and spat them back into the mix to hasten fermentation. Removed to brewing pots, the mash was later mixed with water, strained, and served. Unfermented manioc beer was often an infant's first food after mother's milk. Warmed over the fire by an attentive wife in the hours before dawn, beer was a man's first meal of the day. For parties, beer was allowed to ferment for a few more days to raise its alcohol content.

There was no shortage of well-fermented beer at Huascayacu's New Year party. The community's official registry showed a population of 110, and more than half were present at the house where the celebration commenced. Mature men sat on benches near the door. Women and children clustered near the cooking fire and around the beer pots. A few of the men wore feather coronas or bandoliers of bright seeds across their chests. Women circulated with bowls of beer, serving each man individually. Eventually people began to dance. Tomás had warned me that the Awajún lacked collective dances, that each person danced as he or she pleased. This proved accurate in a general way. Men circled the room, sometimes hopping and turning, each singing his own song and punctuating it with shouts, whistles, or loud guffaws. One or two wore anklets of dried nuts that served as rattles. Sometimes men bunched together, dancing in twos or threes with arms around one another's shoulders. Knots of men broke apart and regrouped. Two circled the house with bamboo flutes that were neither played in unison nor coordinated with the rest of the revelers. Women danced and sang more demurely in the center of the men's circle. The noise was deafening, the sense of cheerful anarchy overpowering. After an hour, someone broke out a battery-powered record player and a handful of 45 rpm records. The music was Andean *huaynos* and tropical *cumbias* to which only the younger people danced, self-conscious and awkward.

During the party I focused on learning people's names. Local custom made that difficult. In Huascayacu, most people had Spanish names as well as traditional Awajún ones. Many had nicknames as well. In the jungle areas of eastern Peru, mestizos favored flamboyant handles, as if to counter the stark simplicity of daily life. One was more likely to meet a Winston, Nixon, Sofocles, Neli, Salomé, or even the occasional Hitler than the conventional Juan or María. This custom had been embraced by the Awajún, among whom were people with names as exotic as Napoleón, Comisario, Hilbertina, Nelson, and Fredesvinda. Because speakers of Awajún had trouble pronouncing certain Spanish consonants and vowels, names were transmogrified almost beyond recognition. Osvaldo became Uspartu; Napoleón became Napurín; Rosinda became Urucínta. Surnames, which were unknown prior to regular contact with Hispanic society, had been imposed by the government. When officials visited native communities to enter families into the land-titling records, they issued surnames based on the names of the parents of the oldest members of a household. If a senior man named Wajajái had a father named Ampám and a mother named Tumús, then his identity document showed his name as Wajajái Ampám Tumús. An additional layer of complexity, about which I was to learn later, was that men might change their name two or three times over the course of a lifetime after participating in murders. An occasional name change made it harder for enemies to target them for reprisal. The tactic of camouflage through renaming was becoming harder to use as names became fixed in official documents.[14]

I returned to my house at around 10:00 P.M., exhausted by the effort to remain sociable amid the din and my limited ability to converse. One of the side effects of consuming quantities of manioc beer, aside from an acid stomach, was the necessity of frequent "undrinking," to use the Peruvian slang of the time. Getting up to empty my aching bladder at 3:00 A.M., I could hear men singing in a house on the other side of the village. All was quiet at dawn, but by 8:00 A.M. festivities had resumed at another house. It continued throughout the day, moving from house to house based on the availability of beer. A couple of colonists from Atumplaya joined the celebration, but they were unable to keep up with the pace of drinking and staggered down the trail toward home by early afternoon. By late that evening, supplies of beer had dwindled, and the 1977 New Year's party faded to black.

Tomás later explained that this was a short celebration by local standards. He had asked women to make only a little beer so that the festivities wouldn't last too long. In his view, several days of nonstop drinking would surely lead to a brawl, a case of wife beating, or some other disturbance. Tomás was a teetotaler but had resigned himself to the prospect that others were going to drink. His goal was to limit the damage.

Tomás, in whose house I took meals and who provided me with daily language lessons, proved to be a mass of contradictions. A trim, fastidious man in his forties, he was old by the standards of other bilingual teachers in the region. His biography seemed like a story from the nineteenth-century American frontier. He had been widowed twice already, and his current wife, Celestina, was at least fifteen years his junior. He had fathered twelve children. Raised in a traditional household in the Awajún heartland to the north, Tomás had been among the first generation of Awajún trained as bilingual teachers by American missionaries. He strongly identified with evangelical Christianity, which he saw as redemptive and modern. Like other bilingual teachers from the Alto Marañón, he thought of his

Alto Mayo students as primitives desperately in need of his civilizing influence.

Tomás's image of starchy rectitude became tarnished in my mind when I learned that he had seduced one of Eladio's daughters, Isabel, a young woman in her teens, during a period when his wife, Celestina, had returned to the Alto Marañón for an extended visit with relatives. The liaison, which continued after Celestina's return, eventually produced two children. Although no one referred to Isabel as Tomás's wife, there was an understanding that he had laid claim to her in some way. The ambiguous marital situation posed no particular problem for Isabel's children. Their grandfather's large household afforded an abundance of caregivers and agemates. As I gained some fluency in the language and came to know people better, I heard amusing stories about Tomás's romantic peccadillos, including one from a man who, while stealthily entering a house one dark night intent on seducing a particular woman, found himself trailing Tomás, who was on an amorous mission of his own.

For all of Tomás's pretensions of sophistication, he was one of the villagers most fearful of sorcery. His wife's persistent abdominal pain led him to shuttle her from doctor to shaman and back during the first months of my residence in the village. Tomás's increasing anxiety about her illness reflected what turned out to be a slow-growing crisis in Huascayacu over a rash of infant deaths and adult illnesses that residents came to see as incontrovertible evidence that homicidal sorcerers lived among them.

Tomás emphasized that in the interest of avoiding gossip I had to be circumspect with village women. That meant, among other things, that accompanying them to their gardens was out of the question. This left me with only a limited range of ways to spend my time. I participated in villagewide events—

parties, formal meetings, communal work, and group fishing expeditions—whenever they took place. I could hunt with the men, assuming that they let me tag along. I soon learned, however, that for an astigmatic suburbanite with limited experience as a tracker and marksman, the Amazonian rainforest was little more than a heavily vegetated theater of humiliation. Even skills in which I had thought of myself as competent, such as axemanship, were of limited use in this new setting. The Awajún made their own axe handles, which were half again as long as their North American counterparts. When attacking a tree, they swung the axe in an elegant overhead arc—nearly a full circle, in fact—that was a wonder to watch but difficult to emulate. I had more success helping out in the fields of maize and rice that Tomás had convinced most of the men to cultivate for sale in town. There, at least, the necessary skills were within reach.

On one occasion I stayed at a temporary camp that Eladio and others had built close to their maize and rice fields, an hour's easy walk from Huascayacu. The group included Eladio's younger brother Kíjik, a widower, as well as Eladio's daughter Lucila and her husband, Lauriano, plus a half dozen children. I set up my mosquito net in Kíjik's shelter. Eladio woke everyone before dawn. Lucila and the other women began to roast green plantains in the coals while Eladio stripped bark from a vine that he would use to make a carrying basket.

At about seven we ate the plantains and boiled howler monkey meat. After a few weeks it had become clear that Awajún cuisine was uncomplicated, to put it charitably. Meat, tubers, and plantains were served roasted or boiled. Gardens attracted agoutis, a species of rodent that could weigh ten pounds or more, as well as a small species of armadillo. Cooked carefully, armadillo meat could be tasty, although I never became fully accustomed to having it cold for breakfast or savoring the layer of fat under the shell, which my hosts eagerly sucked off as if they were eating artichokes. Rustic salt was the only regularly used condiment, although a creative cook might occasionally offer a bowl of crushed chili peppers or ginger into which boiled manioc could be dipped. Now and then there would be a culinary surprise, usually resulting from a discovery on the hunt: edible mushrooms, palm fruits, or polliwogs steamed in banana leaves.

At certain times of year, large red ants were collected by children and roasted in the fire after being spitted on splinters of wood. This delicacy was appreciated by local mestizos, too, who called it "jungle popcorn." A physician in Tarapoto told me that once or twice a year he treated overenthusiastic gourmands who suffered fecal impactions after eating too many of the ants, whose hard exoskeletons were difficult to excrete.

A favorite delicacy—the Awajún equivalent of caviar—was a two-inch-long, tan-colored grub collected from the trunks of rotting palm trees. Served raw and wiggling or cooked and thoroughly dead, grubs were consumed with an avidness I never came to share. In *Tristes Tropiques,* Claude Lévi-Strauss's classic account of his travels in Brazil in the 1930s, similar grubs are described as having "the smoothness and the consistency of butter and the flavor of coconut-milk." He neglects to mention the grub's crunchy head.[15]

The Awajún had their own culinary limits, as I learned after serving pieces of canned Dutch cheese to a group of women and children who stopped at my house for a social call. Almost simultaneously, every bit of the precious cheese was spit onto the floor by my guests, whose expressions suggested that they thought themselves the victims of a disgusting practical joke.

Much of the morning was spent cutting and burning dried maize stalks. Eladio, Kíjik, and the other men worked in a desultory way. Agricultural work clearly was not something embraced with gusto. Their talk was mostly about hunting. At one point Eladio gazed intently at the edge of the field. "Peccary!" he said. "They want to eat the maize but are scared by the smoke." When asked where he saw the wild pigs, he said matter-of-factly, "I don't see them. I smell them."

In this part of Peru the period from January to April is the rainy season, which makes hunting difficult. Meatless days promoted endless talk about game. Because of the difficulty of hunting in wet weather, men fell back on a risky hunting technique: a length of iron pipe with a spring-loaded hammer set to fire a shotgun cartridge when released by a trip wire. These were usually set up a few inches above the ground on an animal trail, often on the edge of a garden, in the hope of bagging an armadillo, peccary, or paca, the last a tropical rodent that often weighs fifteen pounds or more. A distracted walker might fail to notice one of these sinister devices, and cases of accidental shootings were not unknown. It was a good idea to keep one's eye on the path when walking near gardens.

Another way to break the tedium of the rainy season was to organize a fishing expedition, which usually turned into a festive outing. Fishing was done in small streams relatively close to the village or in temporary lakes created when the Río Mayo flooded, then retreated, leaving countless fish imprisoned in forest pools. Although it may be hard to reconcile with today's image of Amazonian Indians as pious protectors of rainforest wildlife, the people of Huascayacu preferred to fish with poison, especially if they couldn't winkle a stick or two of dynamite out of a mestizo colonist in Atumplaya. The fish poison of choice was a tall herb in the aster family called *wasú*, commonly cultivated in house gardens.[16]

Eladio and several of his sons and sons-in-law prepared for a fish-poisoning expedition by piling stacks of wasú that had been cut down with machetes. They then stripped the plants of their leaves, mashed them to a green pulp, wrapped the mash in banana leaves, and loaded it into baskets. Five households of men, women, and children walked a half hour to a stretch of stream with the right qualities. Several boys walked to midstream and dipped the baskets of poisonous mash into the water. Wide fingers of green worked their way downstream through the turbid stream's café au lait. The rest of us waited below holding machetes, nets, fishing spears, and small baskets. Like other fish poisons used in Amazonia, wasú stuns fish when they take it in through their gills. Within a minute, small fish splashed to the surface, their gills flapping spasmodically. Adults and children scrambled through the creek, netting the fish that appeared around them. The few large fish were smacked with machetes or bitten behind the neck to prevent them from escaping. Fish continued to rise for about a half hour, after which we gathered our baskets to walk home. The adventure netted about eight pounds of fish, the largest of which were perhaps ten inches long and the smallest still aspiring to minnowhood. Eating them was an exercise in oral mortification: countless spines, scanty flesh. But they offered dietary novelty at a time of year when meals were mostly limited to manioc, green plantains, and sweet potatoes.

The scarcity of game also led men to kill animals that at other times of year they might ignore. A curious feature of Awajún food preferences was that two of the largest rainforest mammals, the deer and the tapir, were customarily considered taboo. Deer were said to be one of the forms taken by human souls after death. The objection to tapir remained vague, however. These taboos were losing force as access to game-rich territory declined.

One day, my next-door neighbor Kayáp returned from the forest to report that he had killed a tapir at a place an hour away. The animal was far too heavy for him to carry without help, so he had left it where it fell and returned to the village. The next morning, I accompanied Kayáp, his wife, Marleni, Kayáp's brother Tiwijám, and three boys to the kill site. On the way, we experienced the full spectrum of the rainforest's powerful odors, from the smell of rank vegetation in wet places to the pungent, cinnamonlike aroma given off by certain trees.

When we reached the dead tapir, everyone examined it with interest. With a sharp blade, Kayáp carefully punctured the animal's abdomen. There was a sudden rush of gas, and parts of the animal's digestive system ballooned out. The effect was unsettling, and even Kayáp, whose approach to butchering was businesslike, looked momentarily queasy. He and one of the boys cut the hide above the animal's hooves, then sliced up and along the limbs. The hide was peeled back and used as a ground cover to protect the meat from dirt. When Kayáp finally began to remove the entrails, the stink was overpowering. By this time, the entire butchering site was alive with insects. Biting flies, mosquitoes, and sweat bees swarmed over everyone. Marleni built a smoky fire to discourage the insects, but it did little good. Periodically Kayáp's hunting dogs fought among themselves, deranged by the insects and the smell of blood. Kayáp carefully divided the meat into manageable portions, bundled them in palm leaves, and loaded the packets into carrying baskets. Left behind were the hide, the long bones, and all internal organs except heart, lungs, kidneys, and liver.

The arrival of such a quantity of meat was an occasion for dinner invitations to go out from the hunter to other households. The atmosphere was often jovial, especially after a meatless spell. But tapir aroused little enthusiasm. Kayáp invited me to eat the next day, and we were joined by a young man from an outlying household. He politely declined the tapir meat, opting instead for a paltry portion of fish, which prompted a debate about whether the traditional taboo made sense. Kayáp argued that the taboo was misguided, that only deer should be treated as inedible. The visitor stubbornly insisted that traditions were traditions and that in any case he didn't like tapir meat. In the end, Kayáp sold much of the smoked meat to mestizo colonists in violation of a widely flouted law that prohibited traffic in game meat.

All-day rain was favorable for interviewing because it inclined people to sociability. Men stayed at home to make baskets or repair tools, and they were usually willing to chat. If there were ample supplies of beer in the house, invitations went out to other households. My tape recorder became a source of entertainment on these occasions, to the peril of my limited supply of batteries. But I succeeded in recording stories, songs, and instrumental music, which in turn prompted discussions about everything from romance to sorcery.

A friend in Lima had given me old copies of *National Geographic* that I hoped to use as a tool for prompting discussion that would improve my conversation skills. The results were unexpected. When shown pictures of European people in urban settings, the schoolchildren and postadolescent men who were my main conversation partners inevitably asked me their names. The prospect of moving through a world of strangers was still something they struggled to comprehend. A magnified, full-page photo of a mosquito prompted cries of wonder and dismay as my hosts leapt to the conclusion that in my country biting insects grew as big as songbirds.

The most talked-about pictures from *National Geographic* had been taken among another Amazonian people living in Brazil's Xingú region. In common with many indigenous groups of the lower Amazon, men and women of this tribe customarily wore only penis sheaths or G-strings. The Awajún are prudish by comparison: although little boys might shun clothing until puberty, girls were dressed from infancy and as toddlers were sharply rebuked if they revealed their genitals when urinating or bathing. The concept of people living virtually naked scandalized all who examined the magazine, which soon included everyone in Huascayacu. For days afterward, clusters of adolescent boys would slink up to my door after dark and whisper conspiratorially in Awajún, "Brother, let's see the naked women!" I confess to amusement that *National Geographic,* a revered source of images of scantily dressed women for American males of a certain age, was now serving that same purpose in Peru's Upper Amazon. The conversations inspired by the revealing photographs improved my anatomical vocabulary in Awajún, but after a few weeks I tired of serving as village pornographer and concocted a story to account for the magazine's disappearance.

Moyobamba, capital of the Department of San Martín, was founded in 1540, making it one of the oldest colonial settlements in Peru. Its climate was springlike, its views of surrounding mountains enchanting, and its streets well paved and clean— largely, it must be said, because the town had been completely rebuilt after an earthquake leveled it in 1968. There was even electricity now and then. Every few weeks I hiked three hours from Huascayacu, crossed the Río Mayo, walked another hour to San Fernando, then waited for the first of a series of precariously loaded pickup trucks that took paying passengers to Rioja, where I had a post office box. From Rioja it was another hour to Moyobamba. I usually stayed at a small hotel whose owner, Moisés López, a retired police sergeant, let me store a suitcase of clean clothes and personal effects in the back room.

Aside from his hotel business, Don Moisés trafficked in orchids. He had a small garden behind the hotel and took evident pleasure in talking about each plant in his collection. He was a compact, solidly built man with wavy hair and dark skin. He spoke with the lilting cadences of eastern Peru. Consistent with the universal stereotype of police sergeants, Don Moisés's thinking was rarely subtle, and he preferred to follow well-traveled paths in his interpretation of events. He clearly believed my study of Awajún culture to be a cover for something more practical—secret mineral prospecting, perhaps, or the pursuit of sexual conquests based on what he assumed to be the natural ascendancy of white men over native women. His view was shared by many other longtime residents of Moyobamba, who never tired of inquiring about how many blue-eyed "disciples" I had fathered in Huascayacu. Some were convinced that the Awajún carried me around on a litter like a latter-day Inca.

The more recently arrived Andean colonists shared some of these ideas but more often seemed lost in otherworldly dreams inspired by the region's proliferating evangelical sects. A colonist town whose name translates as Second Jerusalem, lying just off the main road to Rioja, was reputed to be organized around a group of "apostles" ruled by a pastor whose word was law. Life in Second Jerusalem was disrupted on several occasions by the intervention of Peruvian police sent to enforce the Ministry of Education's requirement that schools include soccer in their roster of playtime activities. The town's pastor considered games to be sinful and actively prevented government teachers from promoting the national sport.

Once I walked into a colonist settlement to find a group of men standing outside one of the village's cane shacks. They invited me inside to share a glass of aguardiente. Sitting where directed, I found that my bench stood only inches away from a wooden box in which a dead colonist was laid out. The corpse was dressed in a cassock of coarse blue cloth. On both feet were white socks with holes over each mud-encrusted big toe, perhaps for some ritual reason beyond my ken. Candles burned at each end of the coffin. No one said much about the dead man, whose name went unspoken. They mostly stared, stunned and glassy-eyed from the cane liquor, at the gringo who had just emerged from the jungle. The arrival of a truck full of Seventh-day Adventists provided me with an excuse to flee the drunken wake. The visitors, members of a choir from one of the region's towns, disembarked at the nearby chapel. The choir sang hymns vigorously, if not with great accuracy. In his sermon, a young pastor wearing an immaculate *guayabera* shirt reminded us that the world was destined to end soon and that Jesus would come with His angels to collect the saved. Amid the muck and squalor, apocalypse was not hard to conjure up.

Compared to life in colonist settlements, Huascayacu came to feel like paradise despite its endemic biting flies and the enervating boredom of most afternoons. The more I dealt with settlers, the more I worried that awareness of my presence might snowball into one of the heavily embroidered stories that circulated constantly in eastern Peru. It was not unusual to walk into a decrepit shop in Atumplaya and be regaled with reports of recent sightings of the *vaca huilca,* a supernatural cow that breathed fire, or the depredations of a giant feline called *caballo puma,* whose magical howling had the effect of putting entire villages to sleep so that the beast could feast at leisure on the brains of its human victims. Rumors about battalions of gringo engineers, said to helicopter into remote jungle locations for mysterious, sinister "projects," were equally common. Given the possibility that one such story might lead someone to denounce me to the authorities, I endeavored to leave Huascayacu rarely and keep a low profile on my trips to town.

Just when the boredom of those first months became unendurable, something unexpected would happen. One day Kayáp told me that visitors were expected from a community called Kaupán, located far to the north. His wife, Marleni, had already swept the floor, and extra stools were carried in from nearby houses. Eventually four strangers passed my house in single file, each carrying a shotgun. Their cheekbones were painted with red *achiote,* and one wore a corona of toucan feathers. The straps of small woven bags crossed their chests. Their arrival prompted shouting from the adults gathered in Kayáp's house: "It's you?" "Yes, it is I!" "You come?" "Yes, I come!" "Enter!" "I'm entering!" The peculiar call-and-response of Awajún greetings was elaborated and amplified far beyond anything I had previously witnessed. The visitors stood straight, their shoulders thrown back and firearms assertively displayed. After everyone moved into Kayáp's house, the four visitors sat next to each other on a bench. Within minutes, Kayáp, two of his brothers, and their brother-in-law settled on wooden stools positioned directly opposite the guests. Each visitor began shouting rhythmically. Speakers cupped a hand above their mouths or moved an arm out stiffly for emphasis. Conspicuous spitting punctuated long phrases. Each man's opposite number listened intently, sometimes responding with shouted interjections: "Yes!" "That's true!" Then the four men on the host side picked up the chant as the visitors fell silent. The noisy, dramatic back-and-forth continued for perhaps forty-five minutes, then slowed to more normal talk as women bustled about carrying bowls of beer.

This performance was a variation of *enémamu,* a greeting ritual documented by visitors to Jivaroan communities for more than a century. The Finnish ethnographer Rafael Karsten observed enémamu many times during his extensive travels among the Shuar and Awajún between 1919 and 1929. "The most curious thing in this greeting ceremony," Karsten writes, "is the tone in which the men speak and the way in which the whole conversation is carried on." He continues: "It is not the ordinary conversational tone; the Indian who is speaking for the moment *shouts* loudly. . . . During the conversation the host and the guest regard each other with stern looks just as if they were angry or excited, while they speak they hold the hand to

Four visitors from distant community, holding firearms, engage in formal speech with hosts in Huascayacu, 1977.

Photograph courtesy of Michael F. Brown.

the mouth, and after every fourth or fifth word they spit on the ground, sometimes to the right and sometimes to the left. A listener unacquainted with the customs of the Indians might believe that two madmen are conversing. It may be more to the point however to liken them to two lions, doing their best to arouse mutual respect."[17]

Karsten's account conveys the event's intensity, its odd inter-twining of the everyday and the novel to heighten experience. There is danger in visitors. Under the guise of sociability, they may be sizing up the village's vulnerability to attack, perhaps on behalf of some ally harboring an ancient grudge. One might be a hidden sorcerer, bent on finding new victims. More prosaically, the younger men among them might be prowling for attractive girls to seduce. Yet both visitors and hosts are drawn to the encounter: for novelty, for the chance to renew family ties, and for news about alliances or feuds that could affect their well-being. The enémamu gives senior men, Karsten's "lions," a way to show their power. They present themselves as formidable, prepared for combat, unafraid of consequences. Missing from Karsten's description are the treble notes sounded on the edges of the men's bombastic fugue. Clusters of adolescent girls, some with their arms around each other, taking in the performance, whispering and giggling. Boys doing the same but also attentive to a speaking style they would have to master soon enough. Married women moving briskly to keep men supplied with beer, whose quality and quantity measured their value as wives. And the anthropologist, promoted to the status of nonpresence amid so much excitement, at last able to document something important.

The Huascayacu resident who embodied the traditional male virtues displayed in enémamu was Arturo. Arturo, a name that when spoken in Awajún sounded something like "Ásturu," was Eladio's nephew. In his late thirties, Arturo wore his hair long in the traditional style and carried himself with a studied formality already becoming anachronistic among his people. He seemed such an imposing figure that I'm now struck with wonder when I look at photographs of him. They show a serious, solid-looking man whose short stature contrasts with the outsized impression that he managed to project. He inherited some of his toughness from his widowed mother, Inchít, the oldest person in the village. Barely five feet tall, Inchít was creased like a piece of ancient leather and just as tough. I often saw her muscling enormous bundles of firewood or baskets of manioc tubers down one of the village paths.

Arturo's house, which he shared with two wives, a half dozen children, and a son-in-law, was some distance from the school, and he was rarely seen in the center of the village. At first I assumed he was standoffish. But his reserve went deeper, to a growing rift in the community whose full dimensions only became clear after several months. One day as Tomás and I walked to Arturo's house to pay a social visit, Tomás abruptly declared that Eladio, the ápu, and some of his close kin were ruthless killers despite their friendly demeanor. Eladio had murdered in the past, he said, and had moved to Huascayacu to flee the police after one such killing. Eladio and his sons wished others ill—here Tomás spoke in hushed tones—and there was reason to fear that sorcery was behind much of the sickness that afflicted people in the village. One of Arturo's wives suffered from persistent stomach pains. Arturo had already consulted a shaman in another Awajún community, and although Tomás was close-mouthed about the diagnosis, it was not hard to infer that the shaman had fingered someone in Huascayacu as a hidden sorcerer. I had not yet witnessed shamans at work, but it was well known that they were pressured by relatives of the patient to identify the source of illness brought about by sorcery. Arturo had confided to Tomás that he planned to move his family elsewhere.

Tomás called a village meeting the next day. He reminded parents that it was again time to register children for school and to purchase the notebooks and pencils they would need in the coming semester. He lectured them on the importance of agricultural work, which was preferable, he said, to selling game meat to colonists. Finally, he announced his intention to seek a transfer to another community immediately. This sparked an explosive response from Eladio and several other men and women, who began shouting in protest. "We don't want another teacher," they said. In a loud voice, Eladio threatened to burn down the school if Tomás left. "We'll go back to living the way we did before," he said. As the discussion became more heated, Arturo stood and announced that he was leaving Huascayacu because it was a "place of sickness." The unstated implication was that a sorcerer hidden somewhere in the community was threatening the lives of Arturo's family members. The meeting ended with mutual recriminations that I was largely unable to follow because of my still limited command of the language.

That night I was awakened by roosters calling to a false dawn just past midnight. There were clear skies under a full moon, a rare event in those parts. The moonlight cast icy shadows in the house. Lying under my mosquito net, I pondered the animosity and fear simmering beneath the surface of life in Huascayacu. Death was a remorseless enemy here: one out of three infants failed to survive to age five, and many older children and adults were lost to dysentery or snakebite, suicide or murder. Why they would want to compound this heartache by accusing their closest relatives of sorcery was a mystery for which my training had failed to prepare me.

I combed the shortwave bands for news or music, anything to take my mind off this troubling puzzle. A German station was deep into jazz: John Coltrane's "A Love Supreme." Even the static from distant equatorial lightning couldn't mask the power of Coltrane's tenor as it pushed ever higher, propelled by the rhythm section, the massive, blocky chords of McCoy Tyner's piano, and Coltrane's own spiritual hunger. It was music from another world, one infinitely far from the scene of my troubled sleep.

3

Puzzle Pieces

The period from January to April is usually the wettest time of the year in the Alto Mayo, and so it was in 1977. The rains, whose approaching roar could be heard through the forest long before arrival, lingered for days at a stretch. Women used short dry spells to provision their families with plantains and root crops. They returned from their gardens bent double under heavy baskets of tubers, often with a machete in one hand and the other wrapped around a sleeping baby tucked, chrysalislike, into a cotton sling. Men mostly stayed home to work on household tasks. They wove baskets, repaired tools and hunting gear, and, when weather permitted, gathered materials for Huascayacu's new schoolhouse.

With hunting and garden clearing made impractical by the weather, manioc beer flowed liberally. One drinking party was organized by Tíwi, a cheerful, solid-looking middle-aged man who had invited the men of the village to help clear a garden plot. The impressive quantity of beer prepared by Tíwi's wives, Chapáik and Tekuána, had been the talk of Huascayacu for

A woman strains manioc beer prior to serving it to guests, Bajo
   Naranjillo, 1977.

Photograph courtesy of Michael F. Brown.

days. Work was rained out by early afternoon, and people ambled over to Tíwi's to see whether the beer was as abundant as rumored.

Most of the village men were seated on palm-wood benches that ranged along the walls of the house. Women and girls hovered around the beer pots, some sitting on light balsa-wood stools. Chapáik, Tekuána, and one of their daughters moved from guest to guest with constantly replenished bowls of beer. A few of the younger men had their arms around one another, and the mood was jovial. I was not an experienced connoisseur of *nijamánch*, as the Awajún call manioc beer, but it was impossible not to notice that some women's beer was sweeter and smoother than others. Was it the manioc from which it was made? The yeast culture in a woman's pots? The characteristics of her saliva? A mystery. Chapáik's beer was among the best in Huascayacu: foamy and smooth, with a tart aftertaste.

Tíwi was in a talkative frame of mind. He said that he had come to the Alto Mayo as a boy from the community of Kaupán, several days' walk to the north. Orphaned while still young, he became the peon of a mestizo patrón with a coffee plantation upriver from Huascayacu. When the patrón sold out and moved to town, Tíwi allied himself with Eladio, eventually marrying Eladio's sister Chapáik and later Eladio's niece Tekuána. The co-wives, who lived in adjacent houses, got on well, which wasn't always the case with plural marriages. For Tíwi, having two wives was a mixed blessing. Their hard work allowed him to be especially generous on occasions such as this party, which enhanced his reputation. But he also had to build and maintain two houses and take care to treat Chapáik and Tekuána equally. It was a delicate balance that he managed with unusual deftness.

Alcohol is often thought of as a purely destructive force in the New World's native societies, many of which, for reasons still not well understood, failed to weave fermented drinks into the fabric of traditional life. The Awajún were one of the exceptions. They drank mildly fermented manioc beer daily and had developed informal rules about how to manage drinking so that alcohol-fueled conflict was less likely to erupt. Women, who made and served the beer, subtly regulated men's drinking by changing the size of their serving bowls in response to the prevailing atmosphere. Early in the party, women might offer drinkers enormous bowls that held a liter or more. When men became conspicuously drunk or the party took a turn from gaiety to conflict, the large bowls might be swapped out for progressively smaller ones, down to tiny bowls scarcely larger than a thimble. Drinkers grumbled but had little choice save to wait until the next round.

When men lectured their wives, sons, and daughters about the proper way to live, as they were prone to do at thunderous volume in the predawn hours when their captive audience was more interested in sleep, they urged young men to avoid fights at drinking parties by limiting the amount of beer they drank and keeping their distance from others known to be quarrelsome.[1]

Underlying Awajún drinking behavior was adherence to a strict code of personal autonomy. During my travels in the Andes, I found that reluctance to continue drinking past a certain point was interpreted as an insult by the host. The Awajún attitude was different. Polite guests were expected to partake of a bowl or two of beer out of respect for the host's generosity, but anything beyond that was a matter of personal preference. At some point during a drinking party it wasn't unusual to witness a man cheerfully taking leave of fellow drinkers by announcing, "I'm full. I'm going to sleep. Continue getting drunk!" The appropriate response was, "All right, I'll continue getting drunk!" At bottom, autonomy trumped sociability. When a male guest left for the night, he addressed his peers individually, pointing toward each as he walked past. He might similarly address senior women one by one, although it was just as likely that he would bid them farewell collectively.

Traditional wisdom helped to limit alcohol's disordering power, but it was no more foolproof in their society than in ours. Drunkenness accounted for many acts of spontaneous violence. The people of Huascayacu shared tales of fistfights, death threats, accusations of adultery, and even shootings that had erupted at drinking parties in the past. Against this must be weighed the socializing power of beer to hold together a society afflicted by powerful centrifugal forces. The verb *nampét,* "to get drunk," also means "to sing" and "to dance." Drinking, in other words, was bound up in some of the most joyful forms of Awajún self-expression and group sociability. On one sad occasion, Ágkuash, a wizened older man, offered to sell me his last feather corona and a stunning bandolier of bird bones and seeds because, he said, "We don't drink beer anymore." The village was then in the throes of one of its periodic flirtations with evangelical Christianity. So close was the association between drinking and dancing that abandonment of one made the other obsolete in people's minds.

What I remember most about those rainy-season drinking parties was their atmosphere of good humor. Some of this was directed at the resident alien, who served as the butt of countless beer-fueled pranks. When the need to relieve oneself arose during a party, it was customary to say to the host, "Brother, I'm going out to urinate." The ritual response was, *"Ayú* (all right), go ahead and urinate!" Once when I told my host that I was leaving for that purpose, he replied, "Ayú, go ahead and urinate squatting!" The insult escaped me because of my limited command of the language. When I failed to respond with the local equivalent of "Hell no," the assembled men roared with laughter, which continued until someone explained the affront to my masculinity in painful detail. Months later I was able to turn the tables on the jokester through a similar linguistic trick. Such are the small victories of fieldwork.

On another occasion I had the bright idea of asking Tíwi and several other men to tell me about Awajún sexual practices. This sparked stories of increasingly bizarre and anatomically improbable ways of coupling that had most of the men and many of the women laughing to the point of tears. In due course, I was asked to reciprocate by demonstrating how my people, the *kirínku aidau,* did the same thing. If I'd been a contortionist or yoga master I might have been able to top their flights of erotic fancy. As it was, they left convinced that we are as boring in our sex lives as my pedantic questions showed us to be with regard to the life of the mind.

A topic to which my questions returned often in those first months was kinship, a long-standing obsession of anthropologists and an aspect of culture that had the advantage of involving a restricted vocabulary. My starting point was the official village register, a copy of which had been left in Tomás's care. It wasn't an entirely reliable document, however. Birthdates were rough estimates, and some men had changed their names to shake off the taint of past murders. Nevertheless, the register offered a framework for figuring out who lived in Huascayacu and how they were related. From there I could verify people's kinship links and observe how they addressed one another. When complications arose, as they did almost immediately, anomalies had to be explained. As a graduate student I had been indifferent to the formal study of kinship, which had ascended to such heights of abstraction that it eventually reached escape velocity and vanished into space, having threatened to turn anthropology into an obscure branch of mathematics. But the Awajún talked about kinship constantly. Like the rainforest itself, it anchored their daily lives.

The underlying architecture of Awajún families proved to be a method of classifying kin known as Dravidian. Named after a pattern found in parts of South Asia, Dravidian systems are common throughout the world. They divide the universe of people into two fundamental types: kin (or blood kin, as we often say) and affines, with the latter being potential marriage partners and in-laws. On the face of it, that doesn't sound much different from the way Anglo-Americans think about kinship: there are family members, among whom marriage is either forbidden or, if they lie beyond first-cousin range, allowed but discouraged; and there is everyone else, defined as fair game for sex and marriage. The main difference is that in Dravidian systems suitable marriage partners may be as close as first cousins. But these must be cousins of a particular kind: cross cousins, children of anyone your father considered to be a "sister" or your mother a "brother." These are distinct from parallel cousins, children of people your father classified as "brother" or your mother reckoned to be a "sister."

Within this system, siblings and parallel cousins are addressed by the same terms, reflecting their social equivalence. As with true siblings, parallel cousins are theoretically off-limits for sex and marriage regardless of genealogical distance. In contrast, cross cousins are classified by terms that can be translated as "brother-in-law," "sister-in-law," and "cross cousin of opposite sex." In some situations opposite-sex cross cousins are simply defined as "unrelated persons."

It quickly became apparent that the classification of relatives didn't transfer directly to the way people addressed each other in daily life. During a beer-drinking episode in which the subject of kinship arose, one man slyly suggested that I address the girl serving us beer, who was all of eight or nine years old, as "cross cousin." When she brought the bowl of beer to me, I said, "Thank you, little cross cousin," as instructed. A look of revulsion came over her face, and she blurted out, *"Wah! Chu!"* which in this context translates loosely as "Ugh, that's disgusting!" There were guffaws of amusement from the men. My host then dutifully explained that when a man addresses a woman by the term "cross cousin," he is being flirtatious or provocative. A dignified visitor, he said, addresses such women as "sister" in public even though everyone recognizes this as a polite fiction. Women reciprocate in kind.

Other complications arose because Awajún genealogies twisted themselves into knots via plural marriages, frequent divorce, and the remarriage of widows. For instance, if an elderly man left behind a much younger second wife when he died, she might well marry her stepson, thus skewing generations. This meant that a child could be the classificatory "mother" or "father" of a much older relative. Given the clash between kinship terms and the speakers' relative ages, they might opt for reciprocal use of "sister" or "brother" as a more natural way to address one another.

Two key features of Awajún family life began to emerge as the days rolled by. The first was that families were inherently fluid, lacking the stability found in clan systems documented elsewhere in Amazonia and in other parts of the world. The core households of Huascayacu were those of Eladio, his brothers, and their sons. This turned out to be a fluke, however. It later became clear that in other communities the gravitational pull between senior men and their sons-in-law was as great, or greater, than between men and their married sons. Second, the system of cross-cousin marriage was vulnerable to disruption if anyone violated the rules by marrying a parallel cousin or some other category of prohibited kin. Think about it: if a woman marries her parallel cousin, the couple's children are left with blurred family lines that make it difficult to determine whom they can legitimately marry when it's their turn. The only solution is what anthropologists primly call "genealogical revision." In plain talk, that means lying about one's genealogy. In time, the real link fades from memory.

Genealogical questions turned up several Huascayacu unions out of step with the rules. Chapáik, Tíwi's older wife, was the daughter of his paternal grandfather's brother. Technically, then, she was his classificatory "mother" and therefore unmarriageable. Perhaps the cross-sex link—she was his uncle's sister—took some of the edge off the impropriety. Even Eladio and Manúgka, the village's ranking couple, turned out to have an improper parallel cousin marriage well hidden by genealogical flimflam. Months later, while visiting another community, I asked a distant relative of Manúgka's about this. He said that there had been a fuss when she and Eladio eloped decades earlier. But the marriage had proven durable, and after a while people simply stopped caring about the union's irregularity. As my knowledge of local genealogies grew, it looked as if roughly a fifth of marriages violated the letter of the cross-cousin marriage rule. An irony of all this rule breaking was that muddy genealogical lines made it easier for violators to find a defensible genealogical link to their marriage partner.[2]

Villagers were unwilling to turn a blind eye to more serious cases of incest. A senior man who lived in a rugged mountainous area two days' walk from any other household was said to have a long-standing sexual relationship with a daughter, whom he treated as one of his wives. Although no one intervened to stop him, his isolation reflected the disdain in which he was collectively held. Once or twice I even heard people use his name as a code word for incestuous sex.

When I asked Tomás, Tíwi, Eladio, and other men how marriages were arranged, they presented a rosy vision of how things worked, one that emphasized prudent negotiation. In some cases two men decide that their young children should marry eventually. The groom is increasingly integrated into his future bride's household until the couple is old enough for the marriage to be consummated. An older man seeking a bride should approach a woman's father, who is often his uncle, with a proposal of marriage. If the father approves, the man joins the household as a resident son-in-law unless he already has another unrelated wife. The new husband is on trial: if he drinks excessively or shows himself to be lazy and inattentive to the demands of his wife's parents, they may end the marriage and send him away. A powerful incentive for good behavior is the prospect that a man's father-in-law will eventually allow him to marry a younger daughter as well, thus forming the most common type of plural marriage.

Where did the desires of women stand in this high-stakes marital politicking? That seemed murky in the accounts of Eladio and other men. Traditional marriages were arranged for girls of nine or ten, and they might be only in their early teens when they became proper wives. Their immaturity left them with little power to voice strong opinions about marriage partners. By the time they were sixteen or seventeen, most were mothers caring for a child or two and providing garden foods for a growing family. Mature women, especially divorcées and widows, were more likely to have a say in second marriages, although widows had to navigate around the tradition of levirate, the expectation that they marry one of their dead husband's brothers or perhaps a stepson of appropriate age.

The currents of gossip and marital crisis that eddied through Huascayacu offered a picture of domestic life far stormier than the idealized version offered in interviews. Even a few months in the village stocked my notebook with tales of amorous turmoil that ran from the tawdry to the Shakespearean. At the shabby end of the spectrum was the ambiguous relationship between Tomás and Eladio's daughter Isabel. There were also multiple scandals surrounding the affairs of a handsome womanizer named Rubén, currently divorced from Tíwi's teenage daughter Atalina and married to one of Arturo's daughters, Ojelia. One day Tíwi called a village meeting in response to Atalina's advanced pregnancy. She insisted that Rubén had fathered the child after the formal breakup of their marriage. Tíwi demanded that Rubén support the soon-to-be-born infant and take Atalina back as a wife. Defending himself vigorously, Rubén admitted that he had slept with Atalina a few times since their separation but insisted that she was known to have had sex with other men, whom he identified by name. In the absence of convincing denials of Rubén's accusation, the status of their marriage remained uncertain.

The tragic extreme was embodied in a series of events that had taken place two years earlier. Oscar, a young man in his early twenties, seduced the young daughter of his wife, a widow whom he had married several years before. Marriage or sexual relations with a stepdaughter were unseemly but not completely off the map of traditional practices. When his wife learned of the relationship, however, she was unhinged by rage and a desire to punish him. She convinced her daughter to join her in a suicide pact. Together they drank a potent plant poison called *tsúim* and died within hours. Theirs was one of a half dozen recent suicides in Huascayacu, most linked to marital strife.

Around the edges of this turbulence were a handful of liaisons between Awajún and settlers. These were, if anything, even more unstable than their village counterparts because of the cultural and linguistic gap between partners. Some of these relationships, especially ones that predated the titling of Awajún communities, clearly represented the sexual exploitation of Awajún women by more powerful mestizo *patróns*. The few cross-ethnic marriages dating to the late 1970s were harder to classify. I chatted on many occasions with a settler named Ángel who had taken up with María, daughter of a couple who abandoned Huascayacu shortly before I arrived. Ángel, who had the fair hair and light eyes that one sometimes saw among Andean colonists from Cajamarca, seemed out of place among the Awajún, whose language left him staring blankly into space. Perhaps loneliness explained his effusive manner whenever our paths crossed.

Sitting in his house one day while María was off in the garden, he told me that he had actively sought an Awajún wife through a trading relationship with María's father, Utiját. Once when María and a younger sister met him on the trail to guide him to their house, he told María that he was in love with her and wanted to marry. She demurred, Ángel said, because another woman in the village had been deserted by a mestizo husband. Utiját received him warmly, and Ángel curried favor by giving gifts, including ammunition. Left alone in the house with María the next day, he tried to seduce her. Ángel's own account puts his advances in the neighborhood of rape. Some would judge that he crossed the line. María resisted, he said, until he convinced her that his love was sincere. That night they trysted outside the house until their absence was noticed. María's mother was outraged, but Utiját, normally a man of strong opinions, kept to the sidelines. Ángel and María later eloped to the nearby mestizo hamlet of Soritor. After a few weeks the ensuing furor burned out, and they returned to live near María's parents.

It would be tempting to see Ángel's marriage as motivated by a desire to gain access to Awajún land, at the time more plentiful than the modest plots available to settlers. Yet he lacked the cunning that such a plan implied, and there was little evidence that he had garnered influence in the community or

Formal portrait of Kayáp Jiukám, Huascayacu, with his children looking on, 1977.

Photograph courtesy of Michael F. Brown.

found a way to exploit his in-laws. He was more like a rudderless ship drifting aimlessly away from his family's depleted farm in the Andes. What María's family saw in him was unclear. He had no skill as a hunter, and his familiarity with the forest and its resources was modest at best. Perhaps María's father imagined the union as a useful link to the still-mysterious economic power of Peruvian society.

Sexual conquests crossed ethnic boundaries in both directions. Awajún men sometimes boasted of their *japa ampuya,* "little deer" or hidden lovers, in nearby towns. My neighbor Kayáp, Eladio and Manúgka's youngest son, once regaled me with stories of his conquests among the *señoritas* of Moyobamba. "While walking down the street one day," he said, "a girl called to me, saying that she wanted to talk. She agreed to meet in another place, maybe because she was trying to avoid her relatives. We had a soda and chatted for a while. Then we went into a garden and had sex." He gave her 250 soles (roughly the equivalent of US $3.00), although she hadn't asked for money. "We agreed that the next time I came to town I'd walk in front of her house as if I were just passing by. Then she'd make an excuse to leave and join me in a safe place." On the next visit, he bought her an inexpensive ring as a gift. He voiced regret that a shortage of cash prevented him from traveling to Moyobamba to renew the affair.

It was hard to tell whether Kayáp's story was true or just the local version of locker-room swagger. He was a gregarious, charismatic man who spoke more Spanish than most of his peers, so the tale seemed plausible. Similar claims by others were less convincing. Men occasionally alluded to their mestiza girlfriends in public settings when their wives were present. This prompted sarcastic jeers from the women and good-natured ribbing from men. More notable than the content of the stories was the complete lack of deference to nonindigenous Peruvians and the readiness of Awajún men to think of themselves as immensely attractive to women from the supposedly dominant society.

When I asked Tomás about the apparently disordered state of marriage and sexuality in Huascayacu, he ridiculed the villagers as unrefined hillbillies. "This doesn't happen in the Alto Marañón, where I come from," he would say as we discussed the latest scandal over dinner in the relative privacy of his house. I found his claim unconvincing. Tomás had his own philandering to answer for, and regional gossip suggested that other Awajún schoolteachers, most of whom came from distant Marañón communities as bachelors or with wives left behind at a safe distance, soon established new marriages in the villages where they lived and taught.

One factor that affected marital dynamics was the recent move to compact settlements, a pattern that replaced centuries of life in widely separated households. Isolated Awajún households were virtual statelets ruled by petty lords. As the Jesuit father José María Guallart wrote in 1956, male household heads are "true kings, although not despotically so, in their own homes." Despots or not, oral histories attest that men dispensed harsh justice, up to and including the killing of an adulterous wife.[3]

Village life eroded this power. Most houses were located within easy walking distance of one another. Primary schools became a magnet for young men and, to a lesser extent, girls and young women from outlying households. Taking up residence with relatives near the school, they had more opportunities to be drawn into romantic entanglements without their parents' knowledge. Trouble lurked in the schoolhouse and in every quiet corner of the village. As the saying goes, familiarity breeds attempt. The same was true for their parents. As I learned from Kayáp, the accessibility of other houses had turned adulterous "night crawling" into an exciting hobby.

Villagers were aware of the problems of life at close quarters. These extended beyond the romantic sphere to include conflicts over domestic animals—say, when a woman's chicken house was raided by a neighbor's dogs—and dissatisfaction with the dirtiness of clustered settlements, no small matter given the absence of plumbing or latrines. Every community had a few holdouts who built houses far from the village center because of what they described as the hubbub and aggravation of living in daily contact with others. This, in turn, spawned resentment because men living hours from the village were more likely to neglect collective labor required for school construction and other village projects.

During these months I made several excursions to town for mail and emotional refuge. The lack of privacy was wearing to someone accustomed to indoor solitude; in Huascayacu my life was constantly on display. The trips were also quests for kerosene, which had become scarce throughout the region. Heavy rains washed out the highway to the Pacific coast. No roads meant no fuel. Without kerosene it was impossible to read or write during the long equatorial nights, for candles were expensive and nearly as scarce. The shortage was sufficiently acute that airline passengers sometimes included liter jugs of kerosene in their hand luggage during regional flights, a violation of safety principles so brazen that it seems hallucinatory today.

Passing through Atumplaya on these trips, I sometimes stopped to chat with Pancho Vela, a grizzled, sinewy old man who ran one of the hamlet's shops, really just a shack stocked with a few bars of whey-colored laundry soap, dusty cans of sardines, and crates of warm soda. The only beverage option other than aguardiente was Inca Cola, a cloying drink whose electric yellow color invited comparisons to radioactive urine, especially when unrefrigerated. As I downed one of these after a hot walk through the forest, Don Pancho reminisced about his time as a patrón for whom Eladio and other Awajún worked beginning in the late 1940s.

First contact with the Awajún was made by a man who mined salt deposits at a place called Cachiyacu (literally "salt water" or "salt river"). One day he noticed strange footprints in the sand. Thinking that these had been left by "wild" Indians, he set out presents such as mirrors and strings of beads. The gifts vanished. Days later, four Awajún men emerged from the forest. After more gifts changed hands, they began to work for him as peons. Don Pancho's experience was similar. "I was working alone at Cachiyacu and a group of men appeared: Nikitai, Wisú, Domingo, Samarendo, Samajái, and Tagkámash. They said over and over again, *'Mina patrón, mina patrón'* [my patrón], and I agreed. I brought them mosquito nets and shirts, and they brought me meat and mahogany," he said. "And they worked the salt deposits for me. They wore kilts back then and carried palm-wood spears."

Men from other Alto Mayo communities later explained that they pushed south into Cachiyacu fleeing vengeance attacks on the Río Potro. Their numbers were insufficient to defend themselves, so they had little choice but to escape their enemies by settling in remote territory that their fathers and grandfathers had visited only on hunting trips. Eventually they found themselves in need of steel axes and machetes, which is why they decided to make contact with would-be patróns.

Don Pancho insisted that his dealings with the Awajún were fair. They brought him lumber, jaguar and ocelot pelts, meat, natural rubber, and labor. He reciprocated with cloth, steel tools, seed beads, and ammunition for their shotguns and aging Winchester repeaters. From a trading partner in San José de Sisa, a village to the south, he secured a supply of much-coveted *ampi*, curare dart poison, for their blowguns, the last remnants of which were still being used by men in Huascayacu.

The accounts of Eladio and others who worked with Pancho Vela backed up this benign portrait of their relationship. In fact, older men and women talked about the era as if it were a golden age of affluence. Manúgka, Eladio's wife, once showed me the heavy strings of *chaquira*, seed beads, that Eladio had obtained years before when working for Don Pancho. Chaquira (*shauk* in Awajún) is apparently a corruption of "Checo" (Czech), reflecting the source of the most coveted glass beads. By the 1970s they were nearly unobtainable, and Manúgka's treasure trove was the envy of younger women. They hounded me to bring them beads from Lima and were jubilant when I eventually did. My own emotions were mixed. Doling out packets of

Manúgka Tsapík and daughter sewing, Huascayacu, 1977.
Photograph courtesy of Michael F. Brown.

beads to the natives didn't seem consistent with cutting-edge anthropology, even if beads were what they wanted more than anything else.

Don Pancho recalled that his Awajún charges sometimes got into nasty scrapes. "Eladio was blamed for the murder of Samakásh in Yanayacu. Two other men, Andrés and Nino, were also involved. They're dead now. Tagkámash and others showed up in Atumplaya with carbines and began shooting at Eladio, who escaped with his life. He moved his family to the Río Huascayacu headwaters until things settled down."

Now and then Don Pancho, accompanied by a grandson and a pack of hunting dogs, would come calling in Huascayacu. Slowed by arthritis, he no longer took extended treks in the jungle but relished the chance to share some manioc beer with

Eladio. Villagers humored him as best they could when he tossed out questions in Quechua, which he insisted was their authentic language.

If Don Pancho was an example of the generous patrón, his late cousin Estenio Vela embodied the cruel, greedy one. Pancho alleged that Estenio Vela traded goods to the Awajún at extortionate markups, took an Awajún "wife" by force, and attempted to run Pancho out of the region by spreading rumors that he used Awajún to satisfy a hunger for sex with men. Given the values of the time and place, accusing one's cousin of homosexuality was an unpardonable sin. "When he was dying of a stroke," Don Pancho told me with a pitiless look in his eyes, "Estenio wanted me to pardon him. But I wouldn't. 'Let the Lord punish his mouth for saying those things,' I said. And He did. Estenio was unable to speak, and he died mute."

In the early 1970s Estenio Vela attempted to use his influence with local officials to block titling of Awajún lands and the founding of bilingual schools. An Awajún teacher was jailed for two months on trumped-up charges; another was questioned by the police but ultimately released for lack of plausible evidence of a crime. Once the Alto Mayo Awajún had legal titles, they no longer had to put up with Vela's abuses. The era of brutal patronage came to an end, to be replaced by different and more subtle forms of servitude.

One morning I joined Kayáp and other men who were helping their uncle Kíjik weed a garden plot destined for a crop of peanuts. We started talking about personal names, in particular the local predilection for having two names, one Spanish and one Awajún. "Don't I need an Awajún name?" I asked. After reflecting a moment, Kíjik suggested that I call myself Dorénsu (Lorenzo) after the much-respected leader of another community. Kíjik mimed the way people spoke when Dorénsu paid one of his rare visits. "Dorénsu's coming! Dorénsu's coming!" he shouted. "Sit down, brother! Drink! Have something to eat!" Kayáp and other men jumped in, speaking loudly to the imaginary dignitary. But the idea of taking a name already in use nearby was unappealing. I countered with Máyak, the name of Kíjik's deceased grandfather. It had the advantage of being close to my real name, Michael. "Máyak it is, then," said Kíjik.

When we took a break from weeding to drink manioc beer, Kíjik told me to squat down. He snapped a small branch from a nearby tree, broke off a clean piece about four inches long, and rolled it over the top of my head and down my neck and back. "Now you are called Máyak," he said. Then he threw the stick into the bush. Kayáp said that it was a strong name and that I would now have to kill many animals. He had me practice shouting, *"Máyak wíitjai,"* "It is I, Máyak." I never lived up to Kayáp's expectations as a hunter, but the name stuck anyway.

The policies that helped the Awajún secure land titles were put in place by a leftist military junta that deposed Peru's president in 1968. The military government created an agency called SINAMOS to promote economic development and provide services to the poor. (SINAMOS was an acronym for National System of Assistance and Social Mobilization. The name was also a clever pun on *sin amos,* "without bosses.") SINAMOS employed young activists motivated by socialist ideals but often unschooled in the everyday realities of rural communities, especially indigenous ones. By 1977, the agency's influence was on the wane. Yet along with the police and the Ministry of Education it remained an arm of government with which the people of Huascayacu were in frequent contact.

One afternoon an Awajún employee of SINAMOS arrived in Huascayacu. Tomás called a village meeting. The government insisted that village leaders be democratically elected regardless of local tradition. Tomás explained that those present needed to elect an ápu, sub-ápu, secretary, and treasurer. For ápu, Tomás put forward two candidates, Eladio and his brother Katán, who lived some distance from the school and was seen in the village only occasionally. The vote, by show of hands, was seventeen votes for Eladio and two for Katán. Tíwi handily won the vote for sub-ápu. Given the low level of literacy among adults, the positions of secretary and treasurer were harder to fill. Marleni, Kayáp's wife, won the most votes for secretary. She had spent part of her youth as a ward of Pancho Vela in Atumplaya, so she could read, write, and speak some Spanish. Oscar, who had completed several years of primary school, bested Kayáp in the vote for treasurer. The meeting closed with adult members of the community adding their thumbprints or signatures to a document that made the results official.

A week later four government functionaries arrived and called for another assembly to witness notarization of the election results. Then one of the visitors explained, with a bilingual Awajún employee translating, that the Revolutionary Government of Peru had declared the Lima newspaper *El Comercio* the official publication of the nation's indigenous and peasant communities. Huascayacu was obliged to elect a representative to *El Comercio* in case the village needed to communicate with the press. "My native brothers and sisters," he said, "I can't emphasize strongly enough the transcendent nature of this post in the communications sector." Tíwi, who could not attend the meeting, was summarily voted out of his new job as sub-ápu and made Huascayacu's press secretary. As far as I knew, no one in the village other than Tomás had ever seen a copy of *El Comercio*, which was rarely available even in the region's towns.

Awkward encounters with the world of officialdom and *papí* (paper), occasionally flirting with the surreal, evoked both wonder and frustration among the Awajún. Some of the Awajún's core values—generosity, obligations to kin, respect for the autonomy of others (other men, at any rate)—collided with modernity's preoccupation with hierarchy and procedure. Government officials urged them to cease selling forest products, especially game meat, and instead contribute to the nation's progress by growing rice. Yet when Eladio and other men followed this advice and brought their rice harvest to town, they found themselves trapped in a Kafkaesque labyrinth of bureaucracy. Rice could be sold only to a government agency. Producers had to find out when the agency's office was open and then wait their turn for service. The price paid for a kilo of rice depended on an assay of moisture content and impurities that was impossible to verify independently. Farmers were paid by check, but to cash the check they had to find the correct bank and present their national identity document. None of the men from Huascayacu possessed this document. The solution: a special procedure involving an expensive trip to another town for additional paperwork. All this took days. The food and travel expenses ate into a farmer's profits.

"So difficult! So much paper!" Eladio said when I visited him in the Casa del Campesino, a spartan cinder-block building where he and a half dozen other men from Huascayacu camped for a week while they waited to be paid for their rice. They slept on the building's concrete floor and ate little more than boiled plantains. The men from Huascayacu, so poised in the forest, looked diminished on paved sidewalks.

Eladio was upbeat despite the difficulties. He told me about their urban adventures, which included an encounter with a woman who tried to pick up one of the young men, Pokochón. She turned out to be "bad," Eladio said, by which he seemed to mean mentally disturbed. Moyobamba was no metropolis—its population barely reached 15,000 then—but its human panorama was far richer than that of Huascayacu. There was no shortage of grifters, hustlers, and eccentrics.

The mysteries of money were a frequent topic of conversation. The traditional counting method used fingers and toes and therefore topped out at twenty. The expression for six literally meant "one hand done and one finger stuck on." Twelve was "both hands done and two (toes) stuck on." Spanish words for larger numbers were now in daily use. But in common with other powerful forms of paper, money retained a sense of mystery. The behavior of local merchants amplified it. They capriciously refused banknotes judged too faded or torn. This led savvy villagers such as Kayáp to tutor his kinsmen on how to pass tattered money by slipping it into a bundle of newer currency. Another peculiarity of the time was that coins were scarcely to be found in circulation. Inflation had eroded their monetary worth until it was lower than their metallic value. Millions of coins disappeared, illegally melted down for resale on the commodities market or turned into brass washers. For small transactions such as bus fares, Peruvians made change with pieces of candy. This was disconcerting for everyone, but it was especially baffling to Awajún coming to grips with the logic of monetary exchange.

More unsettling in moral terms was the lack of reciprocity that the Awajún encountered in town. On several occasions people in Huascayacu asked me, "How is it that when mestizos come here they expect us to feed them, but when we go to their place they make us pay for food?"

Five months after arrival in Huascayacu it had become apparent that my original plan to study the traffic in ideas about illness and healing across ethnic boundaries, formulated with a different indigenous group in mind, was going nowhere. The Alto

Mayo Awajún had been in regular contact with outsiders for only about twenty years. Their ability to communicate with their mestizo neighbors, many of whom were themselves new-comers to the region, was improving but still limited. Whatever medical exchanges took place went largely in one direction: from the region's shops and rustic pharmacies to indigenous bodies. Many Awajún families had glass and steel hypodermic kits that they used with appalling frequency. No sooner did a child come down with a sniffle than an anxious parent wanted to inject a dose of whatever drug was recommended by a para-medic or, more likely, by a barely literate shop owner hawking antibiotics many months past their expiration date.

The allure of Western pharmaceuticals made sense in light of their experience. Like other Amazonian peoples, the Awajún had endured wave after wave of Old World diseases—everything from measles to influenza—that produced high levels of mor-tality in so-called virgin-soil populations. Now well beyond the stage of acute vulnerability, their memory of past horrors per-sisted. Fear of epidemics made them willing to receive vaccina-tions when offered the chance. It also encouraged an exagger-ated faith in the healing power of injections. No matter that inadequately sterilized needles or unforeseen reactions to po-tent drugs sometimes killed rather than cured.

With my research plan now a shambles, there was no choice but to fall back on the principle of just showing up. This paid off in small epiphanies, disconnected and ambiguous, that hinted at understandings of the rainforest and its creatures that were more complex than was visible on the surface of daily life. One day, for instance, Tomás's son Elvin, a precocious eleven-year-old, casually mentioned that a few weeks earlier he had seen something called an *iwanch* near my house after dark. To make sure that I understood, he also used the Spanish word *diablo,* "devil," to identify the apparition. He described it as larger than a man and dark brown or black in color. It had slid back into the forest when Elvin came closer. "Íwanch look like dwarves from a distance," he said. "But when you get closer they change to giants so large that a man can run between their legs." He claimed to be unafraid of them. A week later he reported that his grandmother had heard an íwanch rattling the pots in their house in the middle of the night. Again, this encounter, such as it was, sparked no great concern.

When asked about íwanch, other people volunteered colorful stories of human encounters with them. But the íwanch's nature became more confused with every tale. They were hideous humanoids entirely covered with dark hair, yet they could present themselves as deer, owls, or metallic blue morpho butterflies. They were known to harass people outdoors at night, especially in the forest. A man named Héctor said that his brother-in-law on the Río Potro once had a fistfight with an íwanch and came away roughed up but alive. "There are male and female íwanch, and they have sex just like we do. Their children are born instantly, right after intercourse, so they have many of them," he said. Others insisted that íwanch were souls of the recently dead returning home to convince the living, especially the young or weak-minded, to join them. A further complication: the figure of the íwanch had been appropriated by American evangelical linguists to represent Satan in their translation of the New Testament. The land of the íwanch, wherever it was, had become mixed up with the Christian image of a place where sinners suffer eternal torment. This jumble of ideas about souls and sinister beings could be either evidence of cultural confusion or elements of a coherent system organized by a deeper logic.

Another window opened when I asked Kayáp to bring a recently killed collared peccary out of his house to be photographed in better light. He refused. When I failed to understand his explanation, his wife told me in Spanish that taking the peccary outside would "flip" Kayáp's luck and spoil the hunting dog he had used to kill it. This turned out to be one data point in an elaborate set of rules governing contacts between wild and domesticated animals. Similarly intricate customs led the parents of newborns to avoid contact with a range of forest animals and plants that possessed inherent powers to harm infants from afar.

Such shreds and patches were most likely all that I would have to work with. Up to that point I had encountered few native intellectuals, individuals whose temperament inclined them to be analytical about their society and its workings. Some of the bilingual teachers possessed this gift by virtue of their formal education and more cosmopolitan experience. But they were scattered in distant communities and only crossed my path now and then. In any case, many of them shared Tomás's dim view of the Alto Mayo Awajún. When I asked them to confirm information that I had collected in Huascayacu, they were inclined to "correct" it by presenting information from the Alto Marañón that they considered more palatable or authentic.

Also absent were dramatic, catharsis-inducing public rituals. In many Amazonian societies, complex rites involving bullroarers, sacred flutes, or masked dancers offer a distilled expression of a people's way of imagining their universe. They also crystallize underlying political currents and internal tensions. The Awajún I had met so far seemed uninterested in religious rituals of the public sort. There was little evidence that their ancestors cared much about them, either. The most elaborate rites documented for the Awajún and other Jivaroans were intended to harness the spiritual power of shrunken heads (tsántsa) taken from enemies in intertribal raids. But the preparation of tsántsa had long receded into the mists of history. Shrunken heads and their spiritual significance were about as relevant to the daily life of people in Huascayacu as the War of 1812 is to contemporary Americans.

The new rituals of evangelical worship were desultory, bare-bones affairs, at least as conducted in Huascayacu. People assembled in the schoolhouse, where they sat in rows behind tables fixed to the dirt floor. Haltingly, they sang American hymns with Awajún lyrics. They listened to Bible readings and a homily given by Tomás or one of the students who had fervently embraced Christianity. People seemed to find the services enjoyable, but they never provoked strong emotions apparent to an observer.

One category of ritual that did arouse keen interest was the healing performance of *iwishín* or shamans. These events were not public, strictly speaking, although a dozen or more people might attend them and everyone in a community knew when they were taking place. Huascayacu lacked a resident iwishín, so I would have to travel to other communities to witness them pursuing their craft. In light of the intense fear of sorcery in Huascayacu and presumably in other villages, healing sessions were the best candidate for a ritual that illuminated Awajún understandings of spirit and matter, sacred and profane, good and evil—assuming that these categories even mapped onto their way of seeing things.

My curiosity was also piqued by a handful of atypical songs recorded in my early days in Huascayacu. People called them *ánen* and were strangely guarded when talking about them. Unlike the social songs performed at drinking parties, which were all about joyous self-expression, ánen were said to change the world in concrete ways. They nourished the plants in a woman's garden. They made a hunter irresistible to game animals. They aroused passion in the heart of a loved one. When asked how ánen could produce these effects, people clammed up or changed the subject. The reactions suggested that I was entering a zone of secrecy and moral ambiguity. Everyone agreed that ánen were beautiful. Less clear was why they were dangerous.

My only choice was to continue seeking a framework that would bind these disparate stories and curious facts into a coherent pattern, assuming that one existed. The rains continued unabated, making travel to other communities difficult. The Río Mayo was in flood, so even getting to Atumplaya involved wading through knee-deep water for hundreds of yards. Mildew colonized my clothes and stood poised to annex my notebooks. A forgettable novel I was reading to pass the time quoted a line from Ralph Waldo Emerson, something about the world being "all opportunities, strings of tension waiting to be struck." Unless I began to make headway soon, rainforest fungi would turn those strings to compost.

4

Jesus versus the Warrior Spirits

Sorcery faded into the background for many weeks, overshadowed by attention to the rice fields and the demands of everyday life. As the rains diminished in May and June, hunting picked up. Men returned from the forest burdened with peccary, armadillo, game birds, and the occasional monkey. Huascayacu's passionless flirtation with Christianity continued, sustained by prayer meetings on Sunday mornings.

Two young men, Jaime and Samuel, led services when Tomás was away. They read Bible passages and taught the congregation songs from the Wycliffe Bible Translators' hymnal. They encouraged children to mime the lyrics by pointing to heaven or stamping their feet as they marched to Jesus. "I reject sin. It's bad, bad," a favorite hymn declared. "God's path is a good path, better, better. This path goes to heaven." The two earnest converts—youths awkwardly trying on adult gravitas for size—quizzed the adults to make sure they understood the sermon about sin and forgiveness. What the small congregation thought or felt during the services was hard to gauge. As much as anything, they seemed to be there because Christianity was modern, even if they never talked about it in those terms. "God, Apajuí, helps us to think better," people would say. There was a genuine feeling that something in their lives was changing, had to change. The destination of the change remained indistinct.

Then witchcraft elbowed its way to center stage again, this time in another community that bordered the Marginal Highway. News came first in trickles and then as a flood, each story adding lurid details.

A prominent senior man, head of a large household, collapsed and died suddenly. The symptoms described by witnesses suggested catastrophic stroke or cerebral aneurysm. For the surviving kin, the abrupt death of a vigorous, middle-aged man was no mystery: the cause had to be sorcery—spiritual murder. The only mystery was the identity of the perpetrator.

Relatives of the dead man prevailed upon a kinsman named Genaro, the Alto Mayo's most active shaman, to take *yáji*, the potent hallucinogenic brew used by healers throughout much of the western Amazon. They hoped that Genaro's shamanic vision would reveal the killer's face. It did. The secret sorcerer, Genaro said, was Pedro, a teenage visitor from the Río Potro area. Pedro's remote home community had no school, and he was living with relatives in the Alto Mayo to complete his primary education. Enraged by what they saw as an unforgivable betrayal of trust, several of the deceased man's kinsmen vowed to take Pedro's life.

Pedro's local kin hustled him onto a truck headed out of the region. Genaro and three other men got wind of the escape and set off in pursuit. In their own hired truck, the posse managed to overtake the vehicle in which Pedro was a passenger. Somehow they convinced Pedro's driver that the young man had to return with them so that a problem could be sorted out back in the village. Whether Pedro went with them willingly was never made clear. The pursuers took him into the forest not far from the highway, disemboweled him with knives until he bled to death, and buried his remains nearby.

The immediate dilemma for the teachers was whether the killing should be reported to the authorities. The region's police investigators were not known for nuance or a willingness to get under the skin of a case involving exotic understandings of guilt and innocence. It seemed likely that they would arrive in force and arrest the wrong people. If the body remained hidden, there might not even be a prosecutable case.

A teacher close to the case eventually sought my advice. Should he report the murder? Would I be willing to do it instead? His request potentially drew me into the matter. It was, on the face of it, a classical dilemma of fieldwork ethics. But to my way of thinking, the specific circumstances settled the ethical question. I had little relevant knowledge. I was privy only to hearsay several steps removed from events. And I shared the Awajún's skepticism about the ability of Peruvian police and courts to sort out the crime in a way that would be just. In the end, the police were never informed of the killing. Everyone awaited an eventual settling of accounts by other means.

Later, when I came to know the men involved and was forced to witness and, to a limited extent, share their fear of reprisal, the full human dimensions of the affair became hauntingly clear. But at that moment, distanced from it by twenty-five miles of rainforest, rice fields, and derisory roads, it felt abstract, like news of an earthquake on the other side of the planet.

Talk of witchcraft elsewhere revived similar fears in Huascay-acu. Soledad, a recently divorced mother whose parents had abandoned the village for other parts, said without hesitation that sorcery was the cause of their departure. The sorcerer in question was Tiwijám, one of Eladio's sons. Tiwijám, she said, was responsible for the illness of her mother, her uncle, and other members of the family. She revealed this while showing me her father's abandoned house. Beams of sunlight, slanting in through the palm-slat walls, illuminated the dusty air. Well-made baskets and fish traps still hung from the crossbeams. On the dirt floor stood beer pots and two handsome *chimpuí*, carved hardwood stools used only by men. The house also ware-housed rusted car parts, fragments of electrical equipment, a battered suitcase, and a dog-eared set of playing cards with pictures of naked women on the back. Soledad's eccentric father, Utiját, was known as a packrat. Why he had carried heavy car parts to a house miles from the nearest road was a mystery. Most likely he planned to salvage the metal for a quirky project of one sort or another.

In many societies, witchcraft accusations are commonly leveled at individuals who are socially marginal or deviant in some way. TiwiJám proved an unlikely target on those grounds. He was average almost to a fault. He lacked his brother Kayáp's good looks and ebullience but was just as hospitable. He got on well with his wife, Simira, and was a dutiful guardian to two children fathered by Simira's first husband, Tii, prior to the latter's murder nearly a decade earlier. He and Simira had lost their share of infants to unknown illnesses. He was neither richer nor poorer than anyone else in Huascayacu.

What made him the focus of suspicion was a healing session he had attended some years before. It was conducted by Genaro, the same healer implicated in the recent murder. While in his trance, Genaro, accompanied by two less experienced iwishín, inspected TiwiJám's body and found tiny, glowing *tséntsak* or sorcery darts. These darts can be used to kill or to heal. Genaro reported that TiwiJám's chest, neck, and mouth were full of darts. They were also visible from his shoulders to his elbows. Genaro sucked one out—a tiny colored ball that he called a killing bead—to confirm their presence. When the darts reached Tiwijám's fingertips, Genaro said, he would become a full-fledged killing sorcerer. His only hope was to begin the arduous process of domesticating this power through months of fasting, constant consumption of hallucinogens, and apprenticeship to a healer.

Villagers speculated about how Tiwijám had come to harbor these darts. Some people proposed that they had been planted there years ago without his knowledge, perhaps as he slept, by a witch named Chamikán, now dead. Others held that the source was a woman named Puwái, who prior to her suicide may have been given darts by her iwishín husband. Still others claimed that Tiwijám had actively sought them on his own. Whatever the original source, Tiwijám had been marked as a man with hidden killing power that he needed to discipline and bring into the light of public scrutiny. But he was unwilling. He hadn't the heart for it, he said. The path of the iwishín was too hard, too full of deprivation and danger.

Later Tiwijám went to another iwishín to see whether Genaro's judgment would be overturned. This iwishín told Tiwijám that he detected no darts but later informed others in secret that Tiwijám was a hidden sorcerer.

This legacy of suspicion erupted in bitter recriminations after Tíwi and one of his wives, Chapáik, took their gravely ill infant son to an iwishín named Táki in the community of Dorado and returned days later with the lifeless baby in their arms. A paramedic had earlier diagnosed the child's illness as anemia, but the medicine he prescribed did little good. Táki took yáji and, once his visions began to intensify, discerned that the real cause of the child's illness was sorcery. "Táki saw that the baby's stomach was filled with something black, like dark clay or pitch," Tíwi said to those gathered in his house. "This black clay is hard to cure. It makes the victim's stomach become bloated until it explodes." They fed the baby mashed gingerroot in water to make it vomit or defecate the substance revealed in Táki's vision. In the baby's feces the iwishín found small pieces of clay, bits of something that looked like rice husk, and fragments of the rough bark of a manioc tuber. This was sorcery, he confirmed. For those who crowded around him in Huascayacu, Tíwi unwrapped a small banana-leaf packet. Inside lay the incriminating evidence. To me it looked fresh, undigested. Tíwi also showed us a lock of the dead baby's hair.

While Tíwi spoke, Chapáik mourned in the odd, singsong keening voice that greeted death among the Awajún. Little children cried in the same distinctive style by the time they could walk. Chapáik would wail, clap her hands softly, and then suddenly break off to add detail to Tíwi's account in a normal speaking voice.

Complicating the drama was news that in a nearby house, Tíwi's daughter Hermina claimed to have taken poison because she was distraught over her half sibling's death. Hermina was a slip of a girl, perhaps fourteen. Sitting on a bench with Margarita, an aunt, she was surrounded by agemates and younger children who watched her with curiosity. Her eyes were red-rimmed and she was spitting frequently. Otherwise, she looked unaffected by whatever she had swallowed. Despite the apparent seriousness of the situation, there was a fair amount of laughing and joking. When Tíwi came to find out what was going on, he thought he saw green leafy matter on her teeth and gums— possibly the poison tsúim, although now Hermina denied having eaten any. Tomás said he was certain that Hermina would die because she had tried to kill herself before. She had swallowed laundry detergent with the improbable English name of Ace, which in Spanish and Awajún is pronounced with two syllables. That attempt had been provoked by an argument with her mother. She was saved that time, Tomás said, but surely she would die now.

There was no ipecac in my medical kit, but I had some mustard that when mixed with warm water might induce Hermina to vomit whatever she had swallowed. Returning with the mustard water, I met two teenage boys coming down the path, laughing and mocking Chapáik's weeping. The atmosphere was festive except in the house of the grieving parents.

Hermina first refused to drink the mustard water but finally agreed after being chided by her father. She swallowed a bowlful. Then she moved to a bed and began to pull her clothes and other small personal items out of a waterproof basket. Tomás pronounced this to be another sign of her imminent death: "She's looking at her possessions. She'll die soon." Hermina began to tear the better of her two dresses into shreds, to general laughter. Soon she was laughing, too, as she sat on a bed with other girls. She drank more mustard water and finally went outside to vomit, with others trailing behind to watch the spectacle. The two young men who had led the prayer service tried to convince her that God was offended by suicide and that she shouldn't try it again. She said that she had chewed part of a tsúim leaf but hadn't swallowed much. There were no signs of poisoning.

Back in his own house, Tíwi announced that there was too much witchcraft in Huascayacu and that he intended to move to another community as soon as he could plant a garden and build a house there. As he spoke, Tiwijám was spotted walking our way. There was soft tittering from those who considered Tiwijám the source of the witchcraft.

On Sunday, five days later, Eladio convened a village meeting. After a brief Christian service, Tomás spoke of the need to complete construction of the new school as soon as possible. It was also important, he said, for the men of the village to build a palm-wood jail that would be used to punish people who shirked communal work or offended community sensibilities. Discussion then shifted to the sorcery problem. Tíwi was leaving; Utiját, Wayách, and Arturo had already abandoned their houses and fields. If things carried on like this, Tomás said, eventually everyone would move away and the community would cease to exist. Referring to Tiwiján by implication but not by name, Tomás said, "Genaro saw a witch here while another iwishín, old Táki, could see nothing. How can this be if a curer sees the truth? The way to settle this is to bring a third iwishín to look at everyone in the village and find the witch." He proposed inviting a mestizo shaman from Rioja, the brother-in-law of an Awajún woman. "If the shaman finds a witch among the men, he'll be forced to leave. If it's a woman, she'll be punished. We'll cut her ear."

People began to argue about Tomás's proposal. Tiwiján, obviously fighting for his reputation and perhaps his life, was prominent in the exchanges. He defended himself vigorously, but his face was etched by worry. Tíwi, Katán, and others dredged up quarrels and unexplained deaths dating back a decade or more. I could understand the discussion only imperfectly because so many people were shouting at the same time. After an hour of accusations and rejoinders, everyone drifted away. Nothing had been settled.

This noisy discord might suggest that the village was always an unhappy place. But the conflict remained puzzlingly episodic. Once the ill feeling had been aired, it dissipated for a time. Tíwi was determined to join the exodus from Huascayacu, but his departure would take months to complete. There were crops for his wives to harvest in their present location, fields to clear and plant in the new one. There was the rhythm of the school year to contend with. After a good day's hunting, men still invited

Schoolboys learning to march, Huascayacu, 1977.
Photograph courtesy of Michael F. Brown.

other households to join them for plates of meat and boiled manioc. Beer parties—less frequent in the dry season than they had been during the rains—continued to be convivial affairs that drew in most members of the community.

At the six-month mark, I was joined in the field by Margaret Van Bolt, whom I had met in the graduate program of my university. A lanky, soft-spoken midwesterner, Margaret had effortlessly aced the department's most challenging courses. But she eventually tired of academic theorizing that struck her as pretentious and detached from real life. After completing a master's degree in anthropology, she left the program to develop her talent for scientific illustration, a skill in great demand at the university. She was also an accomplished photographer. As a couple, we had been through ups and downs. Her visit seemed like a way to clarify a relationship unlikely to survive two years of complete separation.

Margaret's abrupt immersion into the life of an indigenous village in the Upper Amazon must have been a profound shock, yet she adapted to its challenges with good humor, staying far longer than either of us expected. Unburdened by pressure to complete a degree, she was free to focus her attention on things that genuinely interested her. Over the following weeks and months she pieced together the genealogy of Alto Mayo families, eventually achieving knowledge of their family lines that surpassed their own. She made pots with women and learned how to make passable manioc beer. Once she got the hang of the language, she was able to talk to women about fertility, garden magic, and dealing with husbands, matters that were mostly off-limits to me. During her time in the Alto Mayo Margaret was the object of courtly treatment by men and unfailing kindness by their wives and daughters.

The arrival of my *compañera* was the talk of Huascayacu for days. It was rare for a man to live alone in Awajún society. Gender roles were rigid: men did not cook, make or serve beer, work in manioc gardens, or wash clothes when they could possibly avoid it. That meant that single men felt obliged to attach themselves to a household that included at least one adult woman. I had dealt with this by taking meals with Tomás's family and washing my own clothes as discreetly as possible— not that I had enough privacy to keep anything secret for long. Single men were also presumed to be sexual predators. I had adhered to the code of propriety laid out by Tomás months earlier, to the point that some men began to pity me because of my celibate condition. Kayáp was once moved to give me a late-night tutorial on how to seduce Soledad, the appealing divorcée whose unattached status provoked great interest among Huascayacu's men. It was an amusing lesson in Awajún courtship technique but not one I was prepared to put into practice.

If Margaret's arrival had a normalizing effect, it was only temporary. Within days, people wanted to know why we didn't have children. A typical Awajún woman in her mid-twenties would already have had as many as a half dozen pregnancies and, accounting for miscarriages and the high rate of infant mortality, perhaps three children in tow. Our childlessness served as a wearisome talking point for months.

Setting up an autonomous household created new complications. We had to carry a small kerosene cookstove to Huascayacu and provision it with fuel, still scarce in the region. Securing food became a burdensome chore. We were able to supplement canned foods with eggs, peanuts, manioc, plantains, and maize purchased from our neighbors. I packed in blocks of locally made brown sugar, called *chancaca*, for breakfast oatmeal. Chancaca, boiled down from pressed sugar cane in huge outdoor pots, contained so many honeybee parts and bits of other insects that it may, in fact, have been a significant source of dietary protein. A small kitchen garden produced occasional tomatoes as well as radishes of near-Jurassic immensity. The shotgun shells that I distributed to hunters ensured that we were regularly invited to meals with game meat, although Margaret never acquired a taste for monkey, armadillo, wasp larvae, and other Amazonian foods that I had learned to eat in order to survive.

Several government agencies had proposed meeting with Awajún leaders in Shimpiyacu, a remote community with one of the largest land grants of the Alto Mayo. Two boatloads of officials were to travel upriver from Moyobamba, but from Huascayacu travel to the meeting required a day and a half's hike through the forest. On the day of departure, Margaret and I joined Eladio, Kayáp, Oscar, Tomás, and two youths on a path leading out of the village. The muddy trail sucked at our feet. Streams swollen by recent rains could only be crossed by balancing on bridges made of a single slender log, which in one case lay under several inches of fast-moving water. As Oscar walked ahead to scout for game, Eladio pointed out overgrown gardens and house sites abandoned years before. We saw a white capuchin monkey, a game bird called Spix's guan much favored by hunters, and a pair of collared peccaries. The guan and one of the peccaries were shot by Tomás and Oscar, which lifted everyone's mood.

We made camp near a stream about an hour before dark. With great economy of motion, Kayáp and one of the young men threw together two simple shelter frames—one large, one small—and then roofed them with leaves of a palm called *tuntúam*. Leaves from a different species of palm, *shímpi*, served as ground cover. Oscar started a fire, singed the hair off the peccary he had killed, and then carved it into chunks suitable for grilling. He spitted the liver on a stick and set it over the coals. As the meat cooked, the young men talked about their romantic prospects in Shimpiyacu. Eating was serious business, though, and conversation ceased until everyone was sated by the meat.

We broke camp the next day two hours after dawn. Crossing a stream called Sukiyacu, "testicle river," Eladio explained that the name came from a painful accident involving a man who lost his footing and made a hard landing astride a log bridge. By midmorning, there were signs of human presence—an abandoned camp, the ruins of an old house—and the pace increased. Before approaching the first occupied house, the men spruced up next to a small stream. They washed their face and hands, donned clean clothes that had been carried in waterproof baskets, and carefully combed their hair. With red achiote paste, Kayáp and Eladio painted thick stripes under their eyes. The goal was to make a good impression. Unfortunately for Huascayacu's reputation, the pair of kirínku attached to the delegation were too mud-spattered and bedraggled to meet the prevailing standard of personal grooming.

Shimpiyacu had a population almost double that of Huascayacu and was more conservative. Some men still wore *itípak*, the cotton kilts that had been abandoned in Huascayacu in favor of trousers. Houses were built in the traditional oval style and on a grand scale. We were given use of a sleeping platform in the house of a man named Chumpík, whose wife immediately fed us manioc and boiled howler monkey. As the food was being served, Chumpík spoke of life in Shimpiyacu. In response to a question about whether the community had an iwishín, a curer, he responded, "No, we get along here. We don't have a problem with sorcery." This observation, shared almost as an aside, was an instant lesson on the ambivalent moral status of iwishín, whose training and healing activities serve as daily reminders of the ubiquity of sorcerers.

A slight disfigurement of Chumpík's nose marked him as someone afflicted by leishmaniasis, a disease spread by a species of biting fly. Leishmaniasis typically appears first as a skin lesion and then enters a chronic phase that attacks tissue in the nose and throat. In the most advanced form of the disease, a victim's nose may be completely destroyed, leaving only a gaping hole. Various drugs can cure leishmaniasis, but treatment must continue over weeks or months, a requirement rarely satisfied by patients who live far from medical posts and pharmacies.

Conversation with Chumpík was interrupted by news that the government dignitaries had arrived. There was bedlam on the riverbank as men from the Ministries of Agriculture, Health, Nutrition, and Education, as well as the Civil Guards and the Forestry Police, were greeted by the community's ápu and teachers. The visitors unloaded their gear from two boats under the watchful eye of scores of Awajún, young and old. I recognized the Civil Guard officer, Ensign Quiróz, from a previous friendly encounter in Moyobamba. Today he was dressed in a Jungle Jim ensemble, complete with camo jacket, Australian bush hat, knee-high boots, and sidearm.

The guests were taken to a house that the community had built to accommodate them. We joined them for dinner. Their conversation was spiced with tidbits of jungle lore, mostly fallacious. They badgered the teachers for useful Awajún words that they then massacred through mispronunciation or inappropriate use. Ensign Quiróz walked about the village saying *"Pégkeg pujájai,"* "I'm fine," to everyone he met and was puzzled when he got no response. It probably didn't help that he addressed men as "sister" in their language.

The nights at Chumpík's were among the first that I spent in an occupied Awajún house because Huascayacu had provided me with my own. The experience offered nothing like the Western ideal of a good night's sleep. Young children nodded off not long after dark and their parents soon afterward. The sounds of barking dogs, crying babies, or young revelers returning from social visits elsewhere punctuated the night. At about 3:00 A.M., Chumpík's wife, Mamái, peeled manioc tubers and set them to boil. As they awoke during the night, people could be heard talking quietly on their sleeping platforms. Some arose and fanned the fire back to life so that they could warm themselves. At dawn, Mamái brought bowls of warm water that men used to rinse out their mouths. She followed this with warm manioc beer and, later, food.

The quiet bustle of the morning was interrupted by an explosive thump upriver. The officer for the Forest Police, whose job was to educate the Awajún about the nation's conservation laws, was apparently using dynamite to fish in the Río Huascayacu.

After this diversion, blasts from a snail-shell trumpet announced the day's first session. Ápus and teachers from several neighboring communities were in attendance, as were perhaps eighty other Awajún men and women. Through an interpreter Ensign Quiróz reminded them that they were not allowed to steal, beat their wives, or kill one another. Everyone should obey the orders of the community's ápu. Communities were permitted to construct a jail, a *calabozo,* if they wanted to. They could exile troublemakers. But violent crimes were to be dealt with by the police, not the community.

While Quiróz and other officials spoke to the assembled men, a doctor gave a talk on public health to a large group of Awajún women. His remarks focused on child care and sanitation. He urged women to wash their babies daily with soap and water and to powder them liberally with talcum, a product that most women had never seen and in any event weren't in a position to buy. During much of the doctor's lecture, women chatted and giggled among themselves. His presentation to a mixed group of men and women, offered the next day, garnered greater attention. He urged women to stop swallowing the head lice that they harvested while grooming one another because, he said, lice harbor microbes that cause stomach disorders. A hullabaloo immediately arose among the men, who mocked their wives and ordered them to stop eating lice, an activity in which several were at the time avidly engaged. The men's sense of superiority was dented moments later when the doctor criticized their habit of frequent spitting. "A most unsanitary practice," he said. He was unaware that spitting was less a nervous tic than an obligatory, ritualized element of men's formal speech.[1]

A memorable moment in the last of the public events was a talk by Winston Vásquez, a representative of the Ministry of Education. Vásquez expressed disapproval of the way the Awajún arranged their houses. Gesturing toward the surrounding village, he said, "Just look at this community! It's ugly. You need to construct a central plaza, locate government buildings next to it, and then situate houses around it in straight rows. That's what a well-organized place looks like."

The specific phrase that Vásquez used for the urgently needed village square was *plaza de armas*. In Hispanic America, this marks the local apex of civil authority as well as the store of weapons that were used to defend it in colonial times. The apparently innocuous recommendation that the Awajún reorganize themselves around a plaza de armas was a condensed nugget of the central political values of civilization: social hierarchy, centralized governance, and physical separation of rulers from the ruled.

More profoundly still, Vásquez's notion of order was blind to the logic of the Awajún's accommodation to life in the rainforest. In Shimpiyacu and Huascayacu, house sites were chosen for their privacy, good drainage, proximity to water, and other practical considerations. The scruffy mix of packed soil and erratically distributed plants that surrounded most houses was, upon close inspection, a living cache of essential raw materials. There were chili peppers and edible fruits to enliven meals; herbal medicines, including ginger, nettle, and dozens of others, to treat everyday skin infections or muscle pain; trees such as achiote and huito that provided dyes; gourd squashes that served as drinking bowls and beer strainers; and psychoactive plants such as tobacco and angel's trumpet (*Brugmansia* sp.), used in healing. What seemed like a contest between order and disorder, developed and underdeveloped, was in fact a struggle between civilization's need to encode power relations in built space and an Amazonian logic of pragmatism and household self-sufficiency.

It was during house-to-house socializing in Shimpiyacu that I first met Míkig, one of the oldest men in the Alto Mayo. I guessed that he was in his seventies, but there was no reliable way to fix his age. Like other old-timers, Míkig spoke with a deliberate formality that gave him substantial presence, far more than his thin, leathery form could account for. Wrinkles creased his face like lines on a topographic map of the Peruvian montaña. Circles and crosshatches tattooed long ago into his chin, cheeks, and nose had faded to blue-black shadows. His gravelly voice wasn't easy to understand at first. Beneath the formality was a dry wit that had survived the ravages of time. This, along with a penchant for colorful turns of phrase, made him a compelling storyteller. In the coming months I returned to Shimpiyacu several times in the hope that Míkig would pull more stories out of the vast library of his memory. I was rarely disappointed.

Míkig's accounts of his early encounters with non-Awajún people were simultaneously strange and hilarious. He lavished special attention on enigmatic gringos whom he depicted as bosses of the local mestizos. "These gringos were tall and substantial-looking," Míkig said. "They wore special coats, and as they walked the coats sounded like this: *sáku, sáku, sáku*. They were great talkers, and they loved to joke around." The identity of these jovial gringos was a mystery, as was the sound of their coats. Perhaps they were military officers or European-looking government officials from Lima.

Míkig told more serious stories, too. When asked how long the Awajún people had been dealing with sorcerers, he answered, "A very long time. The first witch was named Púnku. Back then, it was easy to become a vision-bearer, a *wáimaku*. One could touch the ant called *tíiship* and become wáimaku." Vision-bearers, Míkig implied, were nearly impossible to kill. They were protected by their spiritual strength. So Púnku, the first sorcerer, set out to undo this. "Púnku bewitched the ant tíiship so that men couldn't use it to obtain a vision. This witch also created malaria and influenza. One day Púnku played with his niece and bewitched her arm and nose, the places where he had touched her. He was evil. They were collecting a fruit called

Formal portrait of Míkig Daichàp, Shimpiyacu, 1977.
Photograph courtesy of Michael F. Brown.

inák. He told his niece to come down from the tree. He tried to have sex with her, and she said, 'Uncle, why are you doing that?' She returned to her house and became ill with fever. Before dying, she told her family of the attempted rape. Púnku had bewitched her, she insisted. The people came to kill Púnku for being a witch. It rained, and then the sun came out. Púnku began to cry, pretending to repent. 'How bad witches are!' he said. 'Why did I do this to my niece?' The people attacked him, speared him to death. When he died, witchcraft declined a little. But it never went away, because he had created it."

Míkig's story touched on a key element of traditional life whose current status was uncertain. In common with other Jivaroan peoples, the Awajún believed that the well-being of men, and to a lesser extent of women, depended on the acquisition of powerful visions. In the past, adolescent boys undertook a vision quest that might last weeks or months. They fasted from desirable foods, eating only a few roasted plantains each day. They slept in special high beds that shielded them from contamination associated with sexual activity, human wastes, and domestic animals. Above all, they consumed mind-altering plant substances: tobacco; juice squeezed from the angel's trumpet, a close relative of jimsonweed; and the bitter, stomach-churning brew *ayahuasca*, made from the Amazon's famed visionary vine. Sitting alone in a forest shelter adjacent to places that harbored ancient warrior spirits called *ajútap*, they sang and fasted and stood their ground against terrifying apparitions unleashed by the hallucinogens. With courage and a bit of luck, they were eventually visited by an ajútap who pronounced them to be ruthless, invincible warriors destined to ravage distant enemies and sorcerers closer to home. People insisted that a man in possession of this kind of vision was transformed almost beyond recognition. His thinking and speech became clear, and he acted with unshakable confidence in his invincibility.[2]

Women, it was said, sometimes sought similar visions. But instead of receiving the power to kill, they saw a future marked by healthy children, gardens dense with manioc stems, and frothy pots of manioc beer.

All the middle-aged men of Huascayacu had sought visions in their youth. But the introduction of primary schools and the arrival of Awajún teachers sympathetic to Christianity put a stop to this. Men expressed few regrets, although elders often grumbled about the misbehavior of youths regarded as sex-crazed because they had never submitted to the privation and self-discipline of the vision quest. In essence, the complaint was that today's young men were psychologically unbalanced because they hadn't taken powerful drugs that would show them how the world really worked behind the façade of everyday appearances.

Míkig shared a story that in compressed form revealed the values embedded in the search for visionary power. "Long ago young men couldn't have intercourse with women because when the woman's 'dirt' entered a man's body he would become pregnant. This dirt, called *shúpa,* is like a child. A youth named Dáwa became pregnant this way. There was a party at his house, but Dáwa could only warm himself by the fire like a pregnant woman. He lay on his wooden shield. To tease him, the partiers sang, 'How can they say that Dáwa is a man? Uh au uh au.' People flipped the shield over to torment him. All he could say was, 'Please leave me alone!'

"His brother said, 'What made you like this? What happened to your courage? I've watched you like this for a long time. Why is your stomach bloated?' His brother picked him up, handed him a small net bag, and said, 'Go to the forest shelter.'

"Dáwa came to the shelter. In another shelter nearby some ajútap spirits were talking. One said to the others, 'Let's see whether he comes of his own free will.' One ajútap, a jaguar, sent the bird *súgka* to look. The súgka said, 'He comes not because of his own desire but because he is pregnant with shúpa.' The jaguar sent the mouse *katíp* to confirm this. The mouse said, 'He comes because he has shúpa.' The jaguar emerged from the shelter with a terrifying sound. Hearing the roar, Dáwa tried to escape. The jaguar ajútap knocked him down. With its paws it squeezed out the shúpa baby in his belly. The baby began to cry, and the jaguar ate it.

"Dáwa received a vision. A great storm arrived, with much wind. His brother, still drinking beer at the party, began to weep because he thought that a falling tree would surely kill Dáwa.

"Dáwa returned to the stream near his house, washed and combed his hair, and entered the house carrying his lance. His stomach had returned to normal size. He spoke of his vision. They killed a hen for a feast and served him manioc beer. They celebrated his good fortune. 'This is why I sent you to the shelter,' said Dáwa's brother.

"They formed a war party. They killed many enemies and took their heads. Dáwa arrived with a tsántsa, a smoked trophy head. He sent a messenger ahead to say that he wanted to perform the special tsántsa dance with the girl who had laughed at him most when he was pregnant. The messenger informed the girl, and she was frightened. 'What will I say?' she asked. She could only speak nonsense like 'Opening his mouth, the man laughs.' She threw herself under a sleeping platform, began to shit polliwogs, and died. She died of shame. Her name was Yancháp."

The story emphasizes the corrupting, emasculating effect that contact with women was said to have on young men, who were pressured to achieve spiritual maturity before they engaged in sexual adventures. It is no accident that the tale shifts immediately from Dáwa's vision to his participation in a killing expedition. Possession of a vision meant not just protection from enemies: vision-bearers were fated to defeat their adversaries and harvest heads for rituals that brought life-giving energies to their families. A man named Héctor once told me, apparently without ambivalence, that his late father's status as a visionary warrior made it easy for him to kill others. "He was small and looked like a boy, but he was a wáimaku. He killed for pleasure, like a hunting dog."

For men of Míkig's generation, warfare and head-taking directed against distant enemies—notably, the Wampis people—had already faded into the past. Their adversaries were family members, sometimes close ones. One of Míkig's neighbors, Santiago, spoke of this in response to a question about past conflicts: "We fought to execute sorcerers who killed even their own family members—their fathers, brothers—by witchcraft. My brother-in-law went to visit in the Río Potro, and there his brother gave him sorcery darts. He came back here having become a sorcerer. A woman died, and he was blamed. My relatives waited for him on the trail. He had gone to fish with poison and returned with his wife. He carried his gun. They began to shoot at him. He ran away, unhurt, but his wife called him back to fight. She said he was a wáimaku, a vision-bearer, and could not be killed easily. He came back and fired his gun, in vain. They killed him. His family wanted vengeance, but they couldn't get it."

Santiago said he had murdered his father's brother after his father died from sorcery. "I killed the sorcerer with the help of others. It didn't matter that he was in our family. He was a sorcerer. He lived in the same place, very close by. His relatives demanded payment, and I paid. But they continued the feud and attacked another uncle of mine. He left the house to defecate. They attacked him as he came in the door. He came in covered with blood, but he was just wounded. He had won. There were four of them, just boys. They didn't defeat us. Again we made an agreement not to fight. They wanted to continue the feud, though. . . . Then the teacher Humberto arrived and the fighting ended."

These histories of murderous visions and fratricidal violence, about which Míkig, Santiago, and other mature men spoke so matter-of-factly, were steadily losing relevance. Warrior values were still in place, but the realities of the colonization frontier were shifting power toward those with new skills: literacy, bilingualism, nimbleness in adapting indigenous cultural understandings to those of Peruvian national society. Evangelical Christianity represented another new avenue of power as well as a challenge to tradition. Young men and a few talented young women were gaining purchase on these assets. Pushed aside were the monolingual middle-aged men who should have been reaching the peak of their influence. They and their incendiary visions of martial virtue were fast becoming obsolete.

5

Four Weddings and a Funeral

Not long after dawn, loud chanting could be heard from the largest room of Utiját's sprawling house in the community of Alto Naranjillo. The percussive refrain *"Esáksaktú najágkita, esáksaktú najágkita"* alternated with constantly changing verses. The chanter was Urucínta, Utiját's wife. A weathered, gray-haired woman who had lost many of her teeth, Urucínta wore a patched dress that had faded to mixed shades of pink. She sat on a wooden stool holding a folded piece of banana leaf directly in front of her mouth as she chanted. The leaf cradled mashed gingerroot, used more widely as a medicine than as a condiment.[1]

The chant completed to her satisfaction, Urucínta explained that the medicine was for her granddaughter. She had become ill after her father encountered one of a score of plants and animals regarded as dangerous to newborns. The means by which a parent's contact with certain forest species could harm a distant child resisted ready explanation. Some people said that these animals and plants left contaminating traces on the par-

Urucínta Chijiáp chanting to medicine held in a banana leaf, Alto
Naranjillo, 1978.

Photograph courtesy of Michael F. Brown.

ents' bodies, which were then transferred to the baby. This didn't explain encounters that were solely visual—say, when a man saw a snake while hunting in the forest. Others believed that when an infant's parent eats one of a small number of taboo game birds, this bird "calls all the dirt that the mother may have eaten when she was pregnant." This "dirt" joins together inside the baby to cause diarrhea. Still others insisted that the soul of an afflicting animal attacks the baby's soul. One elderly woman told a story about a relative named Ampúsh, who one day was hunting with his wife and their infant son. They encountered an agouti, a large rodent distantly related to the guinea pig. It took refuge in a hole. As he prepared to dig it out, Ampúsh saw that the agouti had made a fatal choice: the hole contained a boa that had already wrapped itself around the hapless animal. Contact with boas was considered certain to cause illness in the parents' newborn child. Ampúsh's wife begged her husband to abandon the hunt immediately and return home to begin the appropriate treatment. Ampúsh, figuring that if it was too late to prevent the dangerous contact he might as well secure their dinner, dispatched the boa with a large pole and removed the dead agouti. The baby suddenly began to cry. Spasmodic convulsions twisted its tiny body. Before the couple could initiate treatment, the baby died, its back broken by the soul of the boa.

An infant's persistent diarrhea or unexplained crying led parents to search their memories for animal or plant encounters that might have seemed trivial at the time. When this kind of contact was recalled or even just suspected, they were likely to prepare a plant remedy and activate its power with the chant I had just witnessed. The words of the chant likened the baby to beings immune to contact with dangerous plants and animals. The medicine could be given directly to the child, or the mother might take the medicine in her mouth and then suck rhythmically up and down the infant's arms, legs, and chest to draw out the illness. Concern about dangerous contacts amounted to a postpartum taboo that symbolically marked an infant's vulnerability and incomplete separation from its parents. Nearly a third of children failed to survive to age five, so anxiety about an infant's health was understandable. By the time a child could eat solid food and take its first halting steps, it was considered resistant to parental encounters with dangerous species.

This unexpected opportunity to witness a domestic healing ritual—another instance of stumbling upon something just by being there—came while Margaret and I were guests in Utiját's house. We were scouting for a new living situation. Huascayacu had been a perfect starting place: a compact, isolated, and welcoming village. But its remote location buffered it from the effects of the new highway and the highland immigrants pouring into the region. It also set severe limits on the number of Awajún with whom I came into contact. The recent trip to Shimpiyacu had illuminated the great diversity of knowledge and attitudes among the Awajún. In retrospect, that shouldn't have been surprising. They were a people who valued personal independence, at least where adult men were concerned. It might be going too far to call this a society of iconoclasts, but it was unquestionably a society that allowed room for idiosyncrasy.

Alto Naranjillo was close to three other Awajún communities located near the Marginal Highway. The total population of the four communities was about 550, and there was daily visiting between them. Mestizo colonists had settled just outside the boundaries of Awajún lands, some in fast-growing hamlets and towns. When the highway wasn't washed out by heavy rain or blocked by avalanches, its rutted surface carried a battered caravan of Japanese pickups—most of them dangerously overloaded with produce and passengers—as well as cars, motorcycles, and the occasional double-axle truck ferrying produce and supplies between the Peruvian coast and the larger towns of the montaña.

Community elders in Alto Naranjillo gave us permission to move into a tiny abandoned house. The local teacher, Jeremías, was sympathetic to my work; the ápu, a middle-aged man named Shajián, was harder to read but welcoming enough. The house needed attention, including a new roof, to become habitable. I arranged to hire several young men to help with the necessary work. We would move in within a few weeks.

Urucínta's chant likened her sick granddaughter to beings regarded as notably resistant to harm. Many of these were known primarily from a body of myths that the Awajún call "ancestor stories," or "stories from long ago." These narratives, which probably numbered in the hundreds, represented deep history with a metaphysical twist. Many had an odd, dreamlike quality supported by acute observations of the natural world. Boundaries between animate and inanimate, human and nonhuman, remained startlingly porous. Even when the myth provided a clear explanation of how something came to be, it was likely to include distracting subtexts or weird details whose connection to the narrative was difficult to comprehend.[2]

A case in point was a foundational myth, recounted by Urucínta and others, about the being called Núgkui, a name usually glossed as Earth Mother. The narrative opens by explaining that in ancient times the Awajún knew nothing of domesticated plants or the fire needed to cook them. They survived by collecting wild foods and cultivating balsa wood. The ancestors "cooked" this unappetizing crop, as one storyteller explained with a chuckle, by holding it in their armpits until it was warm enough to eat.

One day a woman collecting snails with her small children saw peeled manioc skins floating down the river. Curious, she walked upstream until she came upon Núgkui, who was washing manioc tubers. Around her were the many crops on which the Awajún depend today: manioc, sweet potatoes, yams, peanuts, plantains, squashes, and other cultivated plants. The woman asked Núgkui if she would share this bounty. Taking pity on her, Núgkui had a better idea. "Take my little daughter with you, care for her well, and she will call all the food you want so that you are never hungry."

The woman carried Núgkui's daughter on her back until they returned home. Just as Núgkui had promised, the little girl was able to call into being anything that the woman needed. If she was asked to bring cooked manioc or clay pots for beer, these things appeared instantly. Food began to pile up in all corners of the house. Returning from a day of hard work, her husband marveled at this abundance. Meanwhile, Núgkui's daughter was kept safe on a sleeping platform, wrapped in leaves or, in some versions of the story, hidden in a cloth enclosure.

The woman made a habit of carrying Núgkui's child—who in many versions of the myth is simply called Núgkui—in a basket as she went about her daily tasks. Eventually, though, the child grew too heavy to carry. The woman decided to leave her at home in the care of her own children while she worked in the garden. "Don't hit her or bother her in any way," their mother told them.

The mischievous children had other plans. As soon as their mother was out of sight, they began to cajole Núgkui to call some íwanch to the house. They had heard a great deal about these monstrous beings and wanted to see them in the flesh. "No! I don't want to," Núgkui protested. "They're frightening, and I can't make them leave quickly once they're here." The children persisted. Eventually she conjured up an army of íw-anch, who appeared in single file and swarmed over the house, sprawling on benches and sleeping platforms. This scared the children out of their wits, and they begged Núgkui to make the monsters go away. As she had warned, the íwanch were slow to respond to her commands. The distraught children threw ashes into Núgkui's eyes. She rubbed them and cried out in pain. To escape from her tormenters, she scrambled up onto the house timbers and then clawed her way through the palm-leaf thatch onto the roof beam.

In the garden, the children's mother noticed that all of the plants Núgkui had provided began morphing into closely related but inedible wild species. "What's happening here?" she asked herself. Racing back to the house, she saw Núgkui singing to tall bamboo plants nearby. "Bamboo, bamboo, take me away so that you can eat my mother's sugar cane"—or, in other versions, peanuts or bananas. A bamboo plant leaned toward the child, rubbing against her and finally taking her away. Faced with the potential loss of the being who had made possible a dietary utopia, the woman began to hack at the woody bamboo stem with her machete.

At this point the story takes a bizarre turn in an alimentary direction. The woman eventually finds Núgkui in one of the sections of the bamboo plant. But it is not the real child; it is a corrupted version formed by Núgkui's intestinal gas, *íki*. This flawed Núgkui is unable to deliver normal foods. When Núgkui calls for food plants, what appear instead are rotten, worm-eaten, or malformed versions of Awajún cultigens. Incensed by this failure, the woman kicks Núgkui, who tries to escape by climbing headfirst into the woman's anus. The head breaks off at the shoulders, leaving a headless body on the ground. The decomposing head remains inside the woman, which is why, the myth concludes, people now pass intestinal gas.

Some versions of the myth end on a more resonant note by explaining that Núgkui later appeared in a dream that led the ancestors to cuttings or seeds of all the plants that had disappeared. But instead of arriving magically, these now could be cultivated only through backbreaking work.

At the most superficial level, the Núgkui myth shares with Genesis the theme of humanity's fall from grace. The prosperity made possible by Núgkui's reproductive power is lost when children demand firsthand knowledge of the grotesque íwanch. Only a few years before I recorded myths such as this one in the Alto Mayo, the French anthropologist Claude Lévi-Strauss had completed a multivolume project called *Mythologiques,* a dauntingly erudite study of myths collected throughout the Americas. Lévi-Strauss tried to show that narratives like the Núgkui story are elements of a unified code that grapples, unconsciously, with fundamental dualities of the human condition. What happens in any one myth must be understood not in terms of its specific plot or characters but by how it relates to *other* myths as part of a total system of relationships. For Lévi-Strauss, the primordial duality with which all New World myths wrestle is the tension between nature and culture. Other oppositions serve as proxies for this opposition: rotten/burned, edible/inedible, subterranean/celestial, ingestion/evacuation. The list of polarities is vast—by the end of the 2,200 densely argued pages of *Mythologiques,* numbingly so. The elusiveness of the project leads Lévi-Strauss's biographer Patrick Wilcken to call it "a kind of Zen anthropology" and "a demonstration of ultimate interconnectivity, a nirvana of thought and nature."[3]

Some elements of Lévi-Strauss's theory rang true when I pondered the Núgkui story. The myth's vivid closing image— Núgkui's head stuffed into the protagonist's anal cavity as the headless body falls to the ground—had a Daliesque quality that was hard to put out of one's mind. In a book called *The Jealous Potter,* a coda to *Mythologiques,* Lévi-Strauss alludes to the Núgkui story and notes a symmetry between myths from other parts of the hemisphere that portray human ancestors consuming wind because it was the only food they knew, in contrast to the Núgkui story, which has ancestors venting decomposed wind. It isn't implausible to think of the child Núgkui as being symbolically consumed and digested by the long bamboo tube, then excreted at the story's end. The myth's alimentary theme received additional support when one storyteller mentioned that Núgkui couldn't defecate. "After eating, she would say, 'I'm going to defecate,' taking with her some ground peanut meal. She would go into the forest, squat, and drop the ground peanuts over her head and down her back, saying, 'I have defecated.' The rest of the people noticed this and said, 'She is throwing away peanuts.' They ate it. Núgkui said, 'You're eating my feces!' "[4]

The experience of listening to people tell myths was hard to reconcile with Lévi-Strauss's analytical gymnastics. Gifted storytellers such as Urucínta and Míkig were completely in the moment, using gestures and dramatic changes of voice to make their stories as entertaining as possible. Often they weren't solo acts. Listeners laughed appreciatively, parroted memorable phrases, and shouted corrections or embellishments. When Núgkui calls to the bamboo for help, the storyteller would sing the child's song, which was likely to be imitated by any children within hearing distance. In other words, myths were a performance to be shared with others.

Some myths seemed to be more focused on everyday social problems than on questions of cosmic order. An example is a narrative shared by a middle-aged man named Cristóbal. He told me that a bird called *puampúa* was a powerful sorcerer who killed many of his fellow birds with witchcraft. (Scientists know this bird as the thrush-like antpitta, which typically forages on the forest floor for ants and other insects.) Tired of the puampúa's sorcery, the other birds united against him. They could not kill him easily, though, because he knew how to hide in holes close to the ground. They enlisted the help of the ant called *katsáip*, which combed the ground for hiding places. Together they killed many puampúa sorcerers, but the most powerful one managed to elude them. Finally they cornered him in a dense thicket. They could hear the bird's mournful cry as he faced certain death. The toucan hacked at the puampúa with its enormous beak. Wounded, it escaped to a hole but was chased out by the ants. The other birds tore it to pieces. "That's what happens to sorcerers today," Cristóbal said.

Many Awajún mythic accounts close by invoking the sun, Étsa, once a person of godlike powers who gave the world much of its present shape. In myths that together form a sun cycle, Étsa ordained that human beings would die and never return to life, that husbands would be jealous of their wives, that some snakes would be poisonous and others not, and that animals would take the forms by which we know them today.

Étsa's role as the principal creator of the present Awajún world was challenged by one curious myth that appears to date from the historic period, perhaps influenced by early Jesuit mission teachings. The story's principal characters are Apajuí (Our Father) and Kumpanám (possibly a corruption of the Spanish word *compañero*, "companion"). Apajuí and Kumpanám lived on opposite sides of the river. Apajuí was amply provisioned with manufactured goods such as machetes and axes. The two men became friends, although Apajuí cautioned Kumpanám to keep his hands off Apajuí's attractive wife (in some versions, his daughter), who one Alto Mayo storyteller said was named María. But Kumpanám so passionately desired the woman that his longing gaze and, in one version, his thrusting hips made her pregnant from the other side of the river—a not quite immaculate conception. This so enraged Apajuí that he abandoned his house and took the woman upriver in a canoe. Along the way, he tossed out enormous wooden crates of trade goods that ultimately became prominent rock formations along the Río Marañón. The name Apajuí was used for God the Father in Wycliffe's translation of the Bible, loading the term with connotations broader than those expressed in the myth.[5]

What was frustratingly unclear was whether these stories remained a vital part of everyday life. They were familiar to adults, but I had no way of assessing how often they were recounted or how they might be used strategically in social situations. There seemed little question, though, that the Núgkui story and others like it showed that the Awajún thought of almost every element of the natural world—from thunder to prominent boulders, from the largest forest trees to most birds, mammals, reptiles, and fish—as having once been endowed with a human identity. This personhood could reemerge unexpectedly, a possibility to which people were wise to remain alert.

A curious feature of myths was that their tellers treated them like elaborate machines that, once started, could be stopped only with great difficulty. After hearing the Núgkui myth a number of times, I found myself wanting to ask detailed questions about Núgkui's role in promoting the growth of women's crops. My queries usually prompted recitation of the entire myth, a process that could last an hour or more. It was difficult to get storytellers to stop the gears of the mythic machinery and reflect on Núgkui's appearance or behavior or special powers. On more than one occasion I found myself in the awkward position of interrupting knowledgeable elders just as they were shifting into myth-telling overdrive. As the story gathered momentum, I would say something like, "Sister, please don't tell the whole story. I just want to talk about Núgkui." Most would respond simply by saying that Núgkui still lived in gardens and could be persuaded to produce abundant growth if the gardener kept her field well weeded and regularly performed songs that made Núgkui happy.

Eladio was eager to talk about the recent miscarriage of Tiwijám's wife, Simira. He had seen the fetus and insisted that its face "looked like a machete," apparently meaning that it was flat and pointed. Many people in Huascayacu had come to examine the fetus before it was unceremoniously buried in the forest.

Miscarriages were blamed on a woman's unfulfilled longing for a particular food. Simira reportedly had felt a strong desire to eat peccary, but Tiwijám was unable to find and kill one. Husbands were under considerable pressure to satisfy a pregnant wife's food cravings to prevent a possible miscarriage. A cruel irony is that asking a hunter for a particular game animal was, under normal circumstances, thought to produce bad luck in the hunt. Men heading out of the village with a shotgun on their shoulder were usually circumspect about their intentions. When asked what they are doing, they said, "I'm going walking."

The notion that unsatisfied desire produced illness took other forms. Eladio and several others insisted that a man whose strong desire for a woman was thwarted in some way could become ill with a condition called *chúki usupágbau,* "vagina miscarriage." This presents itself as intense abdominal pains similar to a true miscarriage. The illness could be cured by asking an old man to prepare a medicinal infusion of hot peppers or fingernail shavings whose power has been energized by performing a special version of the same chant used for sick children.

These beliefs suggested an underlying theory of the emotions: desires must be fully expressed. To do otherwise invited illness. Complicating this was a technology of emotional manipulation, which took the form of songs and charms believed to change people's feelings. After listening to songs that I had recorded in Shimpiyacu and Alto Naranjillo, Tomás said that he and other men had all experienced moments when, having embarked on a long journey, they felt a sudden urge to return home. This, he said, was surely because wives were using magical songs to manipulate their feelings. "A woman finds a secret place in the forest and takes a small amount of tobacco juice or powder through her nose. She becomes intoxicated, just a little. Then she sings her songs, her ánen." Other ánen could block a man's anger when he suspected a wife of adultery and was preparing to beat her: "As a Núgkui woman, I say / It is not easy to take my blood, to make me bleed," asserted one of these songs. "Husband, if you speak harsh words / The ancestors disappeared when the earth opened beneath them / This I will do to you / I'm not easy to bruise / I say this as a Núgkui woman."

More memorable still were ánen said to quell a man's interest in another woman whom he thought to bring home as a second or third wife. They compared the new love interest to demons, vultures, boas, filthy dogs, or worse: " 'She gives me food,' you say / She, she, she gives you dog's excrement served in a bowl / The bowl filled thus, you eat / Oh! Don't eat, don't eat!"

For their part, men secretly countered with their own songs to arouse a woman's passion or calm an older wife upset by the prospect of a younger wife being added to the household. Magic was domestic warfare by other means.

The end of my year in Huascayacu coincided with a communal wedding feast to celebrate four marriages. The brides—Aurora, Elvira, Ilisa, and Hermina—were in their mid-teens; the grooms—Rubén, Samuel, Chijiáp, and López—were a few years older. All were students in the village primary school. For a young man, Rubén already had a dizzyingly convoluted marital history. Formerly partnered with Atalina, a daughter of Tíwi, he had thrown her over for Ojelia, an adolescent daughter of Arturo. Now he was leaving Ojelia for Aurora, his first wife's younger sister. Why Tíwi supported this was unclear. Perhaps he hoped that bringing Rubén back into his household would resolve Atalina's status as a divorced mother. Earlier, Rubén had admitted publicly that he continued to sleep with Atalina now and then. In effect, he was forming a plural marriage even if Atalina's part in it remained ambiguous.

Before the feast, Tomás convened a meeting to mark the official closing of the school year and announce each student's final grades. The occasion ended on a sour note when Tomás criticized the four young couples who had decided to marry before completion of primary school. He wouldn't allow the four men to continue their studies, he said, because they now had to work to feed their wives and the children they would soon bear. The status of the brides went unremarked, presumably because Tomás believed that it wasn't appropriate for married women to attend school. His public criticism of the newlyweds expressed his deteriorating relations with the community, already damaged by his frequent complaint that Huascayacu was a breeding ground for sorcery, lechery, and drunkenness.

At midday the feast began at the house of a man named Comisario. The meat was provided by the grooms, who had killed two monkeys—capuchin and howler—and an armadillo. Men were served apart from the women. Most squatted in front of banana leaves on which soup, meat, and boiled manioc were served. Sitting with the women, Margaret noticed that they received less desirable cuts of meat. After the food had been eaten and the leavings cleared away, someone brought out a battery-powered phonograph and a half-dozen 45s, all recordings of cumbias, then the most popular music of Amazonian Peru. The scratchy phonograph music sucked all life from the event for a couple of hours. Older adults sat out the dances, looking bored and slightly glassy-eyed. The four newlyweds and other young people danced stiffly, the girls in their brightest cotton dresses, the boys favoring the tropical shirts and flared polyester trousers that marked the zenith of male fashion in eastern Peru.

In keeping with Awajún indifference to ritual, the feast offered little that qualified as a wedding ceremony except for the "delivery" of Elvira to Samuel. This consisted of nothing more than Elvira's classificatory brother, Kayáp, bringing her to dance with Samuel, after which Samuel took up residence in the house of his in-laws. The other newlyweds had already been living together for weeks.

Eventually Tomás convinced the partygoers to put away the record player so that traditional dancing could commence. The atmosphere changed immediately. Two of the older men tied on ankle rattles and began to dance back and forth in a straight line through the middle of the house, laying down a rhythm for everyone else. Other men moved in a larger circle with a simple hopping step, periodically reversing direction. Within the great circle of the men's dancing, women paired off to dance their hop-step in tighter circles with arms around each other's shoulders. Both men and women sang at full volume, each person's songs engaging with those of others, often in a bantering style. Men unflatteringly compared women to game birds, which are meant to be hunted and consumed. Chépa, an outspoken widow getting on in years, gave as good as she got. "Your bottom is like a howler monkey's, full of worms!" she sang. "Your penis is well fed, like the nose of the bird *chíwa!*"

Adults began to leave the party at about 8:00 P.M., when the dancing shifted back to cumbias. By midnight, all was quiet.

The next morning, people drifted to the house of Eladio and Manúgka, where preparations were under way for a fish-poisoning expedition. Suddenly there came surprising news: Arturo, who had moved from Huascayacu months before after accusing the community of harboring sorcerers, had arrived with two of his sons, Wayách and Armando, as well as his two wives. Word had it that he was angry about the marriage of Rubén, his former son-in-law, to Aurora. The formalization of Rubén's new union left Arturo's daughter Ojelia in a difficult spot: young, single, and responsible for a toddler.

Everyone waited at Tíwi's house. When Arturo finally appeared, he was at his most formidable: armed with his shotgun, his face painted with broad stripes of red that traced his prominent cheekbones. His sons were similarly turned out. A sober presence at the best of times, Arturo looked especially grim today. When the visitors settled onto stools in Tíwi's house, the tension was palpable. Arturo wasn't someone to trifle with.

After the visitors had been served bowls of manioc beer, Rubén sat on a stool in front of them at a distance of about ten feet. He looked uncertain of his ground. Arturo opened by declaring that he had come to confirm rumors that Rubén was abandoning Ojelia and that he had long neglected her because he was so busy pursuing romantic affairs with others. Rubén, judging that the best defense was a good offense, denied these stories and insisted that he had never bought clothing for Ojelia because she was lazy, rarely working in her garden. He further asserted that Ojelia's children were not his. They had been fathered by others, he implied. To this Arturo responded by saying, "What? Are you not a man? If your wife is having affairs with others, are you unwilling to defend yourself against them?"

After an hour of this, during which Arturo and Rubén were sometimes talking simultaneously at high volume, the conversation came to the question of what was to be done with Ojelia.

Arturo Ampám (right) and sons confront the man who abandoned
    Arturo's daughter for another woman, Huascayacu, 1978.
Photograph courtesy of Michael F. Brown.

At Kayáp's suggestion, Arturo and Rubén agreed that she
should accompany Arturo to his house and stay there until Tíwi
completed his relocation to another community. Once resettled
there, Rubén said that he was open to having her join him as
part of a plural marriage.

When the men put this solution to Ojelia, though, she objected violently, refusing to leave with her father. A shouting
match erupted between Ojelia and her mother. Then Arturo's
other wife, Semona, got involved. She waved a machete as she

dragged the screaming, struggling Ojelia from Tíwi's house. This feminine drama had the odd effect of reducing tension among the men, and Arturo chatted amiably with Rubén. Other men cruelly mocked Ojelia as young children watched her weeping with her mother and sister in an adjacent house.

Perhaps to draw attention away from Ojelia's misery, Semona began a procedure to protect another woman, Oronsha, from a condition called *múntsu dápu*, "breast" dápu. Dápu, a term unfamiliar to me, proved to be a category of mostly minor illnesses or conditions transferred by sight from one person to another. In the case of breast dápu, a woman who had been unable to produce sufficient milk for her baby was obliged to "cure" any pregnant woman with whom she came into contact. Semona served Oronsha beer from a bowl without letting the bowl touch Oronsha's mouth. A second part of the cure required the dápu giver to warm a piece of cloth over the coals and apply it to the pregnant woman's abdomen. Arturo's second wife performed the same sequence because she, too, was said to be an "owner" of dápu.[6]

On the few occasions when I witnessed dápu being treated, the atmosphere was surprisingly lighthearted. Although the Awajún were stoics in the face of personal discomfort and traumatic injuries such as cuts, their behavior when afflicted by disease ran to the other extreme. Even senior men, normally given to presenting themselves as indomitable warriors, were reduced by a sniffle or low-grade fever to melodramatic predictions of imminent death. They complained in a weak, scratchy voice, abandoned their normally high standards of personal cleanliness, and conveyed an impression of utter misery. This may have reflected the legacy of introduced epidemic diseases, whose high rate of mortality was burned into Awajún collective memory. In that context, a low-grade fever could augur fatal illness. Dápu, in contrast, were less freighted with danger. They might best be thought of as a way for women, who were most commonly afflicted, to express solidarity with one another in the face of the burden of bearing children.

As Margaret and I packed our few things in preparation for the move to Alto Naranjillo, Eladio stopped by to give advice. "Be careful there. It's a dangerous place. Arturo has learned that the man Túgki and his sons, Pípi and Aurelio, are sorcerers. Hidden in Túgki's garden is a kind of angel's trumpet plant that made him a sorcerer." Somehow Eladio already knew that Túgki and his family would be our closest neighbors. I asked how Aurelio, a six-year-old who still went about naked, could be a sorcerer. Eladio replied, "Túgki gave him killing darts. He might bewitch someone if he became angry because he's young and irresponsible." The best approach, Eladio counseled, was to confront Túgki directly by demanding that he not bewitch me or Margaret. I had to let him know that I was aware of his sinister powers and prepared to avenge any harm done to us.

Departure from Huascayacu left me with mixed feelings. I was grateful for the community's welcome so many months earlier as well as for the generosity shown to me while I was living there. When people were getting along, their vivacity and good humor were a pleasure to witness, especially in light of an everyday reality that seemed precarious. But pervasive suspicion, expressed primarily through sorcery accusations that were tearing the community apart, had made Huascayacu feel increasingly claustrophobic. I hoped that I was leaving behind this suffocating sense of fear.

Alto Naranjillo offered a new setting and cast of characters. The community consisted of two clusters of houses, one on the highway and the other about a half hour's walk up the Naranjillo, a beautiful whitewater river that tumbled noisily out of the eastern slopes of the Andes. The house loaned by the community was in the older, interior location, adjacent to a half dozen other houses. A similar number of residences, plus the community's primary school, were located next to the road.

The founding of Alto Naranjillo arose from a troubled history. Around 1970, four young men from a place called Unguyacu were hunting together. Two of them began to argue about some trivial matter, and one—a youth regarded as hotheaded and perhaps even mentally unstable—grabbed his weapon and took a shot point-blank at the other, possibly intending to intimidate him with a near miss. His antagonist took some pellets in a shoulder and fell as if seriously wounded. A third man fatally shot the attacker as he fled. The feud that resulted from the shooting led one faction to abandon the community and establish a new settlement on the Río Naranjillo. This group was legally recognized with a title several years later when construction of the highway opened up the region to colonization.

The pivotal figure in Alto Naranjillo had been a senior man named Antonio, who only months before I arrived had been killed in a tree-felling accident. The community's households consisted of his eldest sons, Chímpa and Kúam, and several mature men married to Antonio's sisters and daughters. Of these, the most prominent were Shajián, the village ápu, and his brother Genaro, the most active and accomplished shaman of the Alto Mayo.

Shajián was a different kind of leader than Eladio. In contrast to Eladio's gregarious bluster, Shajián was reserved and deliberate. His enthusiasm and good humor were tempered by restraint, which made him seem both dignified and somewhat elusive. He had long lived in the shadow of his influential brother-in-law Antonio but came into his own after Antonio's accidental death. Alto Naranjillo did not share Huascayacu's recent history of sorcery-related defections, and the role of its resident teacher, Jeremías, was more narrowly professional than had been the case with Tomás.

One reason for Alto Naranjillo's high level of solidarity may have been the prospect of a vengeance raid by relatives of the young man murdered eight months earlier. During a brief exploratory visit, I had failed to notice that the community was on full alert for attackers, who were thought likely to attempt a nighttime ambush in the coming months. Once Margaret and I moved there, though, talk of a possible raid was a daily reminder of the underlying situation. A loud clap of thunder, for instance, would prompt someone to comment that this was an omen of imminent attack. The primary target was Genaro, who had identified the sorcerer in his shamanic trance and also joined in the subsequent killing. Genaro didn't give the impression of being a hunted man, although he kept his shotgun within arm's reach during those months. His recent decision to build a new house on the highway may have been a defensive tactic. It would be more difficult to stage an assassination in a cleared, heavily trafficked location than in a forested, interior part of the community. Genaro had commercial motives for the relocation as well. A growing number of his patients were mestizos from nearby settlements and even more distant towns, among whom he was gaining a reputation as a powerful healer.

Our closest neighbors were Utiját and Urucínta, on one side, and Urucínta's brother Túgki and his wife, Wampurái, on the other. Following the pattern established when he had lived in Huascayacu, Utiját was a collector of rusty iron tools and pieces of scrap metal. So marked was this behavioral quirk that people nicknamed him "Tomanguillo," the surname of the owner of Moyobamba's biggest hardware store. Utiját was an odd character: notably grouchy much of the time yet capable of flashes of offbeat humor that could convulse a houseful of visitors in gut-splitting laughter. A homely man, his face was pockmarked and his nose disfigured by what was probably a case of leishmaniasis that had been treated early enough to achieve a cure.

Urucínta, Utiját's wife, was one of two senior women whose knowledge of plant medicines was relied upon by younger mothers. She was in her late forties but looked considerably older. Like many other Awajún women who survived to menopause, she was sharp-tongued and occasionally quarrelsome but, in her own way, bighearted. She had earned every line on her careworn face. Left a widow with a small child after the murder of her first husband in a feud twenty-five years earlier, she had married Utiját and borne eight more children. Four were dead, victims of either homicide or, as she saw it, sorcery. The large house that Urucínta shared with Utiját was a crossroads of community gossip and ideas about the treatment of illness, conversations sustained by liberal servings of her excellent beer.

Túgki and Wampurái were in a different situation. Misfortune shadowed them both. Túgki suffered from an advanced case of leishmaniasis that had already damaged his throat. His voice was a barely intelligible croak. He swallowed with difficulty, and as a result his body had wasted to a nearly skeletal state. He could still get around and was sociable on his good days but too frail to hunt or cut new gardens. That meant that Wampurái presided over the poorest household in the community. Their three grown-up sons lived with their wives' families and were obliged to work for them. The oldest child still living at home, Pípi, was a teenager unable to provide much in the way of game meat or cash to support his younger siblings. Wampurái's two youngest children dressed in rags when they were clothed at all.

Túgki's downward spiral had begun years earlier, while he resided in another community. His first wife killed herself by taking poison. A few years after marrying Wampurái, he took a second wife who was so young that she hadn't yet developed breasts. She abandoned him for another man when Túgki's illness began to undermine his vigor. It was said, too, that Wampurái routinely beat the younger co-wife, contributing to her flight from the household. Túgki and Wampurái relocated to Alto Naranjillo after concluding that he was being bewitched by his kin. Despite Eladio's warning that Túgki was a hidden sorcerer, I saw little evidence that this notion was given credence in Túgki's own community.

Wampurái had her own tale of woe. Apparently in her late thirties, she was the mother of seven. When she was still a child living on the Río Cahuapanas, her father, Shinkikát, discovered that one of his wives was having an affair with another man. He murdered the adulterous wife by firing his shotgun into her genital area at point-blank range. She was soon avenged by her kin, who assassinated Shinkikát in an ambush. Wampurái spent the rest of her childhood as a ward of her father's brother. Despite the trouble in her life, Wampurái was surprisingly cheerful, breaking into song at the slightest pretext and, when circumstances allowed, sharing her beer with anyone in the community inclined to visit.

The eventful life histories of Wampurái and Urucínta were hardly unique among the Alto Mayo's women. To get a sense of the Awajún's population dynamics, I eventually managed to interview thirteen postmenopausal women about their fertility histories, something that they were generally willing to talk about without hesitation. The mean number of live births of this small sample was slightly more than eleven, and most had also experienced at least one miscarriage. Each of these women had lost several young children to disease and older ones to suicide, homicide, accidents, or illness. Many had also experienced the death of a husband or the collapse of an earlier marriage due to incompatibility. Several had unwillingly shared a husband's attention with a co-wife. Like Urucínta and Wampurái, they tended to have sagging, shapeless bodies acquired from multiple pregnancies and decades of hard work. Yet all were vigorous, tough as nails, and full of barbed opinions about everything happening among their network of kin.

One morning Urucínta asked me to look at a three-year-old girl named Marleni, an orphan cared for by her aunt, Mishít, one of Kúam's two wives. While Mishít and Kúam were away hunting, Marleni had fallen into the cooking fire. Her tiny arm was burned from the elbow to the top of her hand. Only a strip of skin at the wrist, protected by a bracelet of seed beads, had been spared. Some of the burned skin was carbonized. It looked like overcooked steak: black, crusted, and glistening, with angry red swelling around the edges. The pain must have been agonizing.

Urucínta was pounding medicinal ginger to put on the burn. Ángel, the married-in mestizo farmer, intervened with a home cure, milk of magnesia poured on the affected area. Skeptical of this approach, Margaret and I washed the burn gently with soap and purified water to remove ash and dirt. Marleni was stoic, only whimpering a little as the cleaning revealed the wound's contours. A third-degree burn required more care than we could provide.

I proposed that we take Marleni to the government health post a half hour's walk away. Urucínta was hesitant. Just then Kúam and Mishít returned. Kúam berated the child for the clumsiness that led her to fall into the fire. When he calmed down, he agreed to accompany us to the health post. He took his time about it, insisting that Mishít give him beer and something to eat first. Then we walked to the post. The paramedic, unshaven and wearing a filthy T-shirt, was less startled by the injury than by his two gringo visitors. After taking stock of the situation, though, he went to work. He injected an antiseptic fluid into as much of the wound as he could reach, then swabbed it with ointment. He also provided burn dressings. There were no antibiotics available at the post, so I gave Kúam and Mishít a course of tetracycline capsules with instructions on how to administer them.

In a few weeks, Marleni's burn had healed. The strip of healthy skin protected by her bracelet stood out against the extensive scar tissue. "She looks like she's wearing a wristwatch," Kúam said. From that day forward her nickname was Relój, "Wristwatch."

On the last day of 1977, what had started as a quiet night was disturbed by the sound of a snail-shell trumpet from Kúam's house. This was followed by the excited voices of people passing by on the footpath. There was news: Mishít's brother Héctor, a man in his late twenties, had died in Unguyacu, an hour's walk away. His death was said to have come after two days of acute diarrhea and vomiting. Mishít and other close relatives of the deceased left immediately to participate in the mourning and, if possible, find an explanation for his death.

Not long after dawn, Margaret and I walked to Unguyacu. Even a hundred yards short of the settlement the sounds of grief were unmistakable: the keening of dozens of women punctuated by shouts and wailing from men. The tumult failed to convey fully the intense anguish visible in and around the dead man's house. Adults and children milled about outside, some peering inside through gaps in the palm-wood slats. Inside the house, which was divided in half by a partition, fifteen people paced back and forth, the women weeping or screaming, the men talking in loud voices about their sadness and their willingness to avenge the death if it was shown to be the result of sorcery.

The body lay on a sleeping platform in the second room, covered by rags and scraps of blankets. Only the lifeless face was visible, flanked by two burning candles. A copy of the Awajún translation of the New Testament, open to one of the color illustrations, rested on the blankets. At the head of the platform stood a pile of pharmaceutical packets, the drugs that had failed to save his life. A fire smoldered under the dead man's wrapped feet.

Mourning women surrounded the body. One climbed on the platform and kissed Héctor's face, keening in a high-pitched wail. Men walked in from the adjacent room and shouted, as if to the dead man. Because we were relative strangers in this community, Margaret and I were profoundly ill at ease. We left the room after only a few minutes. Approaching the door, we saw a sudden scramble as a female mourner tried to run outside. "She wants to kill herself!" someone shouted. A man grabbed the woman by the hair before she could slip away. She kicked, struggled, and screamed frantically. The most stricken women, including the dead man's widow and sister, were shadowed by male guardians. Once or twice these women made sudden dashes toward the edge of the settlement, but they were dragged back before they could harm themselves. The suicidal behavior was more than ritual drama: family histories included many cases of women who had committed suicide in the throes of extreme grief.

Outside, visitors continued to arrive from other communities. Messengers were dispatched to inform the dead man's extended kin in distant settlements on the Río Cahuapanas. Mishít, alone with Héctor's body, fanned his face while moaning, "My little brother, my little brother." Late in the morning there was a flurry of activity around another house in response to a rumor that Héctor's widow had tried to hang herself there. This proved untrue. A more credible story was that a grieving relative had attacked her for failing to take care of him properly. Others intervened to stop the assault, including a pregnant woman who took a blow to the stomach.

The dead man's relatives debated how to bury him. In the past, adults were often interred in their houses, which were then abandoned and allowed to collapse on top of the grave. It was said that the corpse of a *kakájam,* a senior man whose success as a killer identified him as a vision-bearer, was left seated upright on his wooden stool, lashed to a house post. Young vision-seekers who could overcome their fear of the dead and endure the stench of a rotting corpse would spend a watchful night in the house in expectation that the deceased's vision might pass to them. Resettlement in tightly clustered villages made such customs impractical. When one man suggested burying Héctor in an abandoned house on the edge of the village, others protested on the grounds that they didn't want to live so close to a grave. Burial in the mestizo cemetery in Naranjillo would require a proper coffin and a truck to haul it. That meant money, which no one possessed or was willing to provide. In the absence of other options, Úwek, the dead man's uncle, recruited some youths to help him carve a rough coffin from a trunk of balsa wood. Where it would finally rest was a matter to be resolved later.

Within a day, information about Héctor's medical history trickled into Alto Naranjillo. Some stories described the death as a sudden, catastrophic affair. A more informed version came from a bilingual paramedic, the only indigenous health care worker in the region. She had treated Héctor for chronic dysentery for months. He recovered from a previous acute episode but was showing signs of malnutrition. When the second attack came, she sent an emergency request to the Rioja hospital for medicine to control Héctor's vomiting. What arrived instead was a pharmaceutical used to treat rheumatism.

Héctor's death was tailor-made for accusations of sorcery, but his status as an innocent victim was complicated by the recent murder of the accused teenage sorcerer from the Río Potro. Héctor, too, had been named as an accomplice to the alleged sorcerer, which made him a target. He managed to elude a posse of would-be killers after being tipped off by relatives that an assassination plot was afoot. When the other accused sorcery culprit was murdered a day or two later, interest in killing Héctor seemed to have waned.

Shortly after Héctor's wake, the ápus of the communities near the road met to talk about whether they could trust men originally from the Río Potro who now lived in the Alto Mayo. During the mourning for Héctor one of them had called out, "Brother, now you're dead. If I stay here, I too will die! Better that I return home." Community leaders feared that if these men pulled up stakes, they would take their Alto Mayo wives with them. That would leave the women vulnerable to abuse because of the distance from their natal families and the growing hostility between the two regions. The matter was resolved, at least temporarily, when the men promised to stay put.

Other repercussions of the death took longer to register. Six weeks later, Héctor's sister, Mishít, ate laundry detergent in a halfhearted attempt to kill herself. She eventually vomited up most of it but was left with a sore throat and an aching gut. To explain her actions, Mishít said only that her brother's death had filled her with such sadness that she no longer wanted to live.

The convoluted stories associated with Héctor's final months defied efforts to make sense of his death. Was he killed by a sorcerer from the Río Potro region, perhaps to avenge the death of the young man who had been murdered earlier that year? Or was the sorcery a local matter engineered by one of the men involved in the failed attempt to assassinate him? There were wheels within wheels of grief, mistrust, divided loyalties, and simmering grudges. They overwhelmed people's capacity to assign blame or settle on a compelling explanation. In the end, perhaps the maze of conflicting narratives was more consoling than a banal fact: that the immediate cause of Héctor's death was a pharmacist's error.

6

Trouble in Mind

Genaro's wife, Tumús, served beer as he and I chatted in his house one day. After weeks of biding my time, I finally got up the courage to ask whether he would tell me about his life and work as an iwishín, a healing shaman. "Would you be willing to talk about how you became a healer and what happens when you take yáji? I'd like to record your story," I said. Genaro, a vigorous middle-aged man whose general appearance was indistinguishable from that of his mestizo neighbors, appraised me for a long moment over the bowl of beer, which he then proceeded to empty. "No, my brother," he said cheerfully. "I won't do that."

Genaro's wariness was disheartening. Like many young anthropologists of the time, I had hoped to learn about shamanism and perhaps even apprentice myself to a working shaman. This interest had been fueled by the work of Carlos Castaneda, whose best-selling books on shamanism and sorcery as practiced by the Yaqui people of northern Mexico, beginning with *The Teachings of Don Juan,* had generated broad public interest in these freelance virtuosos of the divine. By the mid-1970s, Castaneda's reputation was clouded by evidence that his books were nothing but engaging fictions. Yet this revelation did little to diminish enthusiasm for the study of shamans and their ancient vocation.[1]

Existing studies stressed the role that Amazonian shamans play in articulating a community's vision of the cosmos. By definition, shamans are individuals whose special gift is the ability to undertake spiritual journeys, usually via soul travel, to the universe's most remote corners. There they find and neutralize the source of a patient's illness. In those parts of Amazonia where shamans and patients together take hallucinogenic ayahuasca and other plant substances for curative purposes, the shaman guides patients through a visionary maelstrom of multicolored anacondas, jaguars with thunderous roars, and other apparitions. Ordinary people experience the spirit world in all its terror and magnificence. Shamanism, in other words, was a heroic vocation. In popular novels about the Amazon, such as Peter Matthiessen's *At Play in the Fields of the Lord* (1965), shamans were contrasted with small-minded Christian missionaries dedicated to the suppression of indigenous spirituality and its replacement by an alien faith. The noble image of shamans was tarnished by occasional reports that some indigenous peoples saw shamanism and sorcery as inextricably bound together. At the time of my encounter with Genaro, these cases appeared to be outliers. It was to be another decade before anthropologists began to acknowledge that in many societies shamans are both healers and spiritual warriors whose actions could spark real-world violence and contribute to an atmosphere of suspicion and fear.[2]

I shared these romantic views of shamanism before my encounter with the Awajún, which explains why Genaro's rebuff was such a disappointment. But the year in Huascayacu compli-

cated my thinking about both shamans and missionaries. I had
to admit that decades of work by missionary-linguists had incal-
culably improved the Awajún's prospects for survival. They had
fostered literacy and bilingualism years earlier than the Peruvian government would likely have achieved on its own. This
was primarily in the service of providing access to the Christian
Bible, but the benefits were undeniable.

I had also begun to collaborate with a nongovernmental organization that received significant funding from the Catholic
Church. The multinational team of anthropologists recruited
by this organization was solely focused on documenting the
Peruvian Amazon's indigenous cultures. Matters of Christian
doctrine or questions about personal faith commitments were
never broached. The research team's director, Luís Uriarte, a
Spaniard and former Jesuit priest, was the most dedicated Amazonian fieldworker I had ever met. Another anthropologist with
links to the organization, an energetic young Spanish Jesuit
named Manuel García-Rendueles, was devoted to recording
Awajún and Wampis mythology and making it available to the
wider world. These experiences forced me to recognize that not
all work supported by Christian denominations was intolerant
or injurious.

As for shamanism, Awajún attitudes proved anything but uni-
versally supportive. Shamans such as Genaro were lionized by
some, feared and shunned by others. Their public healing activities gave them higher moral standing than those believed to
practice sorcery in secret, but the distinction between public
and covert shamanism was murky. A publicly recognized iwishín
could engage in covert sorcery on the side, and the Awajún held
that the ability to kill in secret offered temptations that few
could resist.[3]

In some ways Awajún attitudes toward shamanism were not
unlike American views of gun ownership. Many states allow

citizens to carry concealed firearms; a few allow guns to be carried openly. A segment of the American public claims to find the presence of deadly weapons comforting when the bearers are individuals of known probity. Others aren't so sure. They wonder whether every stranger can be trusted to handle a weapon responsibly. Those who possess licensed firearms stand in a moral shadow, valued in the exceptional instance when their weapon offers protection but regarded uneasily under everyday circumstances because of the risks inherent in possession of a device that through momentary misjudgment or negligence could produce grave injury—and does, with mind-numbing frequency.

The analogy has limitations. Firearms are tools, physical objects. They lack moral meaning in and of themselves. Their efficacy is not questioned, only the circumstances in which they may be possessed and used, some of which are considered legitimate. The shaman's killing darts, in contrast, are what the French sociologist Émile Durkheim called a collective representation. They stand as a shared illusion that can be validated only by knowledgeable experts. To accept their existence is to embrace certain assumptions about reality, including the possibility that one's closest relatives are capable of occult homicide driven by well-concealed spite. The invisibility of the darts makes them more menacing than firearms and, in their own way, more corrosive of social relations.

Why did Genaro rebuff my overture? Although I can't discount the possibility that he judged me untrustworthy, the main reason was probably professional secretiveness. Shamans in Jivaroan societies often apprentice themselves to healers from different ethnic groups as part of their training. Acquiring exotic powers from afar enhances their reputation. Genaro let it be known that he used an undisclosed "mestizo medicine" *(kistián ampi)* in his healing practice, knowledge of which he was said to have acquired from a distant master shaman. He was unwilling to divulge information about this powerful substance or anything else that burnished his reputation.

Genaro was also concerned by matters weightier than an outsider's persistent questions. Because of his involvement in the recent murder, he was marked for death. Life went on as usual, but underneath the veneer of normalcy lay constant vigilance. Reluctance to talk about his life and work doubtless reflected this preoccupation.

Relations warmed after I helped him arrange a shamanic session for a group of young mestizos who arrived at his house looking for "Maestro Genaro" while I happened to be visiting. The four pilgrims, well dressed and apparently affluent, were students on a holiday adventure in the jungle. They had traveled from Chachapoyas in search of a shaman who could treat their minor illnesses and, as they put it, see their fortunes. One asked whether Genaro knew how to read tarot cards. When I translated the question for Genaro, he looked baffled for a moment and then, laughing, said, "I don't know anything about cards, but find out what I can do to satisfy them." Taking yáji wasn't an option; none was at hand. Collecting and preparing the right plant materials involved considerable work and, of course, familiarity with the relevant species and where they could be found. (Genaro generally expected his Awajún clients to bring prepared yáji when they sought treatment.) The visitors asked for Genaro's opinion of two other shamans in the region. He scornfully dismissed them as incompetents. He agreed to treat the visitors if they returned after dark with two liters of cane alcohol, a package of Inca brand cigarettes, and a bottle of *agua florida,* a cheap, diluted cologne widely used in Peruvian folk healing. Flushed with excitement by the prospect of a close encounter with Amazonian mysticism, they left the house in search of the necessary items. Genaro later intimated that he had been well paid for his performance.

With time, Genaro proved willing to share some general observations about his craft, although we never had the lengthy, probing exchanges that I sought. He explained that the key element in the killing and healing abilities of all shamans, both benevolent and homicidal, was a viscous, salivalike substance called *kaag* or *káaji*. It provided the medium in which the shaman held his killing darts. A shaman-in-training obtains his kaag in secret from an experienced mentor while both are intoxicated by tobacco water or yáji. Kaag was described as having a tendency to escape from its new owner. He could retain it only by maintaining weeks of sexual abstinence, a rigorously limited diet, and constant consumption of tobacco water. After a few weeks of this, the neophyte shaman experiments with controlling the killing darts contained in his kaag. When he can direct them efficiently, he begins to withdraw from the fast. Genaro contended that shamans from the neighboring Shawi (Chayahuita) people were especially formidable because they fasted longer than their Awajún rivals.[4]

People seeking sorcery powers could sometimes bypass the acquisition of kaag from another shaman through the use of special varieties of angel's trumpet, ginger, or a sedge called *pijipíg*—the last a plant attributed magical or psychotropic properties throughout much of the Amazon Basin under the name *piripiri*. In the state of intoxication induced by these plants, spirit beings provide the kaag to the aspiring sorcerer. Genaro implied that these beings were spirit sorcerers called *pásuk*, who live a parallel existence, complete with pásuk wives and pásuk children, normally visible only to shamans who have recruited them for purposes of divination, healing, and killing.

Another reputed source of sorcery darts and kaag was the kapok tree, a botanical giant of the rainforest. "The kapok tree has gringos inside, people who look like you, Máyak," a man once told me. To establish contact with these powerful people,

who are called *wíakuch,* the seeker clears a space around the but-
tress roots of the tree and drinks tobacco water. "From high in
the tree comes the *tak tak tak* of the wíakuch's shoes. 'Son, what
are you doing here?' the wíakuch asks. 'I come because I want to
be a sorcerer,' the man replies. 'All right, come inside,' the wíakuch
says." Héctor and others described the inside of the kapok tree
as being like a city, an alternate universe of powerful people
who look European. These wíakuch put darts in the seeker's
mouth and ear. " 'Pai!'" says the wíakuch. 'Now you're ready.'
That's how a person gets killing darts from the kapok tree."

However obtained, darts and kaag serve two purposes. Secretly applied to someone else, kaag draws sorcery darts into the
body with potentially fatal results. In the hands of a healing
shaman, kaag facilitates removal of darts from sorcery victims,
after which the healer absorbs them into his own body, assimi-
lating their power. While a healer is intoxicated by yáji, Genaro
said, sorcerer's darts look like glowing fireflies. The darts take
many forms, and some people contended that they can be sent
great distances to wreak havoc on their victims. Others speculated that a sorcerer lures a victim's soul from his body, assaults
it with his darts, then returns it to its human vessel. The damaged soul fades like a guttering candle unless an iwishín inter-
venes to reverse the process.

Where women fit into this system remained unclear. In the
Alto Mayo one or two women who healed openly for a time had
their careers cut short by suicide or murder. According to Genaro and other men, women are unsuited to the work of the
iwishín because they are vindictive and hot-tempered. "Long
ago," one man told me, "there was a woman who cured with
yáji. When she became angry, she secretly bewitched her own
children. Little by little her husband came to suspect her.
'Because of her, my children die,' he thought. So he and his
kinsmen killed her. Now women don't become healers." As

hidden sorcerers, women are especially feared because of their ready access to beer, used to deliver kaag to victims surreptitiously. Gossip about sorcery sometimes implicated individual women, but people reported few cases in which accused female sorcerers had been killed for their crimes. Men were far more frequently targeted for sorcery murders.

By sheer good fortune I stumbled upon a rare, quasi-shamanic practice: men and women serving as diviners or oracles. While interviewing Míkig, the aged storyteller I had come to know months earlier, I overheard a visiting relative ask him whether her sick relative would die from the abdominal pains that had laid her low. Míkig paused a moment, then produced a loud, stuttering sigh. This meant that the woman was on the path to recovery; silence would have foretold death or at least a long, difficult illness, he explained. Míkig and others insisted that this special ability could also predict an attack by enemies and help sick people identify foods that would make their condition worse. The diviner's peculiar sigh was indistinguishable from a sound that shamans made while healing and which they identified with the activity of their spirit familiars, pásuk. When I asked an elderly woman also known for her divining ability whether the sound came from a pásuk, she denied it vigorously. Her gift, she said, dated from her adolescence, when she took the powerful hallucinogen angel's trumpet as a cure. In her healing vision she was visited by a tiny old man whose own divinatory sigh gave her the power to foretell the course of illness, whether a spouse was involved in an adulterous affair, and other things. The fervor with which she distanced her special gift from the activities of shamans underscored the ambiguous moral standing of shamanism and the reluctance of most Awajún to be identified with it.

Word arrived from Huascayacu that two of the four marriages celebrated in the recent mass wedding had already dissolved.

The aggrieved parties were trafficking in mutual blame and accusations of abuse. Similar conflicts proved just as pervasive in
Alto Naranjillo, especially among younger couples. One morning the village was abuzz with gossip about a fight between
Shajián and his son-in-law Wajajái that broke out after a drinking party. In the middle of the night, Shajián's daughter Yolanda,
a young woman in her late teens, had woken her father to say
that Wajajái had threatened her life. Just as bad, Wajajái had
pronounced Shajián too weak and cowardly to avenge her death
if he should kill her. Confronted by Shajián, the young man
declared that the village elders were all "ignorant burros" whom
he intended to denounce to the authorities. This threat provoked
Shajián's normally dignified wife, Kapári, to begin striking Wajajái's back with nettles hastily pulled from her garden. He
escaped to the house of his parents to sleep things off. Before
dawn the next morning he slipped out of the village for a few
days, ostensibly to visit relatives elsewhere. Although Shajián
publicly declared that he was willing to forgive Wajajái for his
threats and insults, others in the community voiced the opinion
that Wajajái's marriage to Yolanda was doomed.

Wajajái was a twenty-one-year-old struggling to find a place in
the world, which at least partly explained his testiness. He had
completed primary school and spoke Spanish tolerably well. He
held a high opinion of his own talents but had nowhere to apply
them. Nonagricultural jobs were scarce in the region and in any
case were mostly unavailable to Awajún, who lacked the contacts
required by anyone hoping to secure even the most menial employment. Wajajái was expected to provide for his wife and two
small children. His only option was to pursue the same course as
older men in the community: hunting, growing rice as a cash
crop, and negotiating the occasional sale of trees to shady lumber
buyers who cruised the region in search of mahogany and other
hardwoods. He seethed with resentment that his education,

which was modest in the larger scheme of things but advanced for his community, had proved to be of so little use, leaving him no choice but to kowtow to illiterate elders such as his father-in-law.

His fourteen-year-old brother Pípi had sparked an uproar several weeks earlier when he crawled into the bed of his recently married cross cousin Candilaria while her husband was partying in a neighbor's house. She cried out in alarm, and Pípi fled the scene. People in neighboring houses were awakened at midnight by the sound of weeping women and Pípi's mother, Wampurái, calling out, "Pípi's disappeared!" Cooler heads argued that he would most likely take refuge in the household of relatives in one of the communities across the highway and that everyone should go back to sleep.

He was located and brought back for a dressing-down the next day. Everyone in the community assembled in the house of Pípi's parents. As the delinquent stood nervously in the middle of the house, staring at his feet in shame, senior men, including Shajián and Chímpa, spoke sternly of Pípi's obligation to respect married women and avoid drinking to excess. There were two surprising moments. The first came when Chímpa insisted that Candilaria and another girl in which Pípi had shown sexual interest were Pípi's "sisters," not "unrelated women"—that is, they were parallel cousins and therefore off-limits to him. This was untrue in both cases. Both were entirely eligible, although Candilaria's marriage put her in a forbidden category. The disconnect between actual genealogies and Chímpa's sermonette showed how slippery kinship rules were in practice. Equally unexpected were the speakers' references to Pípi's visions, the times when he had taken ayahuasca and tobacco water and angel's trumpet as a boy to help him "think straight." Unlike teenagers in Huascayacu, it seemed, some young men in Alto Naranjillo had undergone the traditional vision quest, although there was no sign that it was still being pursued.

Boys, Shimpiyacu, 1978.
Photograph courtesy of Michael F. Brown.

Candilaria's husband was willing to shrug off Pípi's clumsy attempt at adultery as a juvenile indiscretion. After closing remarks from Shajián, everyone drifted away. At dawn the next morning, Pípi left on a hunting trip with a group of older men.

Shortly after the incident, a document came into my hands that expressed Awajún views of the disruptive potential of sexuality. Prepared in a neighboring village, it bore the boldface title "Internal Regulations of the Community." My interest was aroused. Could this be a people's first experiment with written laws? Although I didn't expect the document to rival the Ten Commandments or the Magna Carta in grandeur, it offered the prospect of witnessing the birth of a new legal order, bringing the ancient lawgiver Étsa, the sun, face-to-face with Max Weber, the German sociologist whose work on bureaucracy, power, and rationalization set the agenda for an important branch of Western social science. Or so I imagined.

The regulations were divided into eleven articles. The first six, loosely translated, sufficiently convey the document's focus:

1. A young unmarried man who has sexual relations with an unmarried woman after promising to marry her, then does not marry her, will be given twenty-four hours in jail.
2. Someone from a distant community who has relations with an unmarried woman will not be allowed to marry her.
3. A married man who has relations with an unmarried woman must marry her.
4. An unmarried man who asks an unmarried woman to marry him may do so.
5. A married woman who commits adultery will receive fifteen days in the community jail and fifteen days of community work. Her husband, if he refuses to take her back, may keep all of her personal goods.
6. A man who fondles a woman in the night will be punished by twenty-four hours in the community jail.

The rest of the laws, but for two, explored variations on the theme of sexuality and marriage. The exceptions included a prohibition on fighting and punishment for men who habitually failed to muster for communal work. Matters of property went unmentioned, aside from the reference to an adulterous wife's personal possessions. That was hardly surprising in light of the Awajún's modest material resources and relative indifference to wealth. More significant, perhaps, was silence about sorcery. I could only infer that the topic was too divisive for anyone even to contemplate bringing it under the control of formal law.

Arturo, the fiercely independent traditionalist who a year earlier had abandoned Huascayacu to escape what he believed to be endemic sorcery, found little peace in his new neighborhood. He was embroiled in a dispute with his former son-in-law Mankúse, who had been given one of Arturo's prepubescent daughters as a wife. Mankúse disliked living under Arturo's thumb and eventually built his own house in another community. His bride was too young and inexperienced to care for him properly. An incompetent wife, regardless of age, harvested only rancor from a husband and his relatives. The girl was miserable. Arturo eventually took her back over Mankúse's objections. His relatives now spoke of punishing Arturo in some way, although what that meant in practice remained unclear.

Meanwhile, Arturo had become the target of sorcery accusations in his new community. A wave of minor illnesses had worked its way through neighboring households. These families, noting that they hadn't suffered much sickness before Arturo's arrival, suspected him of causing this illness. He was blamed for the death of a child in another community where he had lived briefly. Closer to home, the recent suicide of a nephew, the son of a man named Kachúm, was attributed to Arturo's malevolent sorcery or the deranging effect of a love charm owned either by him or his son Armando and to which the suicide victim was said to have come into contact. Arturo's prior relations with Kachúm, his wife's brother, had been cordial, but they deteriorated to the point that Kachúm had threatened to kill him during a recent beer party.

The ápu of Arturo's community came to Alto Naranjillo in the hope of pushing the matter toward resolution. He met with Shajián and Genaro, asking Genaro to inspect Arturo for killing darts. Genaro eventually agreed, saying that Arturo should appear in Alto Naranjillo on a specific day. When the news got back to Arturo, it had been embellished to include the promise that if Genaro determined him to be a sorcerer, he would be killed on the spot by the men of Alto Naranjillo.

No stranger to brinkmanship, Arturo announced defiantly that he would come as scheduled despite the risk of execution. Arriving in Alto Naranjillo with his son Armando on the appointed date, he first visited the house of Shajián, who urged him to tell the truth at the shamanic session that night. Genaro, Shajián said, would see through all lies. Arturo might as well admit possession of killing darts or ownership of a love charm if either story was true. Arturo vigorously asserted his innocence. Shajián then asked Arturo's son whether he owned a love charm. He denied this but produced a hunting charm, which was passed around for close examination by the older men. It was to attract game, not women, he said.

Minute-by-minute accounts of the healing session circulated the next day. Genaro had Arturo strip down to his briefs. Rather than drinking yáji, Genaro used cane alcohol and the mysterious "mestizo medicine" to achieve the required intoxication. He then scanned Arturo's body for sorcerer's darts. None were in evidence. He examined Armando with the same result. He fanned Arturo's body to remove even the tiniest dart. This included using the fan to blow air under Arturo's scrotum, a place favored by sorcerers for hiding darts. "You are not a sorcerer," Genaro announced. Arturo returned to his home the following morning, having been spared execution. For now, the matter was settled.

Returning to Huascayacu for a short visit, I found the village in a glum mood. Eladio's son Raúl and his wife, Rosa, had just left carrying their desperately ill newborn child, a girl. Their intended destination was Alto Naranjillo, where they hoped Genaro would consent to an emergency healing session to diagnose and treat the baby's illness. As the infant's vital signs spiraled downward, they decided to consult a paramedic at the health post in Atumplaya. He gave the baby an injection and pronounced the infant's condition to be grave. And so it was: the child died hours later. The cause of death was probably an infection of the umbilical site, a common affliction when the knife or scissors used to cut the cord had not been properly disinfected.

They returned home with the dead baby wrapped in a cloth. They sat for hours in the house of Raúl's parents, Eladio and Manúgka. Rosa cradled the body of her child. Raúl slumped on a nearby sleeping platform and stared at the floor. He suffered from epilepsy and had bitten his lip during a seizure immediately after the death. They both looked battered and defeated. People talked quietly to the couple for a while, and the atmosphere gradually shifted from grim to lighthearted—shockingly so when compared to the frenzied mourning at Héctor's funeral a few weeks earlier. The death of infants was so routine that only parents seemed deeply affected by it.

As Eladio looked for a pot in which to bury his dead grandchild, he began to clown around. "When it comes time to bury me, you'll need a great big pot," he said, squatting to imitate how he would look squashed into a ceramic jar. Then he pointed at me and said, to general laughter, "And when Máyak dies, we'll need a *really* enormous pot!"

A small group of us walked to the village cemetery. Eladio had a hard time finding it, so overgrown was the path. It proved to be a tiny, forlorn clearing with three palm-thatched shelters. The central shelter had collapsed into a muddy heap of leaves and branches. In the shelter to its left, a grave looked like it had been dug up by animals. The contents were not readily visible, and no one seemed interested in looking too closely.

"Are you there?" Eladio called out jauntily to the dead. He and his nephew Comisario decided to excavate a bare spot in the third shelter for the dead baby. As Comisario dug a hole with his machete, Eladio reviewed the other burials, referring to each of the dead by a kinship term rather than a personal name. The shelter in front of which we stood housed a five-foot-long casket made of balsa wood, with a handle carved on each end. A cover, some kind of stiff tree bark, was secured with palm-wood pins. Eladio said it was the coffin of Ágkuash's daughter, who had died of an upper respiratory infection two years earlier.

Comisario tested the pot in the hole to make sure that it would fit. Unwrapping the dead baby from the cloth in which it had been brought from Atumplaya, Rosa lovingly cleaned its face, smoothed its hair, and slowly bundled it in clean fabric, covering the face and head last. She gently put the bundle in the pot, feet down, body flexed, and then covered the burial with an inverted ceramic bowl. She wept softly in the Awajún's sing-song way as Eladio and Comisario lowered the pot into the grave and covered it with earth.

"Ask the others to take care of the baby," Eladio instructed her. She called out to two of the dead, one whom she addressed as "mother" and the other by name: Aurá, a young woman who had committed suicide two years earlier. "Care for my daughter," she said. "Feed her and keep her company."

Privately, Rosa's sister-in-law told me that Rosa lost the child because her mother, long dead but still remembered as a hidden sorcerer, had bewitched Rosa's breasts many years earlier after discovering that Rosa and Raúl had become lovers. She had opposed the relationship for reasons that no one could recall. This theory was thrown into doubt ten days later when the youngest child of Tomás, the schoolteacher, became seriously ill. In the succeeding weeks, both Raúl and Tomás sought healing sessions with Genaro. Genaro removed healing darts from Rosa and reported that her mother had not been their source. The sorcery came from someone else, whom he refused to name. Tomás and his wife brought their sick baby to Genaro but were too late. The child died before he could treat it. This wave of illness and death only worsened fears that Huascayacu harbored a hidden sorcerer, Raúl's brother Tiwijám remaining the prime suspect.

After several weeks of cautious reserve, Wampurái and Urucínta, the two most senior women among our immediate neighbors, began to warm up to Margaret. They talked to her about managing their gardens, the productivity of which was a matter of constant concern. More demanding still was management of husbands, those temperamental and sometimes violent lords of the household.

They gradually introduced Margaret to the secret life of the garden. Mature gardens, which are typically shaded by banana trees and the towering stems of mature manioc plants, were places where a woman and her youngest children enjoyed a few hours of relative peace. Women described the garden as being alive with forces that men did not fully understand. When recently planted, manioc cuttings were childlike "people" who called out for moisture and attention. They might even appear in a gardener's dream to complain of neglect. If they became thirsty, the plants might "drink the blood" or "eat the souls" of anyone who approached them, including a woman's husband and children. This potentially lethal power was harnessed by women in songs that instruct the plants to eat the souls of enemies who approach the house through a garden to stage a surprise attack. More often, however, women tried to satisfy the manioc people by singing special gardening songs and slaking their thirst with a ritual requiring the use of magical stones called *nántag* or *nántaj*.

The power attributed to nántag expressed Awajún fascination with any stone that appeared in an unexpected place. The geology of Amazonia is radically different from that of my native New England, where thanks to recent glaciations it is impossible to dig more than a few inches without having a shovel strike weathered pieces of schist, quartzite, or dolomitic marble. In contrast, Amazonia is blanketed by vast areas of ancient alluvial soils in which stones rarely lie near the surface. In Huascayacu there was so little stone that men were obliged to carry in heavy whetstones from miles away. Encountering a stone in the soil or the entrails of game animals and fish was sufficiently novel that people were inclined to see it as significant. Imagine a hundred-dollar bill fluttering out of your morning newspaper and you get a sense of it.

Nántag were stones that women inherited from their female elders, acquired in trade from other women, or discovered in the soil while cultivating. They tended to be small pebbles of different colors. Their possession and use were surrounded by secrecy because other women were strongly inclined to steal them. Like the manioc plants whose growth they promote, the stones have a propensity to eat souls. One woman spoke of a young boy who had come into his mother's garden to steal fruit. The woman's nántag were hidden there because she had just planted manioc stems. That night the woman had a dream in which the nántag, in the form of a person, told her, "Mother, mother, I have eaten." In the morning she went to the garden to examine her nántag and found them covered by a small nest of hair. "Who was in my garden yesterday?" she asked her children. A son said, "I came to take fruit because I was hungry." He soon died of snakebite. The narrator closed the tale by saying, "The nántag had eaten his soul." Another insisted that her mother's soul had been eaten by a nántag, which her family eventually smashed to pieces with an axe. "Nántag are terrifying," she said.

The day before a woman plants her manioc cuttings, she brings a clay pot to the garden and fills it with water mixed with the red seeds of achiote. Other mashed plant substances may be added to thicken the mixture and increase its potency. This deep red liquid is "blood" that satisfies the plants' thirst. The nántag are then immersed in the liquid, along with as many manioc stem cuttings as the woman can fit in the pot. Covered with a cloth, the pot is hidden in the garden until planting begins the next morning.

Wampurái, accompanied by her young daughter Yanuná, took Margaret to the garden to watch this. Wampurái and Yanuná painted a streak of red achiote under each eye upon reaching the garden. By identifying themselves this way, Wampurái said, they were protected from the soul-eating power of the stones. As Wampurái and her daughter planted the fresh stems, Margaret was assigned the task of feeding the stems that were already in the ground and beginning to sprout leaves. She was told to scatter the red liquid on these plants while saying, "Drink! Drink!" To keep the manioc plants from becoming lonely, it is wise to interplant them with other edible tubers, such as cocoyam and arrowroot. Women said that these plants, which, like manioc, are "people," carry water to the thirsty baby stems.

Anthropologists have long struggled to understand the roots of magic. How is it that peoples who in many cases possess astonishingly detailed factual knowledge of the natural world can believe in practices that strike us as so irrational? The most influential answer is that practitioners of magic don't confuse the practical with the symbolic. Magic has goals different from those of technology: it is *saying* something rather than *doing* something. In short, people who practice magic are not victims of logical error. It is anthropologists who err by failing to distinguish expressive acts from instrumental ones.

This theory rests on sophisticated thinking about the power of speech acts. When an officiating person pronounces the formula "I baptize thee" or "I pronounce you husband and wife," the words achieve their stated goal, assuming that the proper conditions have been met and the speaker is duly qualified. By this same logic, the magician tries to bring a desired state into being through powerful words: inspire someone's affection, draw game into shotgun range, or hasten the growth of cultivated plants. The magical words (and related magical objects, if they are used) don't *substitute* for practical action; they parallel and intensify it, or so the theory asserts.[5]

Unfortunately, this explanation failed to account for magic as the Awajún understood it. They insisted that it was at least theoretically possible to accomplish practical results through magic alone. This idea was clearly conveyed in the Núgkui myth and other narratives about powerful beings. Núgkui possessed knowledge that brought food out of thin air. Her mastery was lost to ordinary humans, who had no choice but to rely on practical knowledge and hard physical labor to accomplish the same things. But one couldn't rule out the possibility that by acquiring additional knowledge—most of which would qualify as spiritual in the Western scheme of things—people could achieve concrete results that approached those of Núgkui. Attitudes toward magical charms, for example, proved surprisingly pragmatic. If a man found a stone in an animal's entrails, there was reason to infer that it had some kind of powerful affinity to game that the stone's new owner could harness for his own purposes. Men said that in those circumstances, they would keep the stone in a safe place and experiment with its effect. If their hunting improved, they concluded that the stone attracted animals and therefore qualified as a *pusánki,* a hunting charm. If it produced only failure, it was tossed away.

This kind of rough-and-ready experiment hardly meets the procedural standards of laboratory science. Too many variables are in play, and the process ignores the role of chance. Science as we know it depends on writing systems that allow experimenters to replicate tests independently. Until only a few years prior to my arrival, few Awajún were literate. The institutional arrangements central to post-Enlightenment science weren't available to them. Nevertheless, there was no mistaking the experimental attitude that the Awajún brought to their engagement with the world. This helps to explain their remarkable technological achievements and those of other Amazonian peoples. These include the domestication and genetic refinement of important crop plants and discovery of countless bioactive plant preparations, ranging from medicines and hallucinogens to sophisticated poisons such as curare. I am not in a position to prove that the vegetable "blood" applied to manioc cuttings during the planting ritual had some biochemical effect on the young plants, but the possibility can't be ruled out.

Decades after my work in the Alto Mayo, cosmopolitan laboratory science solved a similar mystery. A puzzling feature of Awajún botanical knowledge was the prominent role played in magic and medicine by the apparently unremarkable plant pijipíg. The name encompasses several species of the sedge genus *Cyperus,* a spiky, water-loving plant perhaps best known for the species used to make Egyptian papyrus. In the Alto Mayo, people turned to varieties of pijipíg for many purposes, from treating women's gynecological disorders to acquiring sorcery darts.

The extraordinary powers that the Awajún attributed to this plant seemed anomalous because sedges are not generally known for bioactivity. Beginning in the late 1980s, however, scientists discovered that Amazonian species of *Cyperus* serve as host for members of a fungus genus named *Balansia. Balansia* has been shown to produce alkaloids similar to those found in ergot fungus, source of the chemical precursors to LSD. Distinct clones of piripiri harbor different varieties of fungus. This almost certainly accounts for the range of properties attributed to the plant, including its reputed ability to induce powerful visions.[6]

Similar discoveries may eventually explain something that I witnessed in Huascayacu. My neighbor Raúl was troubled by one of the small horrors of Amazonia, an insect larva lodged in his shoulder. Raúl had become a host for the botfly *Dermatobia hominis,* which lays its eggs on human skin. Warmed by contact, the eggs hatch into larvae that burrow under the top layers of skin and develop there until ready to emerge. The presence of a growing, moving animal under the skin is bothersome. Occasionally it produces a painful inflammatory reaction, although in most cases the larva's own secretions prevent infection.

Raúl asked his brother Kayáp to remove it, and they invited me to watch. This is a tricky business, Kayáp explained. If the worm is poisoned by insecticide or tobacco juice and dies under the skin, there will be a nasty infection. He would have to "call it out." Shirtless, Raúl leaned against the exterior wall of a house while Kayáp brought his face to within a few inches of the red, swollen site on Raúl's back. Kayáp began to make a rhythmic slurping sound, pushing air through saliva between his tongue and palate. After thirty seconds or so, the pale head of the larva appeared through a haze of skin tissue, rising to the surface. At that instant Kayáp expertly squeezed the lesion, bringing out the larva completely intact. Everyone insisted that the larva was responding to the call.

Years later I happened upon a description of the same technique in *Head Hunters of the Amazon,* a colorful account published in 1923 but apparently describing travels that took place late in 1899. The author, Fritz Up de Graff, catalogs how an "Antipa" (presumably Awajún) man named Pitacunga removed a botfly larva from Up de Graff's back. After soaking a piece of cotton with tobacco juice, Pitacunga brought his mouth next to the lesion and "made a funny indescribable noise understood by the worm to be the only tune worth coming out to hear, applying the cotton at the same time. Well, out he came, sure enough (driven out, no doubt, by the nicotine, to whose cleansing qualities I have referred before)." I would have dismissed Up de Graff's account as a preposterous yarn if I had not witnessed it myself.[7]

Empirical confirmation of some aspects of Awajún magic doesn't mean that every detail of indigenous knowledge will eventually be proven effective in scientific terms, any more than we can say that conventional Western medicine is immune to error. If you live long enough, the odds are good that you will be harmed by a medical procedure or pharmaceutical product once highly regarded by competent doctors but later shown to be useless or worse. Nevertheless, scientific validation of many elements of Awajún folk knowledge is a humbling reminder that categories such as magic and science should be applied with caution, if applied at all, when evaluating indigenous understandings of the rainforest and its resources.

Magic is hard for scientists to understand because it is deeply embedded in elements of social life that we regard as irrelevant to achieving practical results. Awajún listeners expressed aesthetic pleasure when listening to recordings of magical songs. If they knew the singer, they sometimes helped each other interpret difficult metaphors and speculated about the song's original source. Arcane language might signal that the song had been influenced by neighboring peoples whom the Awajún thought of as possessing more powerful knowledge of the unseen world. This mix of sentiments is not all that different from the pleasure that many Americans take in the design qualities of the latest smartphone or notebook computer. Good design is both elegant and functional. Often it isn't easy to say where one attribute ends and the other begins.

Magic and the shared understandings that supported it had social consequences as well. Investing the garden with a sense of danger, slight though it might be, gave women a degree of freedom from the relentless demands of their husbands. The longer Margaret and I lived with the Awajún, the more those values were projected on us. When she interviewed women alone, they often asked whether I would become angry because she was out of my sight for an hour or two. Once while visiting a family in Shimpiyacu, my host advised me—half jokingly, but with an accusatory edge—to order Margaret to sit without laughing as she chatted happily with a group of women nearby. "If a man sees his wife enjoying herself, he becomes angry because her flirtatious laughter attracts other men," he said. The traditional solution involved a type of knife called *dawág,* a long sliver of honed steel fashioned from a cast-off machete blade and typically worn suspended from a cord while hunting. My host advised me to plunge a blade into Margaret's thigh to a depth of two finger-widths when no one was looking. She would then leave the gathering "in shame" to tend to the wound in secret.

On another occasion, a middle-aged man laughingly referred to my pocketknife as a "clitoris-cutter." Before the arrival of the bilingual teachers and the establishment of schools, he said, a small blade like mine might have been used by a man determined to punish his adulterous wife. Such extreme forms of spousal brutality were receding into the past, but stories of conventional wife beating were not uncommon. The wife of one man in whose house we lived for a week showed Margaret four places where her scalp had been cut by her husband for one reason or another. A woman's garden was a site of hard work and a constant test of her skill. It also served as a refuge.

The rattling of bundled *sámpi* leaves announced the commencement of the curing session an hour after sunset. A dozen adults and three children were crowded into Genaro's small house next to the highway. The focus of his healing attention was to be Chína, his sister, a middle-aged woman complaining of persistent back pains. She lived in another community not far away. Also seeking attention was Genaro's classificatory brother-in-law Benjamín, whose infant son suffered from what appeared to be an ear infection. Everyone else present, excepting the two anthropologists, was related to Genaro or the patients.

As adults chatted quietly, Genaro sat on a carved stool turned to face the wall, waiting for the yáji to take hold. He removed his shirt and swiveled to face patients and visitors. He shook the leaf bundle, which made a soft rasping sound. He began to sing: "Make me intoxicated so that I can cure those who have come." An eerie sound issued from his chest, a drawn-out, percussive sigh or yawn. It announced the arrival of pásuk spirits that provided him with information from distant places. He hawked extravagantly and spat on the dirt floor to one side. His singing commenced again, backed by the soft percussion of the leaf bundle. The words of his song were compressed and arcane, difficult for me and, I later learned, for many Awajún to understand.

Genaro's daughter brought in a clean banana leaf and placed it on the floor directly before him. China removed her dress and lay facedown on the banana leaf, a blanket covering her hips. Genaro sang, then sighed again. The mother of the sick baby moved to Genaro's right, holding the child in her arms. Those present began to shout: "See everything! Think well! Will anyone die or become ill?"

China spoke in a scratchy, plaintive voice. "Little brother, my back hurts a lot. Look into me. See everything. I'm suffering. What sickness has grabbed me?" Genaro spat noisily, then said, "I'm very intoxicated." Now singing, he called out, "Little darts, answer me with your light! I want to be your friend. There it's shining because of sorcery, not illness. Answer me, I want to talk to you. *Yárua* bird, flying above, colored purple, grab the darts!"

The adults began to shout out questions or talk among themselves. In the dim light of a crude, homemade kerosene lamp, at times it was hard to know who was speaking. A woman asked, "Are the enemies from Pumayacu coming to kill us?" Another: "Is someone going to die?" Another still: "If I'm going to die, tell me! Will my wives be widows with new husbands?"

Genaro touched Chína's hip with his left hand. He leaned over, sucked noisily on her back, and spat something on the dirt floor. He began to sing again. Benjamín called out, "Cure my baby son! His ear hurts. It's full of pus."

Genaro sang, "If they kill me, my brother Shajián will be there to avenge me." He stopped shaking the leaf bundle and said in a normal speaking voice, "Give the baby an injection of penicillin. He has a wound in his ear."

Returning to the visionary, prophetic mode, Genaro reported that enemies in the village of the recently murdered young sorcerer were talking, although he couldn't make out their exact words. Again he emitted a series of percussive sighs: "Huh huh huh *huh*!" Then he said, "Dáse will soon die. I see his soul in the sky."

"That's right," responded a man in the dark house. "Only his body lives. Dáse's soul is already gone. Better he should rest."

Genaro, in a normal voice: "I see my dead father-in-law. I, too, will die. I'll be with him. In a while I, too, will die. . . . Sister, you have a few darts in you."

He shook the leaf bundle over Chína, then sucked on her. "When your body hurts, it makes you weak. I'll cure you, my sister. Your liver looks black. It always hurts."

From the darkness came a woman's voice. "Dáse says that his food has no flavor now. Even meat has no taste for him. Perhaps he'll die soon."

A man shouted, "Look at my sons to see whether they'll get sick!" Another man yelled, "See everything so that those from

Atahuallpa will not kill us!" Chína added her voice to the cho-
rus: "See everything! Why did you kill our enemies from
Pumayacu? They will murder you. Be careful!"

Genaro shifted to a normal speaking voice. His words were
cryptic. "The mirror opens. It is changing."

Turning to the mother of the sick child, Genaro said, "I
know how to cure the child. I'll defeat the illness. His ear will
heal. Give him an injection. I've sucked out some of the illness,
but now he needs medicine. There's another medicine like penicillin in a blue ampule. Buy it. That's all." The woman carried
the child across the room and sat against the far wall.

Genaro fanned Chína with the leaf bundle. "I see that they're
weeping in Shampuyacu. Someone has died. The body is wrapped
in a blanket. I can't see whether it's a man or a woman. They've
cut the dead person's hair. The body has been laid out. Is it a
man or a woman? Tsugkinúwa is crying. She wants to kill herself. Don't let her kill herself! I'm walking where people weep.
They ask the dead person, 'Why have you committed suicide?' I
see that someone will die.

"I'm an orphan, but I never wanted to kill myself. We are
men. We must be strong. I see Taag sleeping. I see his soul in the
sky, his clothing white, luminous. When I die, I won't go to
heaven. I'm an iwishín. My soul will suffer. My brother Taag was
once healthy and strong, but now he is sick and cowardly. He is
thin, suffering from sickness. In the sky he'll be well and happy."

From the darkness, someone in the room observed, "Taag's
wife doesn't want him anymore because he's sick."

Genaro's vision became clearer. "The death will be during a
party. It will be a suicide when everyone is drunk."

"Your niece wants to kill herself," Chína said. Someone else
added, "She'll kill herself because her husband took a second
wife. He'd been having sex with her for a long time. That was
why the ápus let him marry her. But his first wife is angry."

"My niece dies," said Genaro. "She hangs herself."

"My Juanita will get drunk and kill herself," Chína echoed.

Genaro's vision then circled back to the fate of the man named Dáse. Dáse would die, Genaro insisted, because he continued to have sex with one of his wives. From elsewhere in the house a woman shouted, "He wanted to have relations with his first wife, but she refused because it will make him sicker. His second wife said yes. She wants him to die soon." Someone else elaborated on the theme of Dáse's marital troubles: "Dáse claims that young men are always having affairs with his wives. Genaro has promised to beat these wives when Dáse dies. Dáse said that it is right and fitting that Genaro and Wisúm beat them when he dies. Other men have been having sex with them."

Genaro: "I see many people in the house of Takarét. Black people."

Others: "Who could it be? Black people?"

Discussion shifted to the threat of a reprisal attack from Atahuallpa. "We ought to carry our guns with us in case they come," someone said. Genaro replied, "I go without my gun because the road is wide. I can see people coming from far away."

The pace of Genaro's observations gradually slowed, and there was a palpable sense that the event was winding down. Genaro informed Chína that he would need to treat her three more times to remove all the sorcery darts that afflicted her. "I took out a tiny stone, and in your calf you had a bit of grass. The sorcery is recent. It will be easy to cure."

Chína lamented, "Before I was always healthy. Now I am sick. Why? It's sorcery."

"Your son-in-law doesn't take good care of you," Genaro said. "He gives you only a little meat, while he takes a lot for himself. He must take better care of you."

"My son doesn't take care of me, either. He hit me the other day."

The event closed with more talk about ailing kinsmen. Genaro sucked on Chína's back one more time and spat the results on the floor. "I'm done, sister." People said goodbye and drifted to nearby houses where they would spend the night.

This was the first of five healing sessions that I attended in Genaro's house during my time in Alto Naranjillo. For three he used yáji to achieve the necessary trance state. For the others it was alcohol and his secret "mestizo" concoction. The format varied little regardless of the means of intoxication.

The events were not exactly what I expected. Genaro's messages rarely touched on cosmological themes. There was no exploration of the far corners of the universe, no insight about the celestial or subterranean realms. His songs did make use of traditional animal imagery—the jaguar, the spectacled bear, various bird species—and sometimes of mythological figures such as Tsúnki, an underwater being closely identified with the anaconda and regarded as something like shamanism's patron saint. In general, though, Genaro divided his attention between treating the patients before him and issuing pronouncements about current situations and future events. Woven throughout were strands of gossip and morally charged observations about the behavior of specific individuals. These included comments about allegedly adulterous wives, abusive or neglectful youths, and the likelihood that someone would commit suicide.

A striking feature of the event was the energetic participation of others. Genaro clearly presided over the session and controlled its rhythm, but Chína and others in the room were far from passive spectators. They badgered him with questions about all manner of things and demanded that he use his divinatory powers to provide information about the future of their kin and their enemies. Genaro took pains to emphasize the strength of his intoxication and the intensity of his effort to achieve a cure.

Given the moral ambiguity of his vocation, he sought to stave off suspicion that his work on the patient's behalf was half-hearted or negligent, which might convince his detractors that he was an agent of sorcery rather than a bulwark against it.

The quick pivot to discussions of pharmaceutical drugs was another surprise. Perhaps it shouldn't have been. The symbolism of hypodermic injections had strong affinities to Awajún notions of how sorcerers attack their victims: the needle is an inversion of the sorcery attack, just as the iwishín inverts the role of sorcerer by using his own darts to effect a cure. By appropriating the symbolism of Western medicine, Genaro enhanced his reputation as a knowledgeable healer who deployed a broad range of healing techniques.[8]

The ritual's eclectic jumble was worlds apart from the variety of shamanism made famous by Claude Lévi-Strauss in his essay "The Effectiveness of Symbols," perhaps the most influential interpretation of shamanic healing ever written. The essay assesses a shaman's intervention in a difficult childbirth among the Kuna people of Panama. The Kuna ritual focuses almost exclusively on the patient's protracted labor. The healer's chant, heavy with symbolism, leads the afflicted woman on a spiritual journey parallel to her own embodied experience, subtly guiding her emotions to reduce pain and achieve a safe delivery. "The shaman," Lévi-Strauss says, "provides the sick woman with a *language*, by means of which unexpressed, and otherwise inexpressible, psychic states can be immediately expressed."[9]

Genaro's yáji sessions bore little resemblance to Lévi-Strauss's portrait of symbolic order and healing catharsis. Instead of the Kuna ritual's focused intensity, there was a nervous hopping from theme to theme, at times approaching communal free association. Chína and the parents of the sick baby were doubtless comforted by Genaro's insistence that their recovery was certain. At the same time, the shaman's visions left disturbing questions unanswered. Chína's fear of sorcery was confirmed. So who caused this suffering? Chína would recover from her current ailment, but what assurance did she have that the sorcerer wouldn't strike again? Would there be a vengeance attack in response to the murder of the accused sorcerer months before? Who was the dead woman seen in Genaro's vision? What would prompt her suicide? In return for the fleeting consolations of a diagnosis, the removal of deadly sorcery darts, and expressions of support from kin, Genaro's patients found themselves led into a labyrinth of unsettling riddles that stretched far beyond that small roadside house, far beyond that moonless night.

7

Hard Lessons

Eighteen months after walking into an Awajún settlement for the first time, I made the punishing dry-season trip up the Río Huascayacu to interview people in Shimpiyacu and two neighboring communities. Margaret had returned to the United States for several months to visit her family and purchase supplies for the final weeks of fieldwork. I used the time to visit all of the Awajún communities of the Alto Mayo, mindful that after nearly two years in Peru my paltry research funds were dwindling rapidly.

Hiring a motorboat and boatman for the trip upriver was a necessary extravagance. The Río Huascayacu, a tributary of the Mayo, offered only slow torment when the water level was low. Fallen trees, many lying beneath the river's broken surface, tested the endurance of boatman and passengers, who were obliged to wade into the shallows, sometimes with an axe or chain saw, to muscle boats past twisted snags.

My work had shifted from documentation of Awajún life in general to a more sharply focused study of how the Awajún used technology and ritual together to act on the world: to attract lovers, make their gardens thrive, draw monkeys closer so that they could be more easily killed, or cause a husband to lose interest in a woman he wanted to bring into the household as a second wife. The focus was magic, in other words, although I hoped eventually to abandon the term because of the way it stacked the analytical deck. The received wisdom was that magic should not be confused with technology. The only escape from the iron cage of this duality was to think of magic and technology as woven together in a joint process of understanding the world and acting on it, something that the Awajún managed skillfully.

Accompanying me was a young Awajún man named Matías, whom I had hired to help with the translation of complex, richly metaphorical magical songs. Matías had proven to be a proficient translator: bright, comfortable in Spanish, and, even more important, genuinely curious about his culture. Working on Awajún materials together was a process of discovery for both of us. This made otherwise tedious work enjoyable.

Matías had one conspicuous social liability and another that soon revealed itself. The first was that, as a young man from the Alto Marañón, he was an outsider. His kinship links to people in the Alto Mayo were tenuous. He was also better educated and more widely traveled than most of his Alto Mayo counterparts. His clothing reflected the height of mestizo fashion of the time, a tropicalized version of men's outfits in the film *Saturday Night Fever:* flared polyester trousers, loose colorful shirts, shoes with stacked heels. This worldliness made him irresistible to Awajún women, or so local gossip attested. He had promised that during our time in Shimpiyacu he would avoid romantic entanglements sure to provoke scandal and conflict.

Shortly after the boatman dropped us off near Shimpiyacu, we walked to old Míkig's house to pay our respects. The house was full of visitors, many of the men well lit up from the beer that Míkig's wife and other women were serving at a brisk pace. I was received courteously, if a bit more stiffly than on previous occasions. When the room's attention shifted to Matías, the tension became palpable. Míkig asked for the name of his home community and, even more insistently, his father's name. Matías answered that his father was Ernesto. "What is his Awajún name?" Míkig wanted to know. "He's Ernesto," insisted Matías. "He's always been Ernesto." Another man, Shímpu, loudly proclaimed this to be a lie, that his father's name was really Chawík. Shímpu claimed to have learned this after Chawík paid a visit to the region a few months before. Matías stuck to his story. The conversation moved on to other matters, but Shímpu persisted in antagonizing Matías with hostile remarks for the next half hour. Sizing up the situation, I pleaded fatigue, thanked Míkig for his hospitality, and hustled Matías out the door.

As we walked to the house where we were staying, he confessed that Shímpu's suspicion was warranted. His father was indeed named Chawík. Decades earlier, Chawík's uncle had married a woman from the Río Potro area, fathered children, and eventually added sons-in-law to his large household. He was also a practicing iwishín. This proved his undoing: accused of sorcery, he was assassinated. The killing took place while one of his sons-in-law was visiting Chawík's village. Chawík and other kinsmen of the murdered shaman demanded that the visitor guide them to the site of the killing so that they could investigate. He agreed but led them astray on the trail. There was an argument that escalated to violence, then murder. The victim of the second killing was related to Shímpu and other men in Shimpiyacu. Matías's father had warned him to avoid these men because they might want to even the score despite the years that had passed since the killings.

My reaction to his confession was a mixture of shock, irritation, and concern. Although I understood that the Awajún could nurse a desire for vengeance for decades after a killing, I had never witnessed personally the kind of smoldering rage that might easily lead to murder. Harder to fathom—emotionally, if not intellectually—was how this could be directed at someone who had been a trouserless boy of nine or ten when the original killings took place. Irritation was prompted by Matías's failure to disclose the danger that he faced by coming to this community. A desire for salaried work had trumped candor and put us both in a tight spot. We would need to leave as soon as possible—no easy matter given Shimpiyacu's location. We arranged to travel downriver in a dugout canoe with a teacher heading to town in a couple of days. Matías was never out of my sight during that time, and we were able to avoid encounters with men who wished to settle scores with Matías's father and his kin.

After two weeks away from Alto Naranjillo, I returned to find that my immediate neighbors, Túgki and Wampurái, had abandoned their house—gear, benches, and sleeping platforms removed, livestock gone. It seemed possible that they had relocated to the house that Utiját was vacating in favor of a newly constructed one. On my way to the river to wash up, I met Túgki, who looked wild-eyed and more frail than ever. "She's dead," he croaked. "My wife drank poison and died."

The news was difficult to accept. Only two weeks earlier Wampurái had been cheerful and full of life. Now she was dead, leaving several young, motherless children in the care of their ailing father. Túgki led me to the grave inside the abandoned house. There was little to see, just a mound of freshly turned earth. We mourned together for a while, then he returned to Utiját's house, where he and his children were staying until they could find another place to live.

No one seemed inclined to talk about the suicide other than to report the heartbreaking facts. Wampurái had awakened one morning as usual. Her sister-in-law Urucínta came by to complain that Wampurái's dog had eaten one of her hens, which people said "made Wampurái angry at the dog." Wampurái then went to her garden, returned with a basketload of manioc, and carried the tubers to the river to be washed and peeled. While there, she pounded stems of the plant *tímu,* a fish poison that contains the toxin rotenone. She covered the pounded stems in water and drank several bowlfuls of the poisonous liquid. Her daughter Yanuná ran to the house to say that her mother was violently ill. She was carried home and died within hours, presumably of the respiratory depression and congestive heart failure that rotenone induces in those who consume it.

Days before her suicide, Wampurái told Túgki about a dream in which she died and returned to life after three days. Recalling the dream, Túgki objected to prompt burial. The body lay in the house in case Wampurái's vision would come to pass. By the fourth day decomposition made immediate burial necessary. Chímpa, eldest son of the recently deceased ápu, refused to allow Wampurái to be buried in the village cemetery, site of his father's grave. As a suicide, he insisted, she would not go to heaven. Thus the decision to bury her in the house. Several neighbors subsequently reported íwanch sightings and strange noises from the abandoned house. Anxiety grew when one of Chímpa's wives had a dream in which Wampurái's spirit declared her intention to mete out omens of death to passersby, perhaps by screaming or making some other kind of terrifying sound. This so upset Túgki that he opened the grave to confirm that Wampurái was really and truly dead. The body was undisturbed.

Chímpa offered his assessment of the suicide during one of my afternoon social visits. He saw three possible motives. Wampurái might have "killed herself from anger" because her dog had eaten Urucínta's hen. She might also have been angry because Oscar, an unmarried nephew, had rejected Wampurái's suggestion that he marry her twelve-year-old daughter Delicia. The third possibility, which Chímpa admitted was pure speculation, was that Wampurái had become pregnant from an affair with another man and wished to escape Túgki's wrath when he learned of the adultery.

The notion that Wampurái's suicide should be blamed on a dog's misbehavior was widely shared by her kin. It illustrated something I had registered but never thought about before: Awajún theories of human motivations were resolutely shallow, demonstrating a profound reluctance or inability to imagine another person's interior life. This first had crossed my mind months earlier when talking to Genaro about a recent sensational suicide in which a young man in another community had leaned the barrel of a loaded shotgun against his chest and pulled the trigger. "Why did he kill himself?" I asked. Genaro mulled over the question for a moment, then said, "Because he no longer wanted to live." A variation on this theme arose in conversations about misconduct such as adultery. One of the teachers observed, "When we Awajún are caught doing something wrong, we simply deny our guilt." There was no appeal to motivational complexity. People did bad things because they were bad or angry or "without thought," not because they were caught in a web of circumstance that impaired their judgment, which would have been the default explanation of many Americans in similar straits. Although the Awajún were capable of great generosity and compassion, when they were confronted by violence or adultery their moral logic veered toward blunt simplicity.

Hence the reluctance to identify Wampurái's desperate family situation as a factor that might have contributed to her suicide. Her husband was slowly succumbing to the effects of a chronic, life-threatening disease. Because she was an orphan, her kinship connections in Alto Naranjillo were weak. Her adult sons, most of whom had married into other communities, were burdened with family responsibilities of their own. Given that backdrop, Chímpa's theory that she was angered by the failure of her scheme to marry off Delicia to Oscar had a degree of plausibility. This would have brought a mature man into the household. The marriage was improbable, however. Oscar, a handsome, ambitious bachelor in his twenties, had little reason to wed a scrawny cross cousin still a year or two shy of puberty. Amid these difficulties, the incident with the dog may have swept Wampurái past the point of no tomorrow.

Her death was a painful reminder of the chasm separating my study of magic and ritual from the unforgiving realities of everyday Awajún life. Wampurái's suicide was an extreme instance of what the sociologist C. Wright Mills, writing in the 1950s, called "troubles." If suicide were an isolated event, it might be interpreted solely in light of individual psychology. But it was shockingly common. To understand it, one needed what Mills called "the sociological imagination." By this he meant attention to the social circumstances that give rise to particular kinds of pathologies, including acts of self-destruction.[1]

Making sense of the larger suicide picture was no easy matter. Death records didn't exist. Fertility histories contained multiple references to suicide. The possibility that reported suicides misrepresented the actual cause of death could not be ruled out completely, even though most reported cases seemed unambiguous. The number of Awajún to whom I had access was small in comparison to the group's total population. This, along with the difficulty of determining the exact dates of past suicides, made it impossible to meet scientific standards of accuracy.

Nevertheless, quick back-of-the-envelope calculations suggested that the suicide rate in the Alto Mayo was at least ten times higher than that of the United States. The small village of Huascayacu, for instance, had experienced seven suicides in the previous five years. Two were dramatic double suicides in which people had poisoned themselves. More frequent still were failed suicide attempts such as the one I witnessed while living there. Even allowing that many of these attempts at self-destruction were halfhearted and largely symbolic, there was little doubt that suicide had woven itself deeply into the social fabric.

Patterns were difficult to substantiate with such a small sample, but a few things were indisputable. Women of all ages were far more likely to kill themselves than men and also more likely to be involved in failed suicide attempts. The failure rate was partly due to their preference for poison—everything from laundry soap and commercial insecticides to plant-based toxins— the effects of which could sometimes be survived. Among men, suicide victims were mostly in their teens and early twenties. Because they were more likely than women to use firearms to kill themselves, failed attempts were rare.

The local explanation of female suicides emphasized an outburst of strong emotion, typically extreme grief or anger provoked by thwarted desire. A woman felt that her husband was slighting her in favor of a younger co-wife. A domineering father proposed giving his daughter in marriage to a man she disliked. Consumed by grief over the death of a mother, a girl drank a bottle of insecticide after escaping the protective circle of fellow mourners. Where these scenarios differed was in the assignment of blame after death. Rarely was anyone held responsible for grief-related deaths or a daughter's refusal to obey her father, but a husband sometimes found himself condemned by his in-laws if a wife's suicide could plausibly be attributed to his brutality or neglect. This plunged a widower into a world of trouble, even making him a target for revenge murder.

The threat of suicide, explicit or implicit, thus represented one of the most powerful sources of leverage that a woman had at her disposal. I had seen this in action during a recent river trip. A senior man planned to take only the younger of his two wives on a visit to Moyobamba. The older wife planted herself in the canoe as well. After a brief standoff, he shrugged and let her stay. Another man who witnessed the incident later confided privately, "He knew that if he had left her in the village, she might have taken poison to punish him." The tragedy, of course, was that the implicit threat was only as strong as a woman's demonstrated willingness to act on it if her bluff was called. Women who survived serious suicide attempts or who described their motives before dying were likely to say that they wanted to punish their husbands for harsh treatment or broken promises.

People regarded the suicides of young men differently. Men were likely to kill themselves while drinking. Drunk, they might "begin to feel alone, like orphans," people often said. A middle-aged man named Santiago claimed that he could identify the type of youth likely to take his own life. "He is always laughing and doesn't listen to the advice of elders," he said. "My sister's son is like this. He shouts when walking alone in the forest. He laughs alone for no apparent reason. My own brother was the same way, and he killed himself. Men like this are *pujuchmín*, ones who will not live."

Old-timers insisted that the decline of the vision quest accounted for the increase in suicidal behavior among young men. Shímpu, the man who had behaved so threateningly to Matías, once demonstrated to me the kind of predawn lecture that he often gave to his wives, daughters, and sons. The part directed to his sons addressed male suicide and its causes: "My sons, I have never threatened to kill myself. I always went to drink aya-huasca to find a vision. I never thought about suicide. Sons, when you drink, you go crazy and want to kill yourself. You have sex with girls when you are still young. You have never taken bitter ayahuasca, nor have you felt suffering. You do these bad things. You have eaten sweet things since you were babies, things that I never ate. These things have penetrated to your marrow. All your body is sweet. Your thought is weak, vacillat-ing. I hear that you talk of wanting to shoot yourself. What will people say, that the sons of Shímpu want to kill themselves? Men should never think these things. How will you correct your children if you yourself do these things? Are you deaf, without ears? Listen to what I tell you, and do as I say!"

When one contemplated so many suicides, so much heart-ache for surviving family members, the best explanation seemed to lie in a contradiction between prevailing values and the in-ability of some people to live up to them. The Awajún valued personal autonomy, which served as a measure of self-worth. Young and middle-aged women had little control over their own lives. They tended to marry young and be pregnant or nursing for most of their childbearing years. Suicide was an av-enue for communicating demands or punishing abusive spouses in terms that made sense within the context of a highly agonis-tic society. Young men shared some of the women's sense of frustration. They aspired to the autonomy of mature men, but it lay just beyond their grasp. With the rigorous discipline of the warrior's life, including its search for visionary certainty, in sharp decline, the inevitable frustrations of youth too easily gave rise to a sense of hopelessness.

This scheme made logical sense but offered little in the way of comforting certainty. For weeks after Wampurái's suicide and burial, my neighbors asked whether it bothered me to live so close to her restless spirit. "Máyak," they would say, "aren't you afraid of seeing her íwanch?" In truth, I did find proximity to the grave disquieting, although not in the way they imagined. More unsettling than Wampurái's ghost was the recognition that anthropology could do so little to explain how she became one.

Shajián, Alto Naranjillo's headman, stopped by to talk about a bloody feud that had broken out among communities located more than a week's hard walk from the Alto Mayo. He was more animated than I had ever seen him. He said that men from a village near Balsapuerto had murdered someone from Kaupán whom they believed to be a sorcerer. A delegation had arrived to inform their Alto Mayo kinsmen of the conflict and solicit support in the form of fighters and ammunition.

With great relish, Shajián described the chain of events that led to the murder. A man named Kunám, a widower, had visited distant relatives for several days. Kunám was known to have been a practicing iwishín in the past, but he had apparently been cured of his shamanic habit by another iwishín. After his departure, two children died. The grieving parents concluded that Kunám had bewitched the local river, causing fish to die. The children died after eating the witchcraft-tainted fish. A plan was hatched to kill Kunám in reprisal.

Three men came to Kunám's community, ostensibly to propose that he marry the sister of one of them. Kunám's relatives suspected a trap. Nevertheless, the visitors convinced him to accompany them. Arriving at the Río Potro, they fished with lines and caught three rays. As they cooked the rays, something made Kunám change his mind about the trip. Perhaps he had begun to suspect their motives. He announced that he was returning home. His travel companions grabbed their shotguns and fired at his chest and head, killing him instantly.

Shajián Wajai, ápu of Alto Naranjillo, 1978.
Photograph courtesy of Michael F. Brown.

His body fell into the fire and was abandoned there by the killers.

When Kunám failed to return home, his relatives launched a search. They found his charred and decomposing body where it had fallen. Their community and three others decided to band together to exact revenge. In one of the ironic twists that sometimes characterized these vendettas, it was said that Kunám's own relatives had contemplated killing him because they, too, feared his sorcery. They were beaten to the punch by men from Balsapuerto and now felt obliged to avenge the death as a matter of principle.

The delegation visiting the Alto Mayo represented Kunám's assassins, who realized that they were outgunned by their victim's numerous relatives and allies. They had secured commitments of support from men in some Alto Mayo communities, but those in Alto Naranjillo were mostly inclined to avoid direct involvement. Shajián, the ápu, was miffed because the recruiting group hadn't dignified him with a direct request but instead sought his help in a hand-delivered letter.

Later I listened to Chímpa and Shajián discuss the situation. Shajián asked, "How can they come here to ask for help? Who will go to fight with them? It's very far."

"I said that those from Ugkuyacu should go there to investigate," Chímpa replied. "I'm sick right now. If I were from the Alto Marañón, I'd be in bed. Those men are more delicate. I sent word that I can't go to the meeting. Let them come to an agreement and inform me. I want them to explain the situation. I'm not a wáimaku, a vision-bearer, but I am a man. Even though I don't have a vision, I can pick up my gun and load it. I can kill, too."

"They asked me to send ammunition, but I refused," Shajián said. "With these cartridges they could kill someone from my family, or they could kill me."

Chímpa agreed. "Some men are contributing ammunition, but I'm not. I don't have confidence in these people. My brother Kúam acted badly by giving them cartridges. I won't support Úwek [Chímpa's father-in-law]. His son killed my brother. People ask me why I visit Úwek. I tell them that Úwek's family respects me more when I visit. They were the ones who wronged me, not the other way around. I want to avoid problems and live in peace. Since they are acting against my kin, I said I wouldn't donate cartridges. Let them get the ammunition on their own. Cartridges cost a lot and only create problems. Let's avoid this. People say that because I'm married to Úwek's daughters I should help him. But I didn't marry them to seek trouble. Let Úwek fight if he wants to.

"Búkuig, my mother's brother, will go to fight with the other side. He didn't start the feud. If Úwek's family goes against Búkuig, I'll defend him. We are not like the parrot *kayák*. You can kill many of them at once because they roost close together. We are spread out. If one of us is killed, I can call relatives from all over to avenge the murder." Chímpa named a specific man whom he intended to kill if Búkuig died in the feud. The conversation ended with Chímpa asking Shajián to witness that he wasn't taking sides. If Chímpa was obliged to go against his in-laws later, it couldn't be said that he had instigated the conflict.

The conversation was a concise lesson in old-school Awajún politics. Chímpa walked a tightrope of conflicting loyalties: to his brother Kúam, to his in-laws, and to lineal kin on both sides of the feud. He had no choice but to read the conflict against the backdrop of the killing a decade earlier that had led him and others, including Shajián, to separate themselves from Chímpa's father-in-law, Úwek, and relocate to the territory that became Alto Naranjillo. That conflict was eventually settled without further violence, but the failure to meet blood with blood left a lingering sense of incompleteness. The risk was that taking a firm position on a distant killing could destabilize things closer to home, with dire consequences. Kúam, Chímpa's hotheaded younger brother, had rashly put down a marker in the new feud, perhaps with the idea of establishing himself as a man of substance. Chímpa—more experienced, cagier, and with nothing left to prove—was determined to keep his distance.

Túgki's physical decline accelerated after Wampurái's death. Every day he looked more skeletal. In the final weeks of my time in the Alto Mayo, I felt obliged to help. After conferring with his son Wajajái, I offered to take him to the regional hospital to see whether anything could be done to stem the disease.

The three of us rode to Rioja in the back of a Toyota pickup, along with a half dozen colonists. At the truck stop near the town plaza, we shook the dust out of our clothes and walked to the hospital. There was a long wait. Túgki eventually was examined by the hospital's director, a short, balding, officious doctor in a white lab coat. He patronizingly identified Túgki as the "chief of his tribe" to two young residents—both doctors from Lima on national service assignments in a rural hospital—who assisted with the examination. Túgki's lower legs were painfully swollen, suggesting anemia, and there was evidence of a low-grade lung infection. The diagnosis of advanced leishmaniasis came as no surprise.

The doctor gave us a list of five medicines to purchase. It included antibiotics, a diuretic, vitamins, and Repodral, the antimony-based compound that would purge the parasite from Túgki's body. The cost of so many medicines was beyond my limited means. It was certainly beyond Túgki's. When asked to identify the most important drugs on the list, the attending physician sniffed, "All medicines are equally important in a course of medical treatment." Eventually he admitted that only the Repodral would cure the disease. He offered to admit Túgki to the hospital, where he could receive appropriate treatment. Wajajái said that on a previous occasion Túgki had run away from the hospital after finding it lonely and frightening. Better that Túgki return home for whatever treatment could be provided there.

Túgki and Wajajái returned to Alto Naranjillo while I spent the rest of the day scouring pharmacies for Repodral and as many of the other medicines as I could find. It was one thing to prescribe a medicine, quite another to obtain it. Repodral was either sold out or in short supply everywhere. New supplies were expected "next month," which meant "delivery date unknown." My plan had been to purchase the six-month supply that Túgki needed for a complete cure. In the end, I could find only enough for a few weeks. With so few health care workers in the area, there was little chance that Túgki would get the necessary daily injections at the correct dosage. Prospects for his recovery were dim.

Kayáp and I sat next to a fire in front of shelters that the people of Huascayacu had thrown up near their rice fields. Margaret, who had returned from the United States for the final weeks of fieldwork, slept under a mosquito net. Kayáp quietly spoke of the community's plans to cultivate rice and maize more intensively than they had in the past. One of his sons was in secondary school in town, and Kayáp needed cash to pay for uniforms and board fees. Like other Awajún communities, Huascayacu found its lands under threat of invasion by colonists. Sometimes the trespass was inadvertent: boundaries were hard to find in the forest. But there were intentional land grabs as well. The Awajún were on constant lookout for squatters. Some offered to pay rent for farmland, but so far community members had resisted the temptation. There was too great a risk that rent would turn into ownership over time, especially given Peru's unstable politics and waning popular support for indigenous rights.

The Awajún had concluded that the best approach was aggressive cultivation of land adjacent to the front lines of colonization. Communities along the highway had cleared enormous tracts and planted them in rice. This plan depended on ready access to transportation and water that could be used to irrigate the fields. Huascayacu was still too remote to undertake agriculture on a commercial scale. But Kayáp and other men were doing the best they could to emulate their kinsmen in other communities.

I told Kayáp that I hoped his children would continue to learn to make things such as baskets, net bags, and toucan-feather coronas. He agreed but noted that these activities were time-consuming. Materials had to be gathered and prepared; acquiring the necessary skills took years. "I'm not sure we have the time to make those things anymore," he said. Time had become money even for him.

Tiwijám, the man from Huascayacu who was unable to shake his reputation as a hidden sorcerer, finally decided that his only hope was to submit to examination by the iwishín Genaro. He came to Alto Naranjillo with his brother Raúl and cousin Manuel, their wives, and several other relatives. Genaro announced that he would use alcohol and his secret mestizo medicine for the healing session. Tiwijám was sent to the nearby colonist settlement to buy two liters of cane alcohol and a bottle of perfumed water. The event began informally. People were eating dried fish that Tiwijám had provided. He and Genaro began to drink the alcohol while chatting amiably.

As darkness closed in around the house, Tiwijám admitted that sorcery darts might have been secretly planted in him by a man in whose house he stayed as a guest. They had argued during a drinking party, but that night he slept in the man's house anyway. Without responding directly to Tiwijám's story, Genaro gave him more alcohol as well as some of his special medicine. "Only people who are not witches can have visions with this medicine. Because you are my brother-in-law, I give it to you to drink."

A few minutes after drinking the medicine, Tiwijám vomited on the dirt floor. After a quick examination, Genaro pronounced the vomit clear. Tiwijám began retching again, this time violently. He moaned, "I'm dying." A woman snickered. Others shouted, "This is what you wanted! This is why you came here!" Genaro's wife, Tumús, encouraged him at high volume: "You are always accused of being a sorcerer. They might even kill you. You have to stand up to the medicine!"

Genaro examined Tiwijám carefully. "Your witchcraft substance is in two parts inside you. Now you are throwing it out," he said. Tiwijám's violent retching continued while the others talked softly among themselves. One man joked about marrying his widowed mother-in-law, Chépa. Tiwijám said, "If I had been a witch by choice, I wouldn't be here suffering like this. If I couldn't be cured, I wouldn't come here."

Genaro inspected Tiwijám's vomit again, then said, "I'll tell you the truth: Others say you are a witch, but you will be cured. When you get home, eat only sweet potatoes and squash. If you don't follow this diet, you might become as you were before." Tiwijám vomited yet again. "Many people avoid me because they say that I'm a sorcerer," he moaned. He slumped forward, groaning because of the violent contractions of his stomach.

Genaro took off his shirt. The other people present continued to chat informally. There was occasional laughter at someone's lighthearted remark. Genaro rubbed Tiwijám's head and chest with perfumed water. Speaking to everyone, Genaro said, "His witchcraft was ready to grow large, but now he is throwing it out. The medicine that I gave him makes his kaag come together and stay on one side of his body. Then it gets thrown out."

Raúl asked, "With time, could it come back?"

"No, it can't happen," Genaro replied. "They will never be able to say that he is a sorcerer. They can say it, but it won't be true."

Genaro now addressed Tiwijám. "Before, I saw in my vision that you were a witch. I was given kaag like yours when I lived in Áchu with an adulteress. But when I sleep in the same house as my in-laws, I don't secretly make them into sorcerers."

Manuel commented, "I had a brother-in-law who was an iwishín. But he never made me into a sorcerer. That's how good men behave."

"The kaag in his body is changing to water because it has died," Genaro explained. "That's why I gave him the medicine."

Manuel called out, "We remember what you say. It is always said that you are good, that you cure people."

"I don't sleep well because sick people are always arriving to be cured."

Genaro showed Manuel his bottles of medicine. "This medicine won't kill all the kaag. This other one will, but now it is old. It's from the coast, from Chiclayo. There's none around here. The medicine that the mestizos make is stronger than ours. They make you intoxicated, and you see lights approaching like lightning bugs."

Manuel was evidently impressed. "Everyone knows about you. You work like a doctor."

Tiwijám asked to lie down, but Genaro told him that he needed to remain seated for a while longer. He scanned the liquid that Tiwijám had vomited onto a piece of pottery placed near him for that purpose. Genaro claimed to see a powerful kind of killing dart called *busmág tséntsak*. Genaro told Tiwijám to lean forward so that all the kaag would come out. Tiwijám noisily hawked up something, then spit onto the piece of pottery. "Little brother-in-law, I'm dying!" he moaned.

"We can't give him more medicine now," Genaro said. "He has to rest. We'll do it another day. He can't take yáji or the kaag will form again. That's why I gave him a different medicine. It's not possible to mix yáji with this. Tomorrow or another day he can take more medicine. If he doesn't follow my instructions, they may again say that he's a sorcerer. Later you can give him an injection of calcium vitamins and he'll get well." Raúl and Tiwijám's sister Isabel made a bed on the floor with banana leaves. Tiwijám was soon unconscious on the floor, snoring loudly.

As the exhausted Tiwijám slept, Manuel discussed whether he could arrange a healing session for his wife, who suffered from stomach pains. Tiwijám's brother Raúl said that he would need to undergo the same kind of purge as Tiwijám, just in case he, too, had been given witchcraft substance surreptitiously by the same sorcerer.

This was as much reassurance as Tiwijám was likely to get. The session was a double-edged sword for him. He had been certified as a hidden sorcerer, a *túnchi,* but an involuntary one, victim of an evil kinsman who had planted the seed of witchcraft in him as he slept, thus turning one of the most intimate expressions of sociability—sharing a house for the night—into an occasion for treachery. The sorcery substance had been purged and neutralized in front of witnesses. If he followed Genaro's recommendations, his commitment to a complete purging would be public knowledge. The news was certain to circulate widely in the coming weeks. Whether it would be sufficient to dispel the shadow of suspicion under which he had lived for years was anyone's guess.

The last twenty-four hours before leaving the Alto Mayo for the United States were festive. Many of our household goods, as well as gifts that Margaret had brought from home, were given to our neighbors. There were awkward moments as women bickered over who should get what, but in general the atmosphere was convivial. We went from house to house donating family photographs taken with an instant camera. One challenging task was disposing of our rubbish so that it wouldn't end up as litter in the village. The Awajún were unaccustomed to dealing with materials that failed to biodegrade quickly in the tropical heat and moisture. Floors were swept meticulously, but organic trash often ended up outside houses, where it normally seemed to disappear in a matter of days, scrounged by domestic animals or pounded to dust by foot traffic and the equatorial sun. People coveted the highly saturated colors found in bottles and other plastic items. When our empties began turning up as litter or integrated into necklaces and other items of material culture, I felt obliged to dispose of them secretly in burial pits.

In the afternoon, word came that visitors were asking for me at Kúam's house, close to the highway. It proved to be a group led by the son of a wealthy former patrón. Accompanying him were two women, both wearing the denim jumpsuits then in fashion among middle-class women in Lima, and two men, one of whom introduced himself as an anthropologist from Switzerland. They had importuned Kúam and his wives for beer. It was evident from their bloodshot eyes that a prodigious amount had already been consumed.

After dropping the names of some well-known professors from my university and asking about my work, the Swiss declared that because we were both citizens of nations that prospered by expropriating the resources of the Third World, he felt free to speak frankly. Was I here for my own career goals, including the publication of obscure articles for other academics? he asked. Or did I want to help the Awajún? As a Swiss citizen, he said, he was ashamed of the economic power of Nestlé, a Swiss corporation, and its harmful activities in Peru and other developing countries. Was I prepared to sacrifice ambition and join the battle against the imperialist Nestlés of the world? Or was I merely feeding the capitalist machine with information that it would use to exploit the Awajún more efficiently? He was unimpressed that I was already scheduled to publish the results of my work in Spanish. "When you tell people where these Indians live, it only makes it easier to exterminate them," he said. His Peruvian friend jumped in to say that although I might be well intentioned, naive Americans like me inadvertently helped the CIA by publishing our research.

As the conversation heated up, Kúam and his large family crowded around. They couldn't follow the argument but could read the tension. The visitors seemed uninterested in the Awajún and barely acknowledged their presence. Their bored-looking driver, anxious to return to town, stared at his watch. In response to a subtle cue, the visitors suddenly took their leave with the most perfunctory of thanks to Kúam and his wives. As their car receded into the distance, Kúam, curious but with a twinkle in his eye, asked, "Did you want us to kill them?"

The sour end to an otherwise happy day served as a bracing reminder that anthropology was a discipline at war with itself, torn between its scientific mission and its political commitments. The social world that I was leaving was grounded in elemental experiences and sentiments: hunger, death, sociability, suspicion, loyalty, and strategies for wresting a livelihood from the rainforest. Twenty-one months with the Awajún had exposed me to a broader range of human emotions than had my previous twenty-eight years. The visitors who needled me with hostile questions evidently cared more about ponderous abstractions—"primitive communism," "capitalist exploitation," "liberation," and the rest—than about extending common courtesy to their Awajún hosts. The prospect of returning to a university setting in which people routinely trafficked in such bromides was sobering.

The next day dawned clear and hot. Utiját and Urucínta sent us off with more bowls of manioc beer than we were accustomed to drinking at that hour. Helped by a few schoolboys, we carried our gear toward the road. Passing Chímpa's house, we learned that one of his wives, Mamách, was in labor. She was behind a blanket that had been hung as a screen. We could hear her groans as she braced herself on the horizontal bar that women used for support during deliveries. Chímpa went behind the blanket to take a look. "It's coming," he said.

Urucínta was called in and arrived in time to catch the baby as it dropped. She barked out orders—"Knife!" "Thread!"—as the umbilical cord was tied off. "It's a girl," she announced. At the news, Chímpa's face fell. Of his ten children, this was the eighth daughter. He would have preferred another son. After a few moments, though, he was his jovial self. Urucínta brought the baby for us to see. She was wrapped in rags, wrinkled, scarlet-faced, and not at all pleased by her new circumstances. Chímpa asked me to write down the time and date of birth on a scrap of paper: 8:45 A.M., October 20, 1978.

Chímpa, Utiját, and others walked with us to the highway. After a brief wait, we flagged down a large truck going our way. Bags were lifted aboard. Farewells were said the customary way before long separations: "If I die, I won't see you again." The driver closed the back gate, cutting off our view of the half dozen figures silhouetted against the road's shimmering heat.

PART TWO

1980–2012

There are many humorous things in the world,
among them the white man's notion that he is
less savage than the other savages.
                              —Mark Twain,
                                Following the Equator

8

Civilization's Twisting Road

The astonished reaction of my Awajún hosts to *National Geographic* images of unclothed Indians from the Brazilian Amazon speaks eloquently of the range of values and practices found in a region once seen as relatively uniform. A textbook on South American Indians, published in 1959 by Julian Steward and Louis Faron, describes South America's rainforest Indians as having "a fairly homogeneous culture" and living as "simple village people." A half century later, the picture looks radically different. We know, for instance, that communities located along the Amazon were, until shortly after European contact, densely populated and ruled by powerful chieftains who redistributed resources and managed large-scale public works that archaeologists are now uncovering with the aid of satellite imaging and other sophisticated survey techniques.[1]

When Steward and Faron wrote their textbook, early explorers' accounts of large, highly organized Amazonian settlements were widely dismissed as fanciful tales no more credible than sightings of mermaids. Most famous is the chronicle of Gaspar de Carvajal, a Dominican friar. Carvajal accompanied Francisco de Orellana's 1541–1542 expedition, which navigated the full length of the Amazon, battling hostile natives much of the way. Carvajal describes canoe flotillas of 2,000 warriors and "very large cities that glistened in white." The recent discovery of major earthworks in various parts of Amazonia has led scholars to conclude that Carvajal may not have been exaggerating. Some have offered precontact Amazonian population estimates as high as 10 million, although these remain controversial. Such dense populations were vulnerable to introduced European diseases and slaving expeditions. A century after contact, only scattered remnants of these Amazonian polities remained, giving rise to the notion that Amazonia was a cultural backwater incapable of supporting large settlements.[2]

Echoes of complex institutions that subordinate individuals to the greater social whole can be found in some of the region's surviving indigenous societies. The Canela people of central Brazil, for instance, live in large villages for much of the year and participate in a demanding cycle of rituals that knit the community together. Until a few decades ago Canela adults were expected to make their bodies available to one another for sexual pleasure. Women offered themselves to groups of men on ritual occasions, and over time most adults had socially sanctioned sex with nearly all opposite-sex individuals except those declared off-limits by incest rules. According to the ethnographers William and Jean Crocker, the Canela believed that "no one was so self-important that satisfying a fellow tribesman was less gratifying than personal gain."[3]

A less extreme variation on the theme of community solidarity is found among the Mehinaku people, who live in the Xingu Indigenous Park in Brazil. Like the Canela, the Mehinaku perform elaborate community rituals that unite people in good fellowship and shared responsibility. They have also developed what their principal ethnographer, Thomas Gregor, calls a "peace system" that produces a "shared, cognitive understanding of social relations in which nonviolence is expected and even inevitable."[4]

On an axis defined by individualism at one end and communalism at the other, the Canela and Mehinaku would have to be placed near the communal extreme and the Awajún at the individualist. Of the Achuar, Jivaroan cousins of the Awajún, Philippe Descola says that they have "established a form of political organization that safeguards each man's independence without bringing about a total dissolution of social links." That puts them among peoples who have "placed the very highest value of their social philosophy upon the realization of an individual's destiny, freely mastered and within the reach of every man." Descola uses "man" advisedly, given the subordinate position of women in Achuar society.[5]

The historical forces that produced indigenous societies as atomistic as the Awajún and Achuar remain mysterious. Recent research suggests that Jivaroan groups enjoyed mutually advantageous, if sometimes antagonistic, relations with the Inca empire. Some historians now think that the societies from which the modern Awajún emerged were populous and highly organized, bridging different environmental zones and engaging in stable trade relations with groups located both downriver and in the Andean highlands to the west. The Upper Amazonian environment set limits on social complexity but probably constrained development less than once thought. What can be said with certainty is that the Awajún and other Jivaroans have been regarded as stubborn, independent-minded, warlike peoples since the early 1500s.[6]

Social science offers several approaches that might explain such aggressive inclinations, although some can be discounted at the outset. There is little evidence, for example, that a desire for territory lay behind Awajún internal feuding or attacks against other ethnic groups. We know little about the size of the Awajún population in the nineteenth and early twentieth centuries, but the waves of devastating epidemics reported by observers suggest that their numbers were flat or declining. Awajún raids sometimes included opportunistic looting, but this does not seem to have been an important goal. Likewise the acquisition of female captives, widely sought elsewhere in Amazonia. Girls and women captured in raids were sometimes taken as wives and thus integrated into Awajún society. Nevertheless, kidnapping, like looting, seems to have been an impromptu act deemed less important than the primary goal, homicide.[7]

Materialist explanations for Awajún violence are not completely off the mark, however. It has long been known that in many parts of Amazonia the search for comparative material advantage led to sharp upticks in levels of violence after contact with Europeans. Groups with direct access to desirable trade goods had a political edge over those forced to deal with intermediaries. The establishment of missions, which served as conduits for trade goods, unsettled long-standing alliances and trading patterns in ways that often spawned local conflict.[8]

Competition for trade goods, social disruptions caused by disease-related mortality, and the destabilizing impact of introduced technologies are key features of what anthropologists refer to as the "tribal zone," the interface between predatory states and the regions where formerly sovereign peoples have governed themselves for centuries. The tribal zone often becomes a Hobbesian petri dish, spawning new and more intense forms of violence. Trade may put deadlier weapons into warriors' hands, raising the stakes for contending parties. Disorder elsewhere pushes refugees into neighboring territory, promoting either conflict or novel alliances—sometimes both. Outside observers have long mistaken this maelstrom for a traditional pattern, feeding the questionable claim that tribal societies are inherently violent.[9]

The Awajún heartland possesses all the hallmarks of the tribal zone. Spanish freebooters and gold miners, who plundered the region during the early colonial period, most likely destabilized existing political arrangements, as did the Jesuit missions and epidemic diseases that followed them. Western weapons quickly penetrated indigenous societies, increasing the lethality of combat. The challenging terrain favored avoidance of state control and, when circumstances required, violent opposition to it. This combination of geography and hostility kept the Alto Marañón lightly populated until the mid-twentieth century. Writing about his voyage up the Alto Marañón in 1891, Courtenay De Kalb observed, "There are no plantations between Barranca and the mountains,—nothing but a vast wilderness, waiting to be subdued by man! The river winds among its hundred islands, ready to be the burden-carrier of a busy race. But now all is silent, deserted." This was partly the result of Awajún belligerence toward settlers. In 1930 the German anthropologist Günter Tessmann said of Jivaroan peoples that although they were the most quick-witted Indians he had encountered, "it is not possible even to think about the domestication of this sanguinary society." To achieve that, he believed, "would require strict military control for several decades as well as cordial and fair economic relations that avoid any form of exploitation," conditions that he felt were unlikely to be met in either Peru or Ecuador.[10]

Yet the Awajún rarely presented a united front to outsiders. For as long as we have historical records, internal feuding was as common as violent opposition to other ethnic groups or the state. A neighborhood of intermarrying Awajún families might enjoy amicable relations for years at a time, but the death of a strong, unifying leader or persistent accusations of sorcery could quickly blow this solidarity to pieces, with murderous results. Absent an overarching leadership structure capable of imposing peace, reciprocal feuding was hard to stop. This isn't to say that the Awajún were incapable of settling disputes by peaceful means. Influential leaders sometimes negotiated payment of trade goods to end a vengeance cycle. The murder that led to the establishment of Alto Naranjillo, the community in which I lived for much of 1978, was settled this way. In general, however, the political realities of Awajún country prior to the 1950s were based on the rule of men rather than the rule of law. In this respect the Awajún scarcely differed from the people of European descent who settled the edges of their territory, few of whom were known for their commitment to abstract notions of justice.

An agonistic worldview was deeply embedded in every facet of Awajún mythology and spiritual practice. For men, the ultimate aspiration was to acquire a vision of an ancient warrior, an *ajútap,* who would give them the power to kill. A man named Kuimiág once told me that the vision resides in a man's chest and has a bright red color. "It rises to the top of your head when you are about to kill," he said. "It sits there pulsating." The ideal Awajún leader was fearless and controlled in his actions, qualities that rested on self-knowledge of his ability to kill and, over time, sufficient experience of killing for his reputation to carry weight. The Awajún and their immediate Jivaroan neighbors, the Shuar and the Wampis, once put this killing power to work in reciprocal head-taking raids. The severed heads of victims from other Jivaroan groups were turned into tsántsa, shrunken heads, and then celebrated in ways that converted the destructive power of the enemy into a life-giving force that benefited the killer and his wives. Although the religious dimension of killing seems to have withered away long ago in Awajún thought, the logic of revenge has proved more persistent. As recently as the 1970s men discouraged the homicidal intent of others by frequently declaring a willingness to respond to violence in kind. The code of vendetta diminishes in importance with every passing year, but its inexorable logic and the powerful emotions that it evokes still make their presence felt when the Awajún confront violence both from within and beyond the boundaries of their society.[11]

Williams College, where I taught for over three decades, offers many advantages to its students, including a sense of personal safety. Violent crime is infrequent on campus, as it is in the surrounding community, which is mostly rural and noted for its old-fashioned New England civility. Late in the fall of 2011 college authorities were dismayed by the discovery of a four-word threat scribbled on the wall of a dormitory corridor by parties unknown. The graffito, which used a racial epithet, urged death to all African Americans. The campus security office called in the local police and eventually the FBI to investigate what was soon classified as a hate crime. The anonymous nature of the act and the possibility it was the work not of a hateful racist but of a misguided political provocateur made it unlikely that the perpetrator would ever be identified.

Uncertainty about the seriousness of the threat did not prevent the college from canceling classes for a day and organizing an all-campus meeting to denounce discrimination and hate. More notable were messages from the president and dean of students urging faculty to be aware that many students were "deeply shaken" by the incident, which caused them "intense alarm, deep hurt, and complete exhaustion." The college's counseling staff was mobilized to provide anxious students with the support needed to calm their fear of imminent harm.

These events took place as I contemplated Awajún attitudes toward violence. In the 1970s and 1980s, overt and implied threats remained a salient part of their daily experience. Violent death was not a remote prospect but a familiar reality manifested in suicide and murder as well as more ambiguous but equally feared attacks by sorcerers. While collecting genealogies in 1978, I recorded the cause of death of 134 individuals of all ages. Of adult male deaths, 37 percent were attributed to homicide. Among girls and adult women, 58 percent of deaths were the result of suicide. The sample size was too small to inspire great confidence. Yet even allowing for a substantial margin of error and the retrospective nature of the evidence, these numbers show the extent to which violence infused Awajún experience. My Awajún mentors—Eladio, Kayáp, Shajián, Utiját, Míkig, and the rest—would surely consider four words written on a wall to be a laughable threat in comparison to the risks they faced every day of their lives.

The sharp contrast between the two situations suggests the degree to which attitudes toward violence have shifted in much of the developed world. Today when we describe an individual or group as "civilized," we typically refer to behavior characterized by high levels of self-control, respect for due process based on ideas of fairness, and above all great reluctance to menace, injure, or kill other people. For anyone reared in this milieu, the prospect of physical attack is profoundly distressing. Under normal circumstances only officially recognized peace officers may resort to violence. They are obliged, at least theoretically, to follow strict rules of engagement. Of course, even the most peaceful societies distribute physical security unevenly. The poor and the socially marginal are more likely to be victims of violence than are the wealthy. In general, however, mass literacy, affluence, and democracy tend to be associated with declining tolerance for physical aggression

Explaining this shift is a central goal of *The Better Angels of Our Nature,* a study published in 2011 by the cognitive scientist Steven Pinker. Pinker surveys the history of violence beginning with the archaeological record and continuing through the twentieth century. The evidence convinces him that tolerance for cruelty and violence has been in decline for centuries. Pinker acknowledges that the trend has suffered reverses, but even the most extreme exceptions (e.g., World Wars I and II) rank fairly low when death tolls are adjusted for the total world population at the time of their occurrence. In Pinker's population-adjusted mortality rankings, twentieth-century wars fall far below the Mongol conquests or the collapse of Rome. In one of his book's many graphs and tables, the Jívaro—indistinguishable from the Awajún in this context—stand close to the top of the global rankings with respect to the percentage of deaths suffered in combat.[12]

How does Pinker explain this ostensible decline? The rise of states, with their monopolization of force, is one factor—even if, as Pinker acknowledges, the expansionist nature of the earliest states probably intensified violence for a time. Pinker sees movement toward higher levels of peace as an expression of the "Civilizing Process," a phrase he borrows from the German-born sociologist Norbert Elias. Elias (1897–1990) studied the emergence of ideas of personal modesty and refined behavior in European history—everything from table manners and attitudes toward bodily wastes—and saw in them a framework for a new kind of personality and the social institutions that support it. This shaped a sensibility that in less than a century moved execution from the status of a public spectacle (which it was as recently as 1939 in France) to a punitive option banned in much of the world. Likewise the steady shift in attitudes toward corporal punishment and cruelty toward animals. Other factors that Pinker identifies as contributing to a reduction of violence include urbanization, which replaces the bonds of kin and group with a cosmopolitan tolerance for diversity, and the mutual dependence that arises in complex commercial networks.

Pinker's sweeping claims have not gone unchallenged. Although evidence of violence is by no means rare in the archaeological record, some of the cases on which Pinker bases his argument are disputed by experts. For cultural anthropologists, the tribal-zone phenomenon complicates any assessment of violence among tribal peoples in historic times. How do we know whether the high mortality documented by observers was a traditional pattern or an effect of colonialism? As for the steady reduction in violence that Pinker sees in developed societies, critics find it hard to ignore the vast destruction that could be unleashed by nuclear or biological weapons. One major incident involving such lethal technologies could make Pinker's upbeat assessment look like the cheery fantasy that skeptics declare it to be.[13]

By limiting his definition of violence to physical assault, Pinker brackets from consideration a phenomenon that social scientists call "structural violence," referring to the harm done by social arrangements that stunt people's life prospects and damage their bodies and minds. Economic systems that extract resources in environmentally destructive ways or deny citizens access to adequate food and shelter may not need overt physical force to inflict pain. Whether structural violence is more common now than in the past is debatable. There can be little doubt, however, that the inequality on which structural violence feeds is increasing sharply in many parts of the world.[14]

Despite such shortcomings, some of Pinker's findings are persuasive. The Civilizing Process has nurtured ideas of universal human rights and the equality of women while consigning total war, torture, and capital punishment to the margins of acceptable state conduct. Since 2001, Americans have learned that these moral advances are reversible, to our great shame. Still, few will deny that the past two centuries have seen progress toward the reduction of physical violence in many parts of the world. In the historical framework proposed by Norbert Elias, this was accomplished through a radical reshaping of human character. "What is established with the monopolization of physical violence in the pacified social spaces is a different type of self-control or self-restraint. It is a more dispassionate self-control." These emerging emotional constraints, Elias says, were promoted by institutions that reinforced the socialization process so as to produce "a more continuous, stable and even regulation of drives and affects in all areas of conduct, in all sectors of [a person's] life."[15]

For the Awajún, the Civilizing Process has followed a crooked path. By the late 1940s, the cultural and economic basis of Awajún life was challenged on multiple fronts. New roads brought more settlers to the region. Northern Peru underwent militarization in response to a long-running border dispute with Ecuador that sparked clashes between the two nations' armies in 1941, 1981, and 1995. (The conflict was finally settled by treaty in 1998.) Texaco began to explore for oil in the region in 1953. Production of petroleum commenced in the early 1970s and increased significantly when construction of a 500-mile-long pipeline to the Pacific coast was completed in 1977. Oil exploration, well digging, and pipeline construction directly affected Awajún settlements near the Alto Río Marañón and eventually more remote communities on several of the Marañón's tributaries.[16]

In cultural terms, the most significant change was driven by the growing influence of Christian missions and the schools they brought to Awajún country. American missionaries affiliated with the Church of the Nazarene established a mission among the Awajún in the mid-1920s. Nazarene missionaries were able to make only modest headway with the Awajún language until the late 1940s, when they sought the help of the recently founded Summer Institute of Linguistics (now called SIL International), an arm of the Wycliffe Bible Translators, an organization devoted to making the Bible available to speakers of every known language. Work on the language accelerated in 1954 with the arrival of Mildred Larson, a gifted SIL-trained linguist, and Jeanne Grover, a nurse. Not to be outdone by American Protestants, the Catholic Church established a mission station and school at Santa María de Nieva in the early 1950s. Local tensions between the two denominations continued for years, with the Awajún sometimes caught in the middle. Eventually, however, they reached a modus vivendi as well as a degree of mutual reconciliation.[17]

During its early years, SIL's activities among Peru's indigenous peoples evoked considerable suspicion in a nation that strongly identified with Roman Catholicism and feared American meddling. Among the Awajún, however, the foreignness of the SIL, its promotion of a minority faith, and its commitment to literacy in the Awajún language ratified the identity of the Awajún as a distinct people. This contrasted with Peruvian national policies focused solely on cultural assimilation—that is, when the state bothered to notice indigenous Amazonians at all.

SIL linguists and their Roman Catholic counterparts trained a cadre of young, bilingual, literate Awajún—in the early years, nearly all men—who became important leaders at the local level and later in the emerging national and international movement for indigenous rights. Since the 1950s the proportion of Protestants in all sectors of Peruvian society has risen to nearly 15 percent thanks to a high rate of conversion, erasing much of the stigma of a faith with which perhaps a quarter of Awajún identify.[18]

The influence of Christian teaching on Awajún combativeness is hard to assess. Elsewhere in Amazonia, anthropologists have found that conversion may reduce violence by allowing individuals to make an implicit public statement of their intention to withdraw from a cycle of revenge killing. The demands of Protestant conversion—abandoning the consumption of alcohol while dedicating oneself to literacy, Bible study, and regular church attendance—provide visible proof of a convert's commitment, which in turn reassures enemies that his renunciation of vengeance is sincere. Such factors may contribute to Awajún interest in the Christian message, although there is little evidence that conversion has reduced fear of sorcery, which even today provokes local conflict.[19]

Belief in the power of individuals to harm or kill by spiritual means has arisen in societies on every inhabited continent. What makes the Awajún version distinctive are its intensity, persistence, and defiance of conventional explanations from the anthropologist's tool kit. Most anthropologists start from the assumption that sorcery is nothing but a figment of the imagination. Explaining it requires an act of intercultural translation. Sorcery beliefs and practices have real effects, interpreters insist, but they aren't those claimed by believers. Their impact is primarily social. In small-scale societies that lack formal institutions, deviant individuals—the violent, the stingy, the overly assertive, or people who are simply strange—may find themselves targeted by sorcery accusations. The harsh spotlight of public attention often convinces them to change their behavior. In extreme cases, they suffer exile or execution. Belief in the reality of sorcery thus serves to enforce social norms.[20]

Among the Awajún, however, sorcery accusations are so widespread that they frustrate attempts to portray them as a mechanism of social control. Close kin, distant kin, politically powerful individuals, politically vulnerable ones, spouses, children—all come into the crosshairs of sorcery fear. Healing shamans are most frequently accused, a situation that leads them to tread carefully in their relations with others. So, too, are members of neighboring societies, especially the Shawi, whose sorcery powers are believed to surpass those of the Awajún. Beyond that, however, suspicion is remarkably indiscriminate.

Another classical explanation of sorcery beliefs appeals to their explanatory power, their ability to account for misfortunes that would otherwise remain mysterious. A touchstone of sorcery research is E. E. Evans-Pritchard's *Witchcraft, Oracles, and Magic among the Azande,* published in 1937 and based on fieldwork undertaken in the 1920s. The Azande, a people of central Africa, saw witchcraft as a factor in nearly every aspect of daily life. "Witchcraft is ubiquitous," writes Evans-Pritchard. "It plays its part in every activity of Zande life; in agricultural, fishing, and hunting pursuits; in domestic life of homesteads as well as in communal life of district and court; . . . there is no niche or corner of Zande culture into which it does not twist itself." Evans-Pritchard's account depicts a society that achieved orderly management of witchcraft accusations through the use of oracles and court procedures that usually resulted in peaceful settlements. (The impact of British colonial authority on local custom was a factor that Evans-Pritchard refers to only tangentially.) The Azande, Evans-Pritchard notes, didn't use witchcraft theories to explain everything. They had a keen understanding of natural phenomena that served them well in the general course of things. Witchcraft was invoked to explain misfortune—the *why,* not the how, of unhappy circumstances.[21]

Awajún notions of sorcery are both more narrow and less constrained by well-established procedure than was the case among the Azande. Awajún sorcerers are blamed only for illness or, very occasionally, snakebite. Sorcery is about killing or attempted killing. It demands reciprocal violence, both to avenge a past death and to prevent the sorcerer from taking other lives.

Belief in sorcery provides a ready-made explanation for the illness or death of loved ones. In that sense it may offer a degree of solace, especially after vengeance has been achieved. Yet one may reasonably wonder how much emotional comfort can be found in a system that sees everyone, from your worst enemy to the family members on whom you most rely, as potentially conspiring to kill you.

Recent research has drawn attention to the political power of shamanism and the sorcery beliefs with which it is commonly intertwined. Neil Whitehead, who studied "dark shamanism" in Guyana, proposed that sorcerers have come to symbolize "a potent indigenous society and culture that is capable of defending itself against the depredations of the outside world." If this were so for the Awajún, their pattern of sorcery accusations and related acts of retribution might be easier to understand. To date, however, they have treated shamanism and sorcery as internal problems, not as practices that foster cultural pride or express resistance to outsiders.[22]

The view of sorcery that best captures Awajún experience was summarized by the South African anthropologist Monica Wilson in the 1950s. Wilson refers to belief in witches as "the standardized nightmare of a group." By this she means that they represent a projection of people's guilt, fear, or anger onto others. The conviviality and good humor that so impressed me in the everyday life of the Awajún masked a fundamental shortage of trust even in the intimacy of the family. Add to this the Awajún's history of volatile political alliances, new and often lethal epidemics, and the unstable nature of traditional religious authority, and one sees a people who have access to few safe harbors, few sites of existential security. The scarcity of such security may account for the willingness of many Awajún to explore Catholicism, evangelical Protestantism, and other religions that proselytize actively in eastern Peru.[23]

The Awajún's high rate of suicide presents another vexing riddle even if its social logic seems simple. In a highly agonistic society, where threats of violence, explicit or implied, figure prominently in interpersonal relations, women find themselves awkwardly positioned. They share these values but lack the power to impose their will on intransigent men. One recourse is to threaten to kill themselves. This might coerce a young woman's father into agreeing to a marriage more to her liking. For a married woman, it may discourage brutal treatment by a husband, especially given the possibility that her suicide would mobilize her family against him. Grief-related female suicide is awkwardly accommodated by this model, although in some cases women may be responding to the death of a father or brother who stood as a bulwark against a husband's cruelty.[24]

Such high levels of suicide are unknown in neighboring societies whose languages and way of life share many commonalities with those of the Awajún. When I first discussed Awajún suicide at an international meeting in the 1980s, several members of the audience refused to accept the evidence. For them, the data differed too dramatically from the behavior of adjacent peoples to be believable. They insisted that other causes of death must have been misrepresented as suicide. Subsequently, however, the suicide rate has been independently confirmed by others and occasionally headlined in Peru's popular press. It is tempting to appeal to the idea of contagion: that female suicide is a meme, a unit of cultural imitation sufficiently "sticky" that it has managed to endure and replicate in Awajún society. When witnessing Hermina's failed or feigned suicide attempt in Huascayacu in 1977, I saw the replication process in action: she was rehearsing a cultural performance that had become common, almost normal. When coupled with the sense of powerlessness experienced by many young women and, to a lesser extent, young men, the suicide meme has proved disturbingly persistent.[25]

In the Alto Mayo, sporadic feuding continued to be part of Awajún life through the end of the twentieth century. One widely discussed case involved a grandson of Wampurái and Túgki, my Alto Naranjillo neighbors whose lives were shadowed by misfortune. The young man disappeared while visiting relatives in the Alto Marañón and is presumed to have been murdered. His death may have settled accounts unbalanced by the 1977 sorcery killing in which the shaman Genaro played a central role.

Genaro, whose perilous vocation had earned him an ever-widening circle of enemies, met a spectacular end in the early 1990s. The story of his death that circulates today may have been embroidered for dramatic effect, but its basic elements are undisputed. On a visit to Huascayacu to treat a sick kinsman, Genaro fell in love with a girl, the youngest daughter of Eladio, the community's ápu. Genaro's wife, Tumús, would have violently opposed a plural marriage had she discovered the affair, so he is said to have meticulously plotted her death. During a healing session in his house, he collapsed on the floor, apparently unconscious. Tumús began to weep, fearing that he had been killed by one of the formidable sorcerers with whom he regularly did spiritual battle. "My husband is dead!" she called out. "A sorcerer has killed him with his darts." But Genaro eventually revived. Acknowledging that he was under attack by a powerful foe, he told Tumús that if he received two more such assaults, the last one would finish him. "If I die," he asked her, "what will you do?" Tumús pledged to kill herself by hanging or taking poison if Genaro succumbed. "In that case, we'll go to heaven together," Genaro is said to have told her.

Soon afterward he was again felled by a spiritual attack. Again he recovered. A third attack followed days later, leaving him inert and apparently dead. The prophecy of a third and fatal assault fulfilled, Tumús ran from the house, swallowed a bowlful of fish poison, and died. Meanwhile, Genaro had regained consciousness, claiming that his own spirit helpers had ultimately proven stronger than his rival's killing darts.

Tumús's brothers concluded that Genaro had tricked her into committing suicide, but they decided to bide their time before exacting revenge. Their resentment smoldered for years as Genaro relocated to Huascayacu, established a household with his new, much younger wife, and fathered children there. Things went well until a son of Genaro's brother-in-law died. "My child was fine. This brother-in-law of mine, Genaro, he's doing the killing," the bereaved father insisted. Then Dáse, Genaro's uncle, died suddenly in another community. Genaro became the chief suspect. When Tumús's mother, Mariana, was lying on her deathbed, she, too, blamed Genaro for her illness and accused him of attempting to rape her years before.

The accusations coalesced into a multi-community plot to execute him. A party of men ambushed Genaro on the trail to Huascayacu, killed him with multiple shotgun blasts, and buried him in the forest. For a time his kin thought that he had disappeared on a trip to treat mestizo patients in Yurimaguas. Eventually, however, all possibilities but murder were eliminated. With so many people involved in the killing, the full story eventually leaked out. By then, the Awajún had been folded into a national system of dispute resolution that included the election of local justices of the peace. The Awajún justice called a meeting at which he convinced the killers to confess publicly their role in the execution. It was said that even Genaro's brother, Shajián, knew of the plot and declined to intervene. To forestall a reciprocal revenge killing in the future, the guilty parties agreed to compensate Genaro's son with 200 hectares of farmland, a substantial award. There the chapter closed. The Alto Mayo has yet to see a traditional healer emerge whose skills approach Genaro's, although a few men reportedly take vision-inducing plants to treat family members and the occasional client.[26]

Today circumstances have shifted Awajún attention to external threats. In the face of intensifying pressure from outsiders, the Awajún have shown an inclination to follow parallel strategies. Ambitious, educated leaders have thrown themselves into campaigns of political mobilization, fund-raising among international organizations, and public denunciation of violations of Awajún civil and territorial rights. Several of these men have achieved global prominence. They include Evaristo Nugkuag, founder of Peru's most influential federation of Amazonian indigenous groups and winner of the Goldman Environmental Prize and the Right Livelihood Award (popularly known as the "alternative Nobel Peace Prize"); Gil Inoach, an outspoken federation leader and environmentalist; Santiago Manuin, winner of Spain's Queen Sofia Prize for his environmental and human-rights work; and Eduardo Nayap, who in 2011 became the first Amazonian indigenous person elected to a seat in the Peruvian Congress, where he represents not only Awajún and Wampis communities but also thousands of nonindigenous citizens.

There have been occasional outbursts of violence reminiscent of earlier patterns. In 1979, a large party of Awajún forcibly occupied and destroyed a movie set built by the German director Werner Herzog for the film *Fitzcarraldo*. The attack followed failed negotiations about the terms under which filming would proceed, a situation complicated by competing Awajún claims of political authority. Fortunately, the conflict resulted in no injuries or deaths. In 1989, three French tourists and a Peruvian companion were reportedly murdered by unidentified Awajún while visiting a village on the Río Marañón, either because the visitors were trying to videotape without permission or, according to press accounts, because residents believed that the travelers were pishtaco vampires searching for victims. Belief in pishtacos and other kinds of supernatural, predatory beings has spread among Peru's Amazonian peoples in direct proportion to intensifying resource extraction by Peruvian and foreign corporations. Whether pishtaco beliefs figured in the murder of Patchen Miller in 1995 remains unclear.[27]

These cases were dwarfed by an incident that occurred in January 2002, when scores of armed Awajún staged a nighttime assault on a squatter settlement called Flor de la Frontera, located on Awajún land in the Department of Cajamarca. Nine adults and seven children died; many more received serious wounds. For years prior to the attack, leaders of the Awajún community whose lands had been appropriated tried to have the squatters evicted by legal means. Every court ruled in the Awajún's favor, but police efforts to remove the settlers stalled, in part because of a long history of official timidity in response to land invasions by militant farmers. Their legal options exhausted, more belligerent Awajún concluded that the only solution was a full-on assault. To date, only one Awajún has been prosecuted and convicted in response to the attack, whose shocking brutality must be blamed in part on the state's unwillingness to protect Awajún rights in frontier areas.[28]

The most highly publicized recent instance of violence involving the Awajún, a disastrous police assault in which the Awajún were as much victims as protagonists, took place in June 2009 near Bagua, a town of 26,000 inhabitants on the western edge of the Awajún heartland. The clash is colloquially known to Peruvians as the "Baguazo," the town's name intensified by the suffix *-azo,* which implies great size or force. The roots of the conflict lay in the efforts of several recent Peruvian presidents to curtail indigenous rights and open up Peru's enormous Amazonian region to economic development by foreign and domestic capital. Beginning in 2006 President Alan García proposed a series of controversial measures that would have ceded control of significant areas of the Amazonian rainforest to loggers and agribusiness. Many of these tracts already belonged to titled indigenous communities. García's claim was that the new measures were necessary for Peru to comply with a recently signed free trade agreement with the United States. He famously likened the Amazon's indigenous peoples to a "dog in the manger" *(perro del hortelano)*, which neither eats nor allows others to eat. Instead, he advocated replacing "smallholders without technology" with "middle-class farmers who know how to obtain resources, seek out markets and create formal jobs."[29]

Long before these proposed changes came into the national spotlight, the Awajún and other Amazonian peoples confronted a political reality common to most Latin American nations: rights to subsurface resources, including minerals, petroleum, and natural gas, belong to the government, not to the people under whose land the resources are located. A recent study found that 72 percent of the Peruvian Amazon has now been zoned for hydrocarbon exploration and extraction, although much of this remains undeveloped to date. Gold deposits have also been targeted for development in Awajún territory and elsewhere in eastern Peru.[30]

When spirited resistance to the proposed laws slowed their ratification in Congress, Alan García implemented some of them by presidential decree. Indigenous and smallholder organizations across Peru rose up in opposition. They blocked rivers and roads, organized local strikes, and staged occupations of hydroelectric facilities, natural-gas pumping stations, and petroleum pipeline sites.[31]

Matters came to a head in early June 2009. The government had already declared a state of emergency in several parts of the

Awajún and Wampis protesters at a petroleum pumping station near
Bagua, June 2009.

Photo by Thomas Quirynen and used with his kind permission.

Amazon. Interruption of the flow of petroleum and natural gas
was costly, both for the affected corporations and for the national treasury. Government officials resolved to end a blockade
of the main highway that linked Bagua to the Pacific Coast.
Negotiations to reopen the road appeared to be on the verge of
success when elements of the Peruvian police launched a massive operation against hundreds of protesters manning the
blockade—mostly Awajún and Wampis, although other indigenous and nonindigenous protesters were involved as well. The
result was a fiasco of poor planning and badly executed crowd
control: use of tear gas and rubber bullets escalated quickly to
undisciplined fire with automatic weapons supported by heli-
copters and armored vehicles. In the ensuing chaos, scores were
wounded or killed.

Initial radio reports and witnesses' accounts circulating by
cell phone led indigenous protesters elsewhere in the region to

Peruvian police, using armored vehicles and tear gas, begin an assault against indigenous demonstrators near Bagua, June 5, 2009.

Photograph by Reuters/Thomas Quirynen.

fear that a massacre of unprecedented scale was under way. Among those was a group of more than a thousand protesters who had taken control of a petroleum pumping station fifty miles from Bagua. Despite efforts by Awajún leaders and evangelical pastors to calm the crowd's growing agitation, militants eventually executed eleven unarmed police officers whom protesters had earlier taken hostage.[32]

The official record states that the multiple clashes of the Baguazo resulted in a total of thirty-three confirmed deaths, one police officer missing and presumed dead, and 200 injured. It is possible that there were additional, uncounted indigenous victims, including some who declined to seek medical attention because they feared arrest. Most unnerving to the Peruvian public was that more than two-thirds of the reported dead were policemen, including members of an elite special operations unit. The death of so many police at the hands of indigenous protesters armed, at least initially, with palm-wood lances may have forever sealed the reputation of the Awajún and their Wampis allies as the nation's toughest and most intransigent indigenous peoples.

Despite predictable calls for punishment of the "savages" who massacred unarmed policemen at the pumping station, the Baguazo prompted national soul-searching about the direction the country was taking in its Amazonian region. The Peruvian Congress soon passed a law that requires meaningful dialogue with indigenous communities before the government can authorize development projects on their lands. This policy is in no small measure due to the organizational skill of Awajún activists and the stalwart resistance of ordinary Awajún. Relations between indigenous groups and the state remain tense, however.[33]

A sad irony of the Baguazo is that it occurred at a time when the Awajún were working energetically to join Peruvian civil

Two days after the Baguazo, policemen guard the coffin of a fellow officer killed in the conflict. Bagua, Department of Amazonas, June 2009.

Photograph by Reuters/Enrique Castro-Mendivil.

society by participating in the nation's electoral process and developing innovative, culturally appropriate procedures to resolve conflicts in nonviolent ways. In the Alto Marañón, for example, communities have developed protocols for banishing accused sorcerers rather than implicitly condoning their execution. Awajún justices of the peace are using their newfound influence to intervene in feuds before they escalate further. These measures arise in part from discussions among an emerging group of Awajún legal thinkers about how to reconcile Peruvian law with Awajún custom through a process of "intercultural justice." The outlines of this system—if it can even be called a system at this stage of its development—remain hazy. But there is little doubt that some Awajún are prepared to modify traditional practices in order to arrive at nonviolent legal solutions appropriate to their changing situation, provided that the state is willing to concede that the Awajún and other indigenous peoples have a right to manage their own internal affairs in keeping with the principle of self-determination.[34]

An example of a grassroots move toward nonviolent justice was outlined for me in 2012 by Cristóbal Juep, an Awajún who had served in several elected positions, including justice of the peace. In Huascayacu, the community in which I had lived for most of 1977, Eladio's grandson was killed by a mestizo youth during a fight that erupted after a long night of drinking. Members of the community immediately set upon the drunken killer, stabbed him to death, and buried his body in the forest. To cover the reprisal killing, they claimed that the mestizo perpetrator had escaped into the forest after his crime. The vanished mestizo's family doubted the story and demanded an investigation by the regional prosecutor. He issued an order for a dozen armed policemen to proceed to Huascayacu. Juep, then serving as an elected official of the district where the events took place, convinced him that this show of force would only provoke more violence.

Juep called a meeting of Huascayacu's household heads, who eventually admitted that they had killed the mestizo in response to the death of Eladio's grandson. Juep went to the mestizo victim's family and explained what had happened. "Your son didn't escape," he said. "He is dead. When someone kills an Awajún, his relatives are obliged to avenge him. Your son is buried there." He urged the crestfallen father to treat the matter as closed, since murder had been answered by murder. "Otherwise it would have taken months or years to resolve in the courts," Juep said. "From there we went to recover the cadaver. There were police, people from Sanitation, a judge, community leaders. We exhumed the body and signed a death certificate. I brought this to the prosecutor in Moyobamba and told him that the issue was settled. But he shouted at me, told me that it wasn't a matter I could resolve. If he didn't like it, I said, he could reopen the case. I told him, 'There are 700 Awajún armed with shotguns. Take your police there to solve it yourself.'"

More highly placed Peruvian authorities eventually concluded that the negotiated solution was appropriate. "Lawyers came from Lima to give a course to the Awajún in Bajo Naranjillo. People there told them that I had resolved the issue in only a month. The lawyers were surprised. 'In one month?' they said. 'Not even in Lima can we solve a problem like this in a month. It takes us years!' That's how it was settled."

In an analysis of the Awajún struggle for cultural survival, the anthropologist Shane Greene has identified an oscillation between violence and sophisticated politics as one expression of an Awajún gift for what he calls "customizing indigeneity." This process involves making heritage self-conscious and then reshaping it in response to new realities. The Awajún have embraced a reputation as stewards of a warrior tradition. They are a people who have never bent to the will of others, they say, and they aren't inclined to do so now.

An example of strategic customization is the revival of traditional dress and adornments, which were scarcely to be seen during the 1970s and early 1980s. Today one would be hard pressed to find a media image of Awajún who are *not* wearing at least one item of traditional dress. For men it is usually the *tawáas* or toucan-feather corona. For women, it is the *buchák*, a simple cotton dress fastened over one shoulder, which may be complemented by face paint and shell earrings in a traditional style.

The visual marking of identity has been on the rise throughout Amazonia and elsewhere in the indigenous world. "Native

Amazonians who once took pains to hide external signs of indigenous identity behind mass-produced Western clothing now
proclaim their cultural distinctiveness with headdresses, body
paint, beads, and feathers," wrote the anthropologist Beth
Conklin in 1997, observations as true today as when she wrote
them. Global media need visual cues to communicate stories
quickly and in terms readily understood by viewers. The mark-
ers that identify people as indigenous—in essence, a mass-
culture iconography—may be as dramatic as feather headdresses
or as discreet as the bolo ties favored by the Native American
senator Ben Nighthorse Campbell during his service in the U.S.
Congress. The use of traditional dress certifies the authenticity
of indigenous peoples whose physical appearance may not otherwise distinguish them from other citizens.[35]

The tragic events of the Baguazo illustrate both the strengths
and limitations of indigenous customization. The demonstra-
tions preceding the violent clashes of June 2009 wove symbols
of Awajún and Wampis tradition—feather coronas, palm-wood
spears brandished in defiance of the state—together with the
sophisticated use of cell phones and press releases. The Awajún
and Wampis once considered themselves mortal enemies. For
the struggle against state threats, though, they joined forces to
create an organization whose name can be translated loosely as
the Battle Committee of the Amazonian Jívaro Peoples. Once
Peruvian authorities unleashed their assault, the political calcu-
lus of Awajún leaders was overwhelmed by a traditional logic
of violent reprisal. Canny customization was abandoned by
men who apparently felt obliged to avenge kinsmen killed (or
so they believed in the confusion of the moment) in the highway altercation outside Bagua. Reports suggest that some Awajún were dismayed by the cold-blooded execution of police
hostages, an act they regarded as morally repellent and tactically
counterproductive.[36]

On balance, however, the diversity of opinion among the Awajún substantiates a supple notion of custom in a society notable for its dynamism. A long-standing ethic of individualism has, if anything, become more marked in recent decades as Awajún follow divergent paths: toward Christianity or away from it; pursuing educational opportunities that can lead to careers as urban professionals or, alternatively, committing themselves to life in their home communities; actively embracing the market economy or doing what they can to survive without it; struggling to contain aggression or celebrating it in public displays of political militancy. These multiple strategies are held together—loosely, and with a high level of internal dissent—by a steadfast commitment to survival as a distinct people.

A notable feature of Awajún society is that many of the cultural characteristics that lead outsiders to view it as quintessentially tribal are qualities that equip the Awajún to respond successfully to the challenges of economic development at its most rapacious. As a people, they draw on a deep history of strategic thinking and sensitivity to hidden motives. Undaunted by threats, they remain supremely self-confident, a quality often mistaken for arrogance in a part of the world that for centuries expected its Indians to be deferential.

The Civilizing Process as experienced by the Awajún is not that of Steven Pinker's Cambridge, Massachusetts, or Norbert Elias's postwar London, settings noted for stable institutions and durable traditions of deliberative justice. Peru's Amazonian frontier is a different place, a tumultuous one. Sudden changes of government policy whipsaw the region's people and their livelihoods. Agents working for powerful corporations prowl the forest in search of exploitable resources. Conflicts over land erupt with ever greater frequency as desperate colonists try to make new lives for themselves east of the Andes. In areas controlled by cocaine mafias or revanchist elements of the Shining

Path, lethal violence may lie around the next bend in the river. The Awajún are working energetically to master the nonviolent skills that will help them cope with what passes for civilization in their corner of Amazonia. They also keep their weapons close at hand.

9

Boundary Condition

Moyobamba, the capital of the Department of San Martín, had become nearly unrecognizable in the quarter century since I last walked its streets. As recently as the 1980s, Moyobamba was a sleepy place reminiscent of Macondo, the jungle town immortalized in Gabriel García Márquez's *One Hundred Years of Solitude*. But by 2012 its languorous tranquility had surrendered to the tumult of a colonization frontier. The population had grown nearly fivefold thanks to the arrival of colonists from elsewhere in Peru. Roughly paved streets sprawled in every direction, mirrored overhead by a tangle of utility lines. Convoys of motorcycles and motorized jitneys rattled buildings from the predawn hours until midnight. Bars and restaurants, their fronts open to the street, offered competing noise from flat-screen TVs and titanic stereos. When soccer matches were not airing, programming favored impossibly fit blond youths dancing to Latin pop music. Resembling no humans visible on the streets of Moyobamba, the images seemed as alien as messages from Alpha Centauri.

These changes tracked the region's social and economic transformation. The principal highways were now paved. Cell phones, priced for people of modest means to a degree that Americans would envy, had become ubiquitous. A national policy of decentralization had drawn more government offices to Moyobamba, and with them middle-class jobs.

Agriculture was the main attraction. Rice, maize, and cattle had long been important, but coffee now reigned supreme. Improved cultivation practices had lifted Alto Mayo coffee into the top ranks of coffee farmed in an ecologically sustainable way. In the Huallaga Valley, to the southeast, coca production for the cocaine trade generated plenty of hard cash, some of which probably sifted into Moyobamba. The Alto Mayo itself had mostly resisted the lure of coca, although remote corners of the valley were rumored to harbor small plantations.

Protocol required that I introduce myself to local officials before visiting Awajún communities. Functionaries from the regional government went out of their way to praise Peru's new commitment to "pluriculturalism," although exactly what this meant seemed uncertain even to them. Various agencies had hired Awajún and Lamista employees to foster communication with the area's native communities, an encouraging departure from past practice but one whose goals were limited, as far as I could ascertain, to a diffuse notion of "participation."

Given the tensions that persisted after the Baguazo conflict of 2009, it was important that I check in with the Awajún's own organization, FERIAAM (Awajún Indigenous Federation of the Alto Mayo). FERIAAM had emerged from the wreckage of two previous attempts to bring the valley's autonomous Awajún communities into a stable federation. The organization's impressive headquarters included offices, living quarters, and a traditional palm-wood house used for public meetings. FERIAAM's president, Lauriano Saldaña, was indistinguishable from the government officials encountered earlier that day, dressed as he was in a crisp white shirt and dark trousers, a cell phone cradled in his left hand. He quickly briefed me on the situation of the communities represented by his organization. The number of titled communities had grown from nine to fourteen, with a fifteenth lying just across the boundary of the adjacent Department of Loreto. Over the previous twenty-five years, the region's Awajún population had more than tripled and now exceeded 5,000. Much of this growth was driven by an influx of Awajún families from land-poor villages to the north.

The Awajún communities that had been issued land titles together encompassed roughly 140,000 hectares (346,000 acres). Although this might sound like a generous allotment, the region's topography made much of the land unsuitable for permanent cultivation. In the 1970s, native communities bordered on intact rainforest, allowing the Awajún to exploit areas beyond the limits of their titled territory. Now their lands were mostly encircled by colonists' farms, triggering conflict over property lines, water rights, and the colonists' clandestine exploitation of Awajún forest resources.[1]

In June 2006, for instance, a water-rights dispute between the Awajún community of Shampuyacu and the bordering mestizo hamlet of San Pablo led to the murder of an Awajún man. Two days later, the killer died in an Awajún reprisal attack. Mediation by government officials and regional nongovernmental organizations managed to keep the conflict from widening. In August 2010 three members of an Awajún family in Morroyacu were murdered during a home invasion by members of a colonist gang. The motive seemed to be robbery—the Awajún family was said to be in possession of a large sum of money—although a land tenure dispute may also have played a part. Two days later, kinsmen of the Awajún victims killed three presumed perpetrators in response. The prevailing atmosphere was a mix of suspicion,

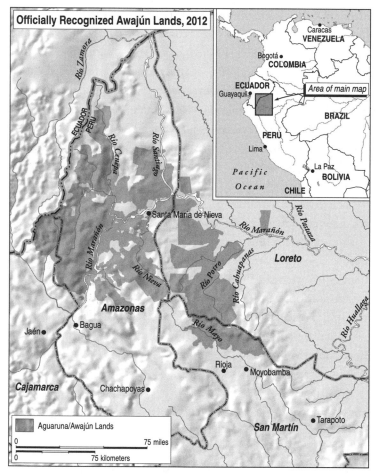

Officially recognized Awajún lands as of 2012. Total titled land
approaches 1 million hectares (3,861 sq. mi.); additional lands
classified as Awajún communal reserves raise the total to approximately
2.25 million hectares (8,687 sq. mi.), roughly the size of New Jersey.
At least forty-five Awajún communities remained untitled in 2012
and are not shown here.

Source: Instituto del Bien Común, Lima. Map copyright © 2014 by Michael F.
Brown.

frontier lawlessness, and unrestrained ambition. The Wild West, in other words, but with palm trees and smartphones.[2]

Lauriano Saldaña proved less inclined to talk about interethnic violence than about the difficulty of convincing his fellow Awajún to present a united front to the government. Instead, communities were more likely to insist on independent decision-making and then, if their plans ran off the rails, lobby FERI-AAM for legal help. Like its predecessors, FERIAAM grappled with the tension between the nation's bureaucratic political culture, which fetishized hierarchy and formal procedures, and the inclination of individual Awajún to pursue whatever course they judged best for themselves and their families.

Reading between the lines of Saldaña's carefully chosen words and the observations of others familiar with the Alto Mayo, it became apparent that the boundary between indigenous and colonist society was becoming more permeable with every passing year as a result of intermarriage, trade, complex leasing arrangements, and shared governance of ethnically mixed settlements. This had not eroded the Awajún's sense of themselves as a distinct people, but it did raise questions about whether current social problems should be seen solely in light of conflicts between indigenous and nonindigenous societies.

On the morning of my scheduled visit to the community of Bajo Naranjillo, long the nerve center of Awajún politics in the Alto Mayo, I received a call from an Awajún acquaintance warning me not to go. "A big dispute has blown up," she warned. "The police have been called in, and it could be violent. You don't want to be there." By later that day the contours of the dispute had become clearer, although there were, as always, subtexts that proved hard to read. An enterprising faction was at loggerheads with their elected leaders over a sand- and gravel-mining business based in the community. The ápu alleged that the business had failed to meet its contractual obligations. The owners insisted that the ápu's campaign against them represented an abuse of authority. When they scheduled a public meeting to demand a change of leadership, the ápu called in the police to maintain order. Fortunately, conflict was confined to some shoving and the exchange of angry words, but tempers remained frayed.

The owners of the controversial business immediately issued a written statement that shed light on the nature of the underlying tensions. It was a declaration of individual initiative worthy of Ayn Rand. "It should be emphasized that the communitarian system of economic activities such as communal businesses, a communal store, a communal pharmacy, communal animal husbandry, communal rotating funds—none has been successful to date. These failures have come about because of an administrative system that defines indigenous communal property as belonging to all and at the same time belonging to no one, giving rise to administrative irresponsibility."[3]

This critique of communitarianism doubtless reflects the views of an emerging Awajún entrepreneurial class. Despite its self-interested quality, however, the document makes a telling point: the current economic adaptation of the Alto Mayo Awajún appears unsustainable. Over the past two decades many of the Awajún have become landlords. Thousands of hectares of community land were subdivided into family portions suitable for leasing to colonist farmers. The attractions of leasing are obvious. Few Awajún are familiar enough with advanced agricultural techniques, including management of temperamental coffee trees, to undertake it successfully. Leasing land offers easy, reliable income. Detailed information on household wealth is unavailable, but those Awajún fortunate enough to control desirable farmland have been able to parlay leases into incomes well above the regional poverty line, sometimes outstripping the salaries of local professionals. Of course, by leasing lands on which they once farmed, hunted, and gathered raw materials, they have made themselves almost completely dependent on purchased goods.[4]

The spectacle of formerly marginalized indigenous people serving as landlords has an undeniable charm. It arouses some of the same emotions that the Ojibwe writer David Treuer reports after watching white bellboys scurrying to move the luggage of wealthy Native American guests as they check into an Indian-owned casino resort in Minnesota. "Everything is pleasantly backward," is how Treuer puts it. But many thoughtful Awajún regard the leasing arrangements as reckless. The presence of colonists' homes and families on Awajún land ignites petty conflicts almost daily and interferes with transmission of Awajún language and culture to the next generation. Dividing tribal lands into private or quasi-private holdings, a practice typically regarded by outsiders as civilizing, has over the long run nearly always made indigenous peoples more impoverished and vulnerable.[5]

More troubling still is the possibility that Awajún land titles will be weakened and eventually lost. Peru has a long history of land reform based on the principle that those who work the land acquire rights in it. Now that colonists have been farming Awajún lands for many years, it seems unlikely that they will peacefully walk away should Awajún owners someday decline to renew their leases. The majority of Alto Mayo colonists come from the Department of Cajamarca, a region noted for land-rights militancy. Despite Peru's current infatuation with free-market policies and privatization, the government has shown little stomach for enforcing land rights in the face of colonist invasions. The lessons of the 2002 massacre at Flor de la Frontera are not lost on those Awajún inclined to look past their current prosperity. They believe that they must extricate themselves from the land-leasing business as soon as possible. Let the

Awajún learn to cultivate coffee themselves, they say. Native communities should serve as incubators of indigenous businesses, not as resources that benefit outsiders.

With Bajo Naranjillo temporarily off-limits because of the dispute, I visited other settlements. My first stop was the municipality of Awajún, the name given to a district created in 1984 to encompass four indigenous communities as well as the colonist hamlets and undeveloped rainforest around them. Awajún's brightly painted town hall faced a construction site from which an elaborately paved plaza de armas was starting to emerge. The rest of the settlement had the thrown-together look characteristic of the Amazonian frontier: rutted streets, piles of rubble, half-built brick buildings capped by stems of rebar reaching toward an equatorial sky.

The town's mayor, Fermín Yagkitai, had been elected despite the Awajún's minority status within the district. He represented a new breed of politician who openly asserted an indigenous identity while reaching out to mestizo constituents. During our conversation he was interrupted several times by aides and secretaries with important messages. Compact, well-groomed, and pudgy-faced, Yagkitai seemed comfortable in his skin—the skin of a natural-born politician.

Not far from the Awajún municipal center was the community of Shampuyacu, now anchored by an impressive administration building of its own. It included, among other resources, a half dozen Internet kiosks that could be rented by the hour. After an obligatory discussion with the community's ápu, I finally was able to get past official encounters to conversations with ordinary Awajún, including some old acquaintances. I had brought snapshots of local people from the late 1970s and early 1980s to give away to their families. The effect was galvanizing. Soon a lively crowd gathered around the photos to laugh at the unfashionable clothes worn by their kinsmen back then. Others re-

Fermín Yagkitai, mayor of Awajún Municipal District, May 2012.
Photograph courtesy of Michael F. Brown.

membered relatives now dead. The list of memorable people lost in the intervening years grew longer and more disheartening as the conversations unfolded. Utiját, Raúl, Manúgka, Urucínta, Takarét, Kuimiág, Robinson, Shajián, Genaro, Arturo, Míkig, Santiago—they and many more were gone now. Most had died of natural causes, some still relatively young by the standards of developed-world life expectancies.

Alto Naranjillo, a community in which I had lived for nearly a year, proved surprisingly hard to locate. On the highway where I had once attended healing sessions in the house of the iwishín Genaro, colonist shops now stood. Billboards advertised Orange Grove Villa, with building lots "only 500 meters from the highway," as well as a housing estate called Paradise of the Valley. I soon learned that surveyors had determined that land immediately adjacent to the road, which the people of Alto

Naranjillo had once believed to be encompassed by their land title, lay outside the community boundaries. Colonist houses and gardens now ringed the community.

Near Alto Naranjillo's modest meeting house I found Chímpa, father of the baby girl born on the morning of my 1978 departure from the village. He was now an aged, shrunken version of his formerly robust self, although he retained much of the cheerful ebullience that marked his character then. My arrival was unexpected, and Chímpa did a double take. As soon as I addressed him in my rusty Awajún, however, he lit up and began to grab passing children, explaining animatedly that I was "Brother Máyak, the kirínku who lived here long ago."

My conversation with Chímpa, and later with a village official, Abel Chumapi, offered a portrait of a beleaguered community. The Awajún population had grown by 400 percent over the past thirty years. The community was leasing out 1,800 hectares, roughly half of its titled lands, to colonist farmers. The Awajún cultivated their own fields on the remainder. Forest resources had declined greatly. Wild game could scarcely be found; people now depended on domestic poultry and whatever dried fish or canned meat they could purchase in shops. The Awajún lived in constant fear of land invasions. To limit more subtle forms of infringement, the community denied property and voting rights to mestizos who married Awajún. Employment prospects in the area remained poor, even for Awajún who completed secondary school.[6]

The most unexpected story concerned Román, son of Shajián, the community's ápu during my time there. Román and his extended family had joined a fast-growing millenarian group known as the Israelite Mission of the New Universal Covenant, founded by an Andean prophet and visionary in the 1950s. The Israelitas, as they are known colloquially, live in settlements organized around a communitarian economy and a regimented ritual cycle. They are easily identified by their Old Testament dress. Male Israelitas let their hair and beards grow long and wear flowing robes; women wear full skirts and head scarves similar to the Islamic *hijab*. To prepare for an awaited time of tribulation, tens of thousands of Israelitas are colonizing sites in Amazonian Peru and neighboring countries. Román and his family had joined a group of Israelita pioneers founding a new settlement in far eastern Peru near the Brazilian frontier. The idea of independent-minded Awajún finding personal satisfaction in an authoritarian religious movement seemed incongruous, but apparently the Israelitas have been actively seeking Awajún converts. Some have answered their call.[7]

This news, as well as the declaration of Albertina Nanchíjam, sub-ápu of Shampuyacu, that she worshipped with a group of Baha'i converts in her community, suggests the broad range of religious influences to which the Awajún are now exposed. Eastern Peru is home to dozens of evangelical Christian sects, some espousing millenarian or apocalyptic theologies. The Baha'i faith is represented in small numbers. The same region has also seen a steady rise in so-called shamanic tourism, spiritual seekers from North America, Europe, and Asia traveling to Amazonia to experience the spectacular visions induced by ayahuasca under the guidance of indigenous and mestizo shamans. The sacramental use of ayahuasca figures centrally in two new religions, Santo Daime and União do Vegetal, which have spread from Brazil to Peru, Colombia, Venezuela, and scattered outposts in North America and Europe. This may, in turn, be fueling an evangelical backlash. In 2011, Peruvian newspapers reported that fourteen indigenous shamans, all Shawi from the Balsapuerto area on the fringes of Awajún territory, had been murdered by mestizo *matabrujos*, "witch killers." The killings were said to be engineered by fanatical Christian converts who wanted to end the practice of "satanic arts" in their community.[8]

A poorly understood aspect of culture change in Latin America is why some indigenous peoples have proven impervious to new religious influences while others gravitate toward them in significant numbers. The circumstances of the Awajún's introduction to evangelical Christianity identified it in their minds with literacy and individual self-improvement. Many recognized that certain traditional practices, including wife abuse and feuding, gave rise to suffering and social disorder. Yet even when the Awajún embraced an alien faith, their own drive and self-assertion tended to surface eventually. Robert Priest, an anthropologist who studied Awajún conversion to evangelical Christianity, reports that leaders of Awajún congregations came to resent the external influence of the Kansas-based Church of the Nazarene, the most important Protestant denomination in Awajún country. This led to a split that culminated in the founding of the Aguaruna Evangelical Church, which was entirely controlled by the Awajún. About half of Awajún Protestants shifted to the new church. When I asked Albertina Nanchíjam about her attraction to the Baha'i faith, which originated in Iran, she insisted that unlike evangelical Christians, whose religion requires them to renounce many aspects of traditional Awajún culture, the more ecumenical Baha'i respect local custom, allowing her to be both Baha'i and Awajún.[9]

In many ways my return to the Alto Mayo proved heartbreaking. A quarter century of change had robbed the region of its piquancy and distinctiveness. The inevitable deaths of so many Awajún elders, whose experience bridged the era of independent life in the forest and the new reality of coffee cultivation, crowded roads, and store-bought food, was the biggest cause for melancholy. It would be only a slight exaggeration to say that Awajún communities such as Shampuyacu and Bajo Naranjillo have taken on suburban qualities. A fair number of Awajún now live in concrete-walled houses and cruise the roads on motorcycles or in pickup trucks. Their everyday clothing is identical to that of their mestizo neighbors. They still work their fields and hunt when they can, but young people mostly look to cash-crop agriculture and town life when planning for the future.

But to portray the current situation in a wholly negative light would be to surrender to personal nostalgia. In economic terms the Awajún of the Alto Mayo are doing substantially better than most indigenous peoples in Amazonia. That helps to explain why so many Awajún migrate to the Alto Mayo in search of opportunity. They have carved out a space for themselves in regional politics and managed to forge alliances with nonindigenous neighbors when they share common interests. They continue to value their language and culture. New religious influences have exacerbated divisions within their society, but history has shown that over time the Awajún are likely to take control of alien faiths and reshape them to suit core Awajún values.

One dark cloud is the tension fostered by economic inequality. The subdivision of communal lands into family-owned plots suitable for leasing to outsiders set the stage for the emergence of marked differences in wealth. Newly arrived Awajún migrants and residents of communities with less desirable lands inevitably resent the affluence of more fortunate kin. Inequality has not yet proved so divisive that it prevents the Awajún from presenting a united front when the state threatens their collective interests. Yet over the long term it is likely to prove a corrosive force in a society once ill-disposed to hierarchy. The Alto Mayo situation bears an uncanny resemblance to the circumstance of late-nineteenth-century Indian Territory in Oklahoma, where steadily growing divisions between rich and poor Indians encouraged destructive legal meddling by the federal government.[10]

The people of the Alto Mayo enjoy exceptional circumstances. In the Awajún heartland to their north, land remains scarce and economic opportunities limited. Thousands still subsist primarily through hunting, fishing, farming, and the collection of forest resources. Hardy Awajún pioneers continue to push into unoccupied rainforest in search of land and game; some have been noted as far afield as the Alto Río Utiquinía in east-central Peru. Others are choosing to stay put and fight to expand their community lands and protect their forests and rivers from the impact of petroleum and gold-mining operations. Although hardly typical, the recent history of the Alto Mayo may be a harbinger of things to come for other Awajún as they wrestle with economic development and a changing political landscape in their increasingly crowded patch of Amazonia.[11]

Eduardo Nayap, a slender man with chiseled features, talks with the careful diction of someone accustomed to speaking in public. Today he is the Awajún most familiar to Peruvians thanks to countless newspaper profiles and television interviews. In 2011 Nayap was elected to the Peruvian Congress from a district in the Department of Amazonas after a lightning campaign that took his opponents by surprise.

I interviewed Congressman Nayap in May 2012 in his office in central Lima. At the time of our meeting, his election was still dogged by accusations of electoral fraud, complaints dismissed by a judge several weeks later. That Nayap had tallied 100 percent of the votes cast in some Awajún and Wampis communities prompted suspicion, although possible irregularities at the polls were less salient than was the outrage of better-established candidates whose ambitions had been thwarted by a political novice scarcely known in Peru. Nayap ran on the ticket of Gana Peru (Peru Wins), an alliance of left-of-center, nation-

Congressman Eduardo Nayap after swearing-in ceremony, Lima, 2011.
Photograph by Congreso de la República del Perú.

alist parties that included the successful presidential candidate Ollanta Humala.[12]

Photographs of Nayap's official swearing-in ceremony show him wearing the kind of hybrid outfit now favored by indigenous politicians worldwide: a conservative suit and tie accompanied by a toucan-feather corona and a colorful bandolier of seed beads. For our meeting, only the suit was in evidence. Also present was a similarly dressed aide who fielded telephone calls and queries from the congressman's secretary as we spoke.

Nayap's biography is unusual. Born in 1956 in a village in the Alto Marañón, he benefited from his father's long association with American missionaries from the Church of the Nazarene. At the age of seven he was sent from the jungle to the coastal city of Trujillo in pursuit of education and fluency in

Spanish. His dream was to study medicine at a Peruvian university. The government offered no scholarship support for indigenous students, however, and Nayap had little choice but to accept an invitation from the Nazarenes to study for a degree in theology at a seminary in Costa Rica. After completing his studies, he worked for various nongovernmental organizations in Costa Rica while serving as a professor of Bible studies and pastor of an evangelical congregation.

Commenting on his binational experience, he explained that despite more than thirty years in Costa Rica he had maintained close contacts with relatives in Peru and had visited the Alto Marañón as often as possible. What convinced him to give up his comfortable situation in Costa Rica for the uncertain prospects of a political career in the country of his birth? "The Baguazo," he said. "It was a profound blow. It made me passionate about fighting for my people. I felt like a traitor to live so far away." He decided to return home and stand as a candidate for Congress. His candidacy papers were submitted at the eleventh hour, and he had no time to raise money. Once committed to running, he spent weeks convincing Awajún and Wampis leaders to vote solely for him rather than splitting their votes among candidates representing nearly a dozen different political parties. He also campaigned hard for the mestizo vote. "I took time to visit the largest towns and the smallest villages. I went to mestizo settlements that had never been visited by a candidate. Many of the Spanish-speakers said, 'Let's go with him. We want a change.'"

Nayap mentioned two areas of particular interest. The first was the quality of education available to his Awajún and Wampis constituents. He lamented the low standards of schools in his district. Although the government had made a good-faith effort to hire enough bilingual teachers to meet burgeoning demand, their training was inadequate. "Many indigenous students complete their secondary education, but when they have to compete with other students for places in the university, none are able to enter." The congressman's focus on schools was emblematic of an Awajún hunger for education matched by few other Amazonian peoples.

Equally important to Congressman Nayap was prompt implementation of the new Law of Prior Consultation, passed in 2011 in response to the Baguazo tragedy. This established norms for negotiating agreements with indigenous communities affected by resource extraction concessions awarded by the state.[13]

Peru's unaccustomed prosperity, fueled by GDP growth that exceeded that of Brazil in 2010, was based on rising world demand for minerals and petroleum products. Export agriculture was also enjoying success, if on a more modest scale. Uprisings such as the one that led to the Baguazo threatened this growth by casting doubt on Peru's ability to protect capital projects and convince its citizens that economic development would benefit anyone other than foreign investors and Lima's moneyed class. Perhaps, legislators hoped, consultation with indigenous communities could turn opponents into stakeholders. A year after the law was passed, however, Peru was still struggling to define its scope. What had seemed clear when viewed from afar became blurred when trudging through the weeds. Who holds decision-making power in indigenous communities marked by decentralized leadership? Could people with little prior exposure to alien policies and processes be expected to give fully informed consent? In view of the state's non-negotiable assertion that it owned subsurface resources, was meaningful consultation even possible when indigenous peoples were confronted with proposals involving mining or the search for oil and natural gas?[14]

Nayap insisted that the Awajún, the Wampis, and other Amazonian peoples had the right to define the terms of development on their lands. "I'm not asking for extra consideration for being indigenous. No sir. I'm a Peruvian, and this is Peruvian territory. We're looking for prerogatives merited by anyone in Peruvian territory. That's what we're fighting for. The Law of Prior Consultation is an advance for us. It signifies a claim, a framework for respecting our rights. It permits us to demand respect and dialogue with the state."

Asked how he reconciled his commitment to evangelical Protestantism with his fight for the survival of Awajún culture, elements of which were long deemed objectionable by missionaries, Congressman Nayap's answer sounded well rehearsed. "I'm not a denominational theologian. I'm more ecumenical," he said. This ecumenical orientation led him to the conclusion that his people's traditional spirituality was compatible with biblical teaching. Although foreign missionaries insisted that they were bringing God to the Awajún, Nayap saw things differently. "There is no lie bigger than this. We lived with God. We had God. God was with us. Biblical language, themes of salvation, can be recontextualized so that indigenous people can be Christians without ceasing to be indigenous. I'm not going to transform myself into a white man to achieve eternal salvation."

Perhaps fearing that he had gone too far in stressing his indigenism, Congressman Nayap asserted his interest in fighting for all his constituents, regardless of ethnicity. "I'm working for the whole region of Amazonas. The roads are in terrible condition, which discourages travelers. This doesn't apply only to indigenous communities; it also applies to towns in my district. This is our reality, and it's my duty to confront these issues. I'm doing it happily, with great optimism, dreaming that we'll achieve many good things."

A pivotal moment of my 2012 trip, a point at which it became clear that the Awajún world I had known was fast becoming something else, came while interviewing Fermín Tiwi, an outgoing, university-trained legal expert who works for an NGO focused on indigenous issues. Tiwi looked at me quizzically and said, "*Doctor*, has anyone ever told you that you look a lot like Eric Clapton?" This unexpected turn led to a conversational detour into Tiwi's passion for music, especially his Awajún rock band Ikámia (From the Forest), which had recently uploaded videos to an Internet video site.

Cosmopolitanism and cultural hybridity were threads woven through Tiwi's biography and those of three other university-trained Awajún whom I interviewed. Their backgrounds shared much in common with Eduardo Nayap's life story. Their parents had been educated in Roman Catholic or Nazarene schools. All had been raised as Christians, although their current feelings about Christianity leaned toward ambivalence. As secondary school students, they had been sent by their parents to cities far from Awajún country to improve their fluency in Spanish. Their daily existence as university students in the capital was mostly hand-to-mouth owing to precarious funding. All had learned how to hustle employment in a capital still inhospitable to indigenous Amazonians. Without exception, their shared ambition was to use their education to earn a decent living while benefitting the Awajún people, a variation on the theme of doing well by doing good, but with an eye firmly fixed on cultural identity.

Felipe Shimbucat, a soft-spoken, slender man in his twenties, described the circumstances that led to his law studies at the National University of San Marcos, the oldest institution of higher education in the Western Hemisphere. Like his father, Shimbucat was educated at a Jesuit mission school. "The Jesuits," he said with a laugh, "gave me the habit of being studious." But his respect for Catholic values did not prevent him from a period of fasting and consumption of hallucinogenic ayahuasca in search of a vision in accordance with Awajún tradition. "The vision grabs you, not to harm you but to make you more competent. This is the Awajún world. The vision makes you think straight. You see your future wife, your fields. It has changed in one way, though, because now you see your future education."

Shimbucat's quest was for ways to reconcile the laws of Peru with Awajún custom. He imagined the creation of tribunals that would deal with crimes committed by indigenous people while outside their community. These tribunals would combine indigenous judges and experts in Peruvian national law to assess the alleged infraction and determine an appropriate penalty. He acknowledged that there are limits to the state's ability to honor native custom. Yet the state continues to favor nonindigenous peoples over indigenous ones, a situation that he aims to see reformed.

When asked whether there was one key lesson from his experiences, Felipe Shimbucat said, "I've seen that some think of us, of indigenous people, as an obstacle. Here in the city you have to develop and adapt. The condition of being indigenous doesn't mean that one is inferior. You have to think about what you can contribute to science, to humanity." This contribution, he said, requires the kind of hard work celebrated in Awajún tradition.

The future of Awajún anthropology may lie in the hands of people such as Wilson Atamain, a thirty-year-old university graduate of mixed Shuar-Awajún descent. Atamain's father, who was born in the upper reaches of the Río Morona, was educated at a Nazarene school in northern Peru and worked as a pastor until he migrated to the coffee-growing lands of the Alto Río Mayo. Atamain was educated in Awajún schools until he came to Lima to study anthropology at San Marcos. His parents provided some support, but he was obliged to take contract work when he could find it. He had worked on a short-term basis for various NGOs, one of which sent him to study indigenous communities on the Río Pastaza in northern Peru, work that he found satisfying. At the time of our interview he was actively looking for a job and hoping to pursue an advanced degree in cultural anthropology.

Atamain spoke bluntly about what he felt was a crisis afflicting Awajún youth. They were moving away from traditional culture and toward a more cosmopolitan education, thinking that this would be rewarding. Now they increasingly find themselves in what he called a "spiritual void" characterized by poor economic prospects and cultural rootlessness.

Dina Ananco, a woman of mixed Awajún-Wampis descent, presented a thumbnail biography similar to Wilson Atamain's, although her university education led her in the direction of literature rather than social science. As a young girl her Wampis mother fled to a Catholic boarding school to escape an arranged marriage to which she objected. Educated there by Spanish nuns, she eventually married an Awajún man who had trained as a teacher. They tried living in an Awajún community for a time, but Ananco's mother never felt welcome. The family eventually relocated to a Wampis community on the Río Santiago. Ananco and her five siblings came to understand and speak both languages.

Ananco, who appeared to be in her late twenties, was dressed simply in pressed jeans and a plain blouse, complemented by fashionable glasses. She was soft-spoken but poised. She explained that she now lives with a man from the Shawi indigenous group who is studying administration at the university. They share a small rented room with their two-year-old son.

"My father always wanted us to study," she said. Her mother felt the same. "The first way to convince us to study was to show us the garden, what it would be like if we didn't study. She took us to the garden every day to plant maize or whatever." Laughing, Ananco insisted that this backbreaking work had traumatized her. "So my mother always said, 'If you don't want this to be your life, you've got to study.'"

One after another, she and her siblings left their village on the Santiago to study in a Catholic secondary school in the town of Jaén and then on to professional training elsewhere. One of her sisters now works as an accountant; a brother has nearly completed a training program in agronomy. Despite some financial support from her father and an older sister, Ananco's university experience in Lima was one of financial and emotional struggle. A rented room in Lima proved too cramped and noisy to allow serious study. A scholarship promised to her by an indigenous organization failed to materialize. At San Marcos, she initially hid her indigenous identity for fear that others would regard her as exotic or strange. Eventually, though, she was elected to a leadership position in a group organized by indigenous students from the Amazon. This eventually led to a job writing press releases and reports for an indigenous-rights website based in Lima. She completed her bachelor's degree and now plans to pursue a postgraduate degree in literature.

Dina Ananco's appraisal of the situation of women in Awajún society was colored by her mother's early escape from the threat of an arranged marriage. Traditionally, Ananco said, a woman was valued only to the extent that she maintained the good image of her husband. "We call this complementarity now, but I'm not so sure. She was expected not to damage a man's pride. It is surprising and curious: the woman was given great importance and at the same time . . . nothing. You are everything and at the same time nothing." The frustrations arising from this predicament account for the high rate of female suicide, she insisted.

Despite this gloomy assessment of the place of women in her society, Ananco was convinced that change is in the wind. "There are female leaders of indigenous groups here in Lima. They're constantly battling for space. They are given responsibilities with the hope that they'll fail. Once they could be dismissed because they weren't as well educated as men. But that's changing now."

The challenges do not end when Awajún men and women complete their training. "I worry about Awajún who finish their education and then can't find employment. You've left your community, and it seems like madness to have done so. But you've done it for a reason. You have to be persistent. We Amazonian people need professionals."

For all their cheerful determination to succeed, Dina Ananco and the other university graduates I interviewed seemed like people dangling between two worlds. Prospects for suitable employment in the heart of Awajún country remain limited, so ambitious young professionals must seek jobs in Lima or other locations far from home. There they are likely to enter into romantic entanglements that cross ethnic lines, complicating their relationship to Awajún society. It is possible that such cultural border crossing will promote cultural assimilation, but recent history suggests otherwise. The sense of cultural difference and even of cultural superiority that one finds in many urban Awajún remains undiminished by formal education. Instead, they nurture the hope that they will achieve a critical mass of cosmopolitan Awajún better positioned to fight for the rights of their kin back home.

When Peruvian friends with knowledge of contemporary indigenous affairs were asked to name the most imaginative Awajún political thinker on the scene today, they were likely to mention Gil Inoach. Inoach, who served a term as president of Peru's largest indigenous federation, AIDESEP (Interethnic Association for the Development of the Peruvian Rainforest), recently stepped out of the political arena to pursue consulting work and formal training as a translator. When we met in Lima to talk about his life, it was obvious that envisioning a future for the

Awajún remained a task to which he still devoted considerable energy.

Inoach is a compact man whose square face and wire-rimmed glasses project both thoughtfulness and strength of purpose. His description of childhood in the Alto Marañón hewed to a familiar pattern: an austerely evangelical father who valued literacy and self-discipline; time at a secondary school on the Peruvian coast to achieve fluency in Spanish; thwarted ambition when lack of family resources made it impossible for him to attend university. Inoach had no choice but to become an ordinary householder in his home community, Sachapapa. "It was the first year of the university of life," he said. Apprenticing himself to an uncle, he was drawn into the rhythm of agricultural work and came to enjoy it. His literacy and bilingualism led him to leadership roles in the community, first focused on the marketing of rice and then on efforts to defend Awajún lands and civil rights as the pace of Amazonian colonization accelerated. In the 1980s, he rode the wave of indigenous organizing that produced increasingly sophisticated native federations at the regional and then national level. Awajún leaders were disproportionately represented in several of these organizations because of their assertiveness and superior education.[15]

Indigenous organizations in Latin America are notoriously volatile. Their leaders must spend time in distant capitals far from the people they represent. Their financial needs are pressing, their resources modest. A sudden change of policy at a funding agency, a major disagreement about strategy, a rumor back home that a native leader is living the high life in Lima or Quito or Bogotá—any one of these can plunge the organization into crisis. Gil Inoach was a weary veteran of federation politics, which may partly account for his view that their era is now ending. He declared that the Awajún and other Amazo-

Awajún bilingual teachers, Moyobamba, 2007.
Photograph by Graham Gordon and used with his kind permission.

nian peoples must take the next step by pushing for integrated territories and greater sovereignty. "The Awajún should have their own system of government under the principle of the right to self-determination. How we structure that—as a central government with ministers or instead look to Awajún models from the past—is something that we need to discuss. On this basis, we'll formulate policies of development, resource management, zoning our territories, and so on." It remains unclear how the Awajún can reassemble a unified nation from more than two hundred separate and sometimes noncontiguous communities, although Inoach said that he and others had already begun surveying territory in pursuit of that dream.[16]

The literacy that made this organizing possible was the fruit of Christian missionaries and their schools. Inoach was critical of both Catholic and Protestant missionaries because so many of them devalued Awajún knowledge and stood in the way of the indigenous struggle for recognition. Yet he took pains to acknowledge the missions' beneficial impact. "The influence of these religions has helped to create internal peace. For example, we Awajún used to kill one other, an eye for an eye. If I think that family thus-and-such killed my nephew, then I can avenge that death. . . . We had to flee from one place to another. For example, the people who migrated from Cahuapanas and Potro to the Alto Mayo—the old man Dáse and the rest—were fleeing from this kind of problem." Foreign missionaries and the bilingual teachers whom they trained were instrumental in reducing the frequency and intensity of this internal violence.

Inoach also conceded that the literacy promoted by missionaries had been a vital tool for the Awajún. "You come to know yourself because you have the capacity to register your own thoughts as you write them. They gave us this tool. With this you can create your own space and project yourself. You are the owner of your own expression, owner of your words. Once we learned to speak Spanish, we could speak directly to the state."

Inoach's political ideas were infused with spiritual idioms favored by other cosmopolitan Awajún. When discussing the 2009 Baguazo conflict, he mentioned that the young Awajún who manned the highway blockades were as tough as any warriors of the past, yet they fought without the spiritual support of the vision quest. "What did they lack? The spirit of the ajútap. For a moment we almost broke, we almost failed because the old men did not want to proclaim their vision. They said that they were now evangelicals and that to proclaim their vision was to condemn themselves to hell. In the old days we proclaimed our visions and we won the war. But now no one wants to do it."

"Proclaiming a vision" was a rite that traditionally took place immediately prior to a raid. Members of a raiding party shared the story of their encounter with an ajútap spirit and their acquisition of its killing power. Paradoxically, the ritual proclamation seems to have both focused the warrior's strength and neutralized the vision's future potency, forcing the warrior to seek a new vision before initiating another round of hostilities.

As Inoach and other Awajún thinkers cast about for language with which to frame their political aspirations, they often gravitate to the theme of visionary power. They commonly identify a mythical personage named Bíkut as one of their people's greatest teachers. Bíkut seems an unlikely hero for the present moment. Myths identify him as a young man who consumed staggering amounts of angel's trumpet, the dangerously deranging hallucinogen related to jimsonweed. This transformed him into a warrior of unparalleled ruthlessness. Bíkut's visions purified him so completely that he sensed when anyone around him had been tainted by sexual contact. After summarily killing several close kin for their impurity, Bíkut was lashed to a house post for the protection of the community, to be turned loose only when an expert killer was needed to defeat enemies. Bíkut eventually met a violent end in one of these battles, and three new varieties of angel's trumpet sprang from his corpse, one of which today bears his name.[17]

Published texts of the Bíkut myth, as well as versions that I recorded in the 1970s, portray him as a dangerous scold—half killer cyborg, half humorless ayatollah—who was respected for his uncompromising discipline but impossible to live with in a world of ordinary mortals. More recently, however, the Awajún have reimagined him as a beneficent sage or, as one Awajún communiqué put it, "the philosopher . . . who delivered the knowledge and ability to understand different worlds through the use of angel's trumpet and ayahuasca." This shift parallels the expressed desire of Gil Inoach and others to revitalize the traditional vision quest in a new form that sheds its association with violence. In addition to killing visions, the Awajún have long believed in *tajímat* (prosperity) visions. "The ancient version of tajímat signified abundance: to be a visionary, to have well-behaved children, to have gardens, to be a hunter and a fisherman, to be respected for one's reputation, to have wives and a large house," Inoach said. A modern tajímat is different. "What we're looking for is to become a people with our own system of education, developing our own technologies, a people who express their understandings to persuade the world of the value of protection and conservation, of the values of development and reciprocity."[18]

This is the credo that Gil Inoach and others hope to resurrect and embellish. "We have good customs and bad customs," he told me. "It's time to choose foreign technologies that strengthen our identity and system of internal governance. We need to accept these and undo and discard technologies that harm our way of life. That's the way the world is."

"The Awajún," Inoach went on, "have an agenda under way, bubbling like manioc beer as it ferments." He closed our conversation with a series of rhetorical questions that underline the scope of Awajún ambition. "Why shouldn't an Awajún come to ally himself with the world's scientists, to take his message and understanding to the world? Why can't a modern Awajún live in a community with technologies of communication, with a luxurious house built of his own wood? Instead of coming to learn here, in Lima, the world will go to the Awajún to learn at good universities, with great healers, that have prestige, that conserve our knowledge, that protect our understandings. This is the modern vision that we seek, the modern tajímat."

Historical accounts tend to portray the Awajún as distinctive when compared to other native peoples of the Amazon. Some portraits are disapproving. They condemn the Awajún's rebellious spirit and violent inclinations, which made them poor candidates for enslavement. Others offer more favorable appraisals. Humboldt found them vivacious. Tessmann declared them "sanguinary" but clever. Orton saw them as brave and hardworking.

The more perceptive observers responded to qualities that today account for the outsized role that the Awajún play in South America's indigenous politics. The marked individualism of Awajún society imbued adult men with a degree of autonomy and a sense of self-importance startling to outsiders. Ambition was highly valued, yet men were obliged to refine their strategic thinking and rhetorical skills if they hoped to mobilize the support of others possessed of similar ambition. Their religious commitments were flexible and portable; not for them the burdensome obligations of communal rituals and formal leadership. They had room to move in response to circumstances, and move they did. Centuries of survival in a tough neighborhood—within easy reach of aggressive Andean empires and then, in the postcontact period, the depredations of conquistadors, slavers, and patróns—schooled them in the art of resistance. Pugnacity and suspicion served them well for much of that time.

By the mid-twentieth century, however, the picture had become more complicated. Diffuse hostility no longer worked as a survival strategy; outsiders were too numerous, their power too overwhelming. Awajún were drawn into the cash nexus, which demanded unfamiliar habits of mind. A desire for literacy, the value of which soon became apparent even to the most unrepentant warrior, brought their children into schools and, through schooling, into new modes of thought and self-discipline. Internal feuding continued, but more sophisticated Awajún thinkers saw how feuds weakened communities that needed to stand together against the state. Whether acceptance of the Christian message by many Awajún was a cause or an effect of this shift remains unclear. More certain is that Christianity allowed the Awajún to forge links to powerful allies both within and outside of Peru. It also provided a framework with which the Awajún could reassess their own values and practices.

Tensions between the Awajún and the state grew in the 1990s as the collapse of Peru's leftist insurgency revived a stagnant economy. The state committed itself to a policy of economic growth funded by foreign capital and managed by local technocrats. The Amazon provided a perfect testing ground for an especially draconian version of neoliberal economics. Far from the prying eyes of the press and mostly populated by people with weak ties to centers of power, the Amazon invited excesses of ambition, as it has since the first Spanish conquistadors explored its western edge in the sixteenth century in search of gilded cities.

Today the Awajún stand in the front lines of groups opposed to Peru's plans for the nation's rainforest region. Stalwart and enterprising, they do not oppose modernity, as critics such as former Peruvian president Alan García have alleged. Their demands for better schools and support for sustainable approaches to resource use and agriculture show that they embrace change. They are better thought of as "off-modern," a label expressing the sensibility of groups that spurn conventional, straight-line models of progress in favor of what the historian T. J. Jackson Lears describes as "economic strategies rooted in their particular circumstances, customs, and traditions."[19]

This ambitious, adaptive creativity gives rise to new predicaments. Traditional values were strongly oriented to an assertive form of male individualism that left few opportunities for women to develop their own potential. The overall Awajún literacy rate is thought to be somewhere between 60 and 75 percent, but female literacy lags significantly behind that of men, mostly because girls are kept home from school at a higher rate than boys and leave it at a younger age. The frequency of female suicide strongly suggests that many Awajún women find their life situations deeply frustrating. NGOs such as UNICEF and CARE are focusing attention on the conditions of women's lives in Awajún communities. The concern of outsiders may have played a part in the establishment of FEMAAM, the Federation of Women of the Alto Marañón, a group focused on the needs of indigenous women, including health care and education. The number of women seeking professional opportunities in education and health care is on the rise, suggesting that the society has reached a crossroads in gender relations.[20]

The ambitions of some Awajún, in combination with the agricultural potential of fortunate communities such as those of the Alto Mayo, are laying the foundation for a class system. The full implications of this remain uncertain. Perhaps the rise of a prosperous minority will fuel the educational and entrepreneurial aspirations of Awajún youth. It will likely give Awajún people greater access to communications media and increase their political influence at the national level. Yet history teaches that extreme social inequality can poison the well of community solidarity. Class antagonisms could eventually render the Awajún more vulnerable to manipulation by outsiders and imperil their hopes for greater sovereignty.

Similar uncertainty surrounds Awajún political militancy. The violence of the 2009 Baguazo had a tonic effect on Peru. Some good has come from the tragedy: indigenous concerns were taken more seriously, and the nation gestured toward reconciliation in multiple arenas. Nevertheless, there are doubtless many Peruvians—among them, one suspects, elements of the national police force—who yearn for an opportunity to settle scores.

In the introduction to his monumental study of the Jívaro, *The Head-Hunters of Western Amazonas* (1935), Rafael Karsten pondered the fate of the Awajún, the Shuar, and other Jivaroan peoples in a changing world. His prediction was that "this exceptionally interesting Indian culture will soon be a thing of the past."[21] History has proven him mistaken. In three generations the Awajún have shifted decisively from the values of a warrior culture to a new kind of indigenous hybrid that aggressively seeks out educational and economic opportunity while maintaining a high level of self-confidence and a clear sense of collective identity. Their population is large and growing, their language still widely spoken. They remain a thorn in the side of the Peruvian state because of their opposition to policies that seek to turn the Amazon into an immense industrial park. No longer the headhunters of Karsten's account, they nevertheless remain resolutely Jivaroan: committed to defending their land and their right to govern themselves, still driven by a steely determination to live on terms of their own choosing. Dina Ananco, the young, college-educated activist, put it best. "It's not as if you can fight as a warrior now," she said. "You fight with your knowledge. That is our work today."

10

Looking Back

This book's final chapters were drafted in surroundings that could hardly be more different from the world familiar to the Awajún. Framed by the window was a portrait of New England winter: trees stripped by October's leaf drop, drifts sculpted by January's winds, ornamental grasses desiccated and askew. Only the occasional chatter of chickadees or the squeak of boots on dry snow broke the boreal silence. In reflective moments, I have wondered why someone from such an austere place should be among those fated to document moments in the life of the Awajún, an exuberant people in an exuberant natural setting. Only chance brought us together. No planning involved.

The impromptu quality of the encounter would be unlikely today. Anyone attempting to do similar work would face ethical vetting by the institutional review board of his or her home institution. This would be followed by months of negotiation with host-nation authorities and the indigenous community's own gatekeeping organization. Only when these obstacles were overcome could real work begin. It is not an undertaking for the impatient or the improvisationally inclined.

Another challenge is the impact of globalization on even the remotest locations. Migration to plantations, urban worksites, and jobs abroad complicates the question of what constitutes "home." Migrants commonly share new ideas and experiences, thus transforming notions of how the culture of home fits into the larger world. Anyone studying the Awajún today might feel obliged to follow them into the cities where some of their young people are pursuing advanced education and their leaders have established offices close to the ministries and NGOs whose activities influence life in the hinterlands. If research funds sufficed, it would be useful to accompany Awajún leaders to global forums in Lima and occasionally as far afield as Geneva, Paris, or Washington, where they make their opinions known through speeches and press conferences. Likewise the journeys of Awajún evangelicals to Christian training centers, where they deepen their understanding of biblical teachings and strategies for attracting converts. All of these sites and situations shed light on what it means to be Awajún now.[1]

History would have to be attended to. Since the 1980s anthropologists have recognized that societies cannot be adequately understood by examining them only in the present. Their current practices may reflect not an ancient cultural orientation but a survival strategy dating back only a few decades. A fieldworker now might feel obliged to spend as much time working in archives as studying everyday life in face-to-face communities.

Despite its virtues, immersion is rarely the steady march toward complete understanding that ethnographies from earlier eras made it out to be. I have described crises that remained unresolved, suspicions that were allayed only provisionally, vengeance that was postponed until later or perhaps forever. All ethnography harbors zones of uncertainty. I witnessed only one adult funeral, for instance, and not even all of that. I might just as easily have witnessed none. I had ready access to a single shaman, whose approach to healing was regarded by his clients as somewhat idiosyncratic. I lived in or visited eight Awajún communities, but these are only a small fraction of the more than 200 that have now secured official recognition. In one memorable interview, a man shared a childhood memory of his family's behavior during a major earthquake. He recalled that his parents and other adults spent hours dancing naked out of a conviction that this would save their lives and prevent the earthquake from recurring. The recollection stretched credulity in light of Awajún prudishness regarding women's bodies. The story's accuracy was impossible for me to verify and may always remain so.[2]

More perplexing than these challenges is a wave of disciplinary self-doubt that has still not crested. My encounter with an opinionated European colleague as I departed from the field in 1978 was a portent. Anthropology's critics portray the discipline as an expression of the need to inventory, classify, and ultimately manage the human resources that the West had drawn into its sphere of influence. They argue further that the colonial project and its Enlightenment foundations consigned non-Western peoples to another category of humanity that could serve as counterimage to the West's own utopian fantasies.[3]

These charges have produced tension between those who see the discipline's primary mission as scientific and others who insist that anthropologists have an overriding ethical obligation to struggle against inequality. For the latter, devoting time to the study of unfamiliar customs and beliefs such as those I have described here is akin to documenting wallpaper patterns inside a burning house.[4]

Unfortunately, denunciation has a powerful tendency to colonize the imagination at the expense of nuance. I have no quarrel with the proposition that injustice merits sustained attention and, when possible, energetic efforts to set things right. The difficulty comes in drawing lines, making distinctions. Denunciatory accounts lean toward a blunt-force vocabulary, with "ethnocide" and "cultural genocide" being the preferred terms of art. Sometimes this strong language is warranted. Amazonian oil-drilling and gold-mining operations that wantonly poison the environment deserve condemnation. Other situations are marked by greater ambiguity. Proselytizing by missionaries, for instance, is routinely condemned as ethnocidal. Strictly speaking, this is accurate: the goal of most missionary work is to kill certain indigenous beliefs and replace them with others. It is indisputable that missionaries have sometimes resorted to manipulative practices to win converts. But there are many contemporary cases in which conversion appears voluntary and indigenous peoples are energetically pursuing their own evangelization efforts. From what position can an anthropologist assert that converts are deluded in their choices?

Another problem of politically engaged research is that its rhetoric needs victims and heroes, or better yet, heroic victims. This requirement may lead to frustratingly thin accounts. Telling details are ignored in favor of portraits of Amazonian peoples as rainforest-worshipping, feather-wearing, tropical Dalai Lamas. A tendency to oversimplify morally complex situations, which may be a legacy of polarized Cold War intellectual debates, continues to be something against which fieldworkers struggle with varying degrees of success.[5]

To their credit, the Awajún have mostly resisted the siren call of Noble Savage rhetoric. Many realize that their reputation as a combative people would be difficult to conceal. If anything, they celebrate and embellish it. In the past decade they have proven militant enough for their aggressive profile to remain credible.

Stepping back from the specific circumstances of an embattled people, one faces questions from the shadowy territory lying between ethics and epistemology. Who granted anthropologists the authority to study societies of which we are not members? Reframed in more disputatious language, the question becomes, by what right does an academic from the developed world, implicitly representing a powerful nation and a hegemonic scientific tradition, presume to speak for a tribal people who never invited this attention and who may have only a limited understanding of what it means for their collective welfare?

Such questions have preoccupied the discipline for decades. Anthropology's classical period, defined by the work of such foundational thinkers as E. E. Evans-Pritchard, Bronislaw Malinowski, Ruth Benedict, and Mary Douglas, was marked by a self-confidence that today registers as arrogance. The anthropologist, as Malinowski announced in the introduction to his masterwork, *Argonauts of the Western Pacific,* introduces "law and order into what seemed chaotic and freakish." Malinowski and his peers held that only trained anthropologists possess the skills needed to tease out the structure of everyday life in exotic places, an order inaccessible to the subjects themselves. This robust certainty sheared open like a seismic fault in the late twentieth century, to be replaced by radical doubt—doubt about anthropology's claim to unique understanding of other people's experience.[6]

In Malinowski's time, an anthropologist could reasonably assume that research subjects were unlikely to encounter the publications that emerged from fieldwork. Global circuits are tighter today. Many indigenous people are literate and multilingual; an increasing number are university educated. They read our work, criticize it, sometimes even appropriate it for their own purposes. This hall-of-mirrors effect gives rise to unanticipated conflicts. Anthropologists once were likely to say that indigenous peoples lived in exquisite balance with their environment. Subsequent research has made that assertion harder to defend even if there remains little doubt that traditional subsistence systems are far less destructive of the environment than are industrial ones. Yet the rhetoric of perfect harmony with nature, often coupled with claims that amity and democracy reign supreme in Amazonian societies, has become a tool that indigenous leaders use to make a case that their rights should be respected. The anthropologist with evidence to the contrary may be in an uncomfortable position.[7]

One response to this dilemma is to reimagine ethnography as part of a long conversation in which the anthropologist represents a single voice among many. A fair number of anthropologists find it liberating to abandon the notion that their assessment of something as complex as another culture should be treated as definitive. This leaves them freer to try new approaches to research and writing, seek innovative ways of collaborating with the communities they study, and contribute to more rewarding intercultural exchanges. I am confident that in the near future Awajún anthropologists—perhaps Wilson Atamain, the anthropology student whom I interviewed in 2012, or someone like him—will become part of the conversation.[8]

At the most elementary level, the work of anthropologists has brought greater global visibility to peoples whose continued existence Amazonian nation-states were inclined to disregard. The demographic collapse of indigenous societies brought about by the introduction of Western diseases and the abuses of the rubber boom made it easy to miss the recovery that many of these groups experienced in the twentieth century. Whether Amazonian societies were represented sympathetically or with adequate subtlety by every anthropologist may be less important than was accumulating evidence that the region sustains tens of thousands of people who still speak their own languages and live according to customs distinct from those of the majority population.

Often ignored is the value that anthropologists' accounts have acquired for indigenous peoples themselves. Years ago I invited a young, Ivy League–trained Mohawk political scientist to speak to students in a class. He mentioned that people in his community were trying to reconstruct Mohawk worship as it had existed before the rise of the Longhouse Religion, an early nineteenth-century adaptation of Iroquoian religious practices to the rising influence of Christianity. "How do you know what worship was like so long ago?" a student asked. "We use oral histories, missionary diaries, and anthropological studies," he replied.

There is another virtue of ethnography that bears consideration. I refer to the effect that long-term immersion in an alien social world has on ethnographers themselves and, via their books, articles, and classroom lectures, on others. The painful process of retraining mind and body is humbling. "In any hard discipline, whether it be gardening, structural engineering, or Russian," Matthew Crawford observes in *Shop Class as Soulcraft*, "one submits to the things that have their own intractable ways."[9]

For me, dealing with a new language was the hardest part. I had to wrestle with agglutinative verbs that stretched longer and longer as new morphemes muscled their way in. Interrogative words, the anthropologist's best friend, seemed to have mutated, like Darwin's finches, into an infinite number of variations. I desperately sought ways to make the learning process endurable. A dozen times a day, small children would look through the slats of my house wall and ask, *"Yatsujú, pujámek?"* The question is conventionally translated as "Brother, are you there?" although its literal meaning is "Do you exist?" This is an example of what linguists call phatic communication, semantically empty exchanges that establish interpersonal connection. Out of sheer perversity, I would sometimes reply in the negative, "No, I don't exist." My interlocutors would pause to ponder this strange news. "You lie!" was a common response, although children accustomed to the game would one-up me by replying, "Well, what happened to you?" or "Where did you go?" That inspired increasingly surreal exchanges about travel to the moon or disappearance into the bowels of a hungry anaconda. Speaking to dignified adults was another matter. The struggle to formulate sophisticated sentences continued throughout my time there—and with it the recognition that I had taken on an assignment for which I had only modest aptitude.

I also had to learn to use a machete, properly fold palm leaves destined for a house roof, identify plants previously unknown to me, dance in the approved manner, and walk in the forest without making too much noise. The point is not that I could become as good at these activities as my Awajún teachers, an unlikely prospect. It is that submission to a disciplined apprenticeship and the experience of repeated failure create new habits of mind. What are these habits? The primary one is willed suspension of interpretive judgment, a radical form of self-distancing. You are obliged to abandon prior understandings of how the world works and, to steal a phrase from Gregory Bateson, recalibrate your understanding of the differences that make a difference. Another is humility. Much of what you already know will be of little value. You have no choice but to start over: with language, rules of deportment, expectations about how bodies are held, used, adorned, fed. Allied with that painful self-reinvention is the obligation to listen, which challenges a core value of scholars, whose vocation celebrates the ability to speak with authority. The process enlists the ethnographer's hosts as well. The very awkwardness of the encounter may change their understanding of what they do and why. It may nudge the more analytically inclined to seek a rationale for practices that normally require no explanation.[10]

When it goes well, the ethnographic encounter is uniquely productive, leading to insights and standards of verification that take it beyond the forms of journalism or travel writing to which it bears a passing resemblance. Even then, how do you know whether you know enough? In a manner reminiscent of Zeno's Paradox, the closer one gets, the more elusive complete comprehension becomes. Although it might appear that this problem will be solved when the Awajún have produced their own anthropologists, it is not necessarily so. An Awajún ethnographer will have an easier time with the language than an outsider, but he or she will still have to struggle to achieve the self-distancing required for the most acute observation. This is by no means impossible for an insider, but it is challenging.

To praise the virtues of ethnography is not to claim that anthropology holds a monopoly on truth. But in a world drawn to absolutist ideologies and addicted to nonstop multimediated chatter, a discipline that gives first priority to attentive listening and close observation of others has much to recommend it. That we sometimes fail to meet the highest standards of the profession says more about human frailty than it does about some profound flaw in the mission itself.

Beyond the search for a deeper understanding of cultural diversity is the simple matter of bearing witness: chronicling a people's aspirations, virtues, shortcomings, and troubles when few others are in a position to do so. Thinking about this, I am reminded of an upriver trip I made with two Awajún families decades ago. A rare cold front had blown in from somewhere. The outboard motor on the dugout canoe died and then defied all efforts to restart it. A journey that normally took three hours would most likely take six or eight, perhaps more. Bone-chilling rain swept the river. Sliding toward self-pity, I noticed a tiny girl standing ahead of me in the dugout. Waiflike, covered only by the thinnest of cotton dresses, she shivered as rain poured off her body. She bore the discomfort with stoic grace. A few minutes later, one of the men poling the canoe cracked a joke that made everyone laugh, a cheerful mood sustained for the rest of the wearisome trip.

A small thing, a fleeting moment, that exemplified the grit and tenacity of the Awajún people. They have survived more than a century of steadily intensifying contact with outsiders, advancing against currents that have overwhelmed less resilient and inventive indigenous societies. Their difficult journey continues. I count myself fortunate to have witnessed part of it.

NOTES

SOURCES ON THE AWAJÚN AND
RELATED SOCIETIES

ACKNOWLEDGMENTS

INDEX

Notes

INTRODUCTION

1. The circumstances of the attack are told in greater detail in Tim Cahill, "A Darkness on the River," *Outside,* November 1995, 84–96, 168–169.

2. John Hemming, *Tree of Rivers: The Story of the Amazon* (New York: Thames and Hudson, 2008).

3. Jared Diamond, *The World until Yesterday* (New York: Viking, 2012), 6.

4. Roger Sandall, *The Culture Cult: Designer Tribalism and Other Essays* (Boulder, CO: Westview, 2001), viii.

5. Robin Fox, *The Tribal Imagination: Civilization and the Savage Mind* (Cambridge, MA: Harvard University Press, 2011), 67.

6. Ibid., 310; Anthony Giddens, "The Nature of Modernity," in *The Giddens Reader,* ed. Philip Cassell (Stanford, CA: Stanford University Press, 1993), 294.

7. Rafael Karsten, *The Head-Hunters of Western Amazonas: The Life and Culture of the Jíbaro Indians of Eastern Ecuador and Peru,* Commentationes Humanarum Litterarum, vol. 7 (Helsingfors: Societas Scientiarum Fennica, 1935), 78–83.

8. For details of the bioprospecting controversy, see Shane Greene, "Indigenous People Incorporated? Culture as Politics, Culture as Property in Pharmaceutical Bioprospecting," *Current Anthropology* 45, no. 2 (2004): 211–237.

9. Key sources for understanding this convoluted dispute include Patrick Tierney, *Darkness in El Dorado: How Scientists and Journalists*

Devastated the Amazon (New York: W.W. Norton, 2000); Robert Borofsky et al., *Yanomami: The Fierce Controversy and What We Can Learn from It* (Berkeley: University of California Press, 2005); Alice Dreger, "Darkness's Descent on the American Anthropological Association: A Cautionary Tale," *Human Nature* 22 (2011): 225–246; Emily Eakin, "Who Are the Real Savages?" *New York Times Magazine,* February 17, 2013, 32–37, 51–53; and Thomas A. Gregor and Daniel R. Gross, "Guilt by Association: The Culture of Accusation and the American Anthropological Association's Investigation of *Darkness in El Dorado,*" *American Anthropologist* 106, no. 4 (2004): 687–698. Works that contest Chagnon's factual claims about Yanomami violence include R. Brian Ferguson, *Yanomami Warfare: A Political History* (Santa Fe, NM: SAR Press, 1995), and Bruce Albert, "Yanomami 'Violence': Inclusive Fitness or Ethnographer's Representation?" *Current Anthropology* 30 (1989): 637–640. Aspects of the controversy are addressed in the documentary film *Secrets of the Tribe,* directed by José Padilha (HBO Documentary Films, 2010).

10. Fernando Santos-Granero, "The Enemy Within: Child Sorcery, Revolution, and the Evils of Modernization in Eastern Peru," in *In Darkness and Secrecy: The Anthropology of Assault Sorcery and Witchcraft in Amazonia,* ed. Neil L. Whitehead and Robin Wright (Durham, NC: Duke University Press, 2004); Janet Wall Hendricks, *To Drink of Death: The Narrative of a Shuar Warrior* (Tucson: University of Arizona Press, 1993); Clayton Robarchek and Carole Robarchek, *Waorani: The Contexts of Violence and War* (Fort Worth, TX: Harcourt Brace, 1998); Beth A. Conklin, *Consuming Grief: Compassionate Cannibalism in an Amazonian Society* (Austin: University of Texas Press, 2001). For an argument that anthropologists' representations have had little impact on the way the Yanomami and other Amazonian groups are treated by nation-states, see Raymond Hames, "The Political Uses of Ethnographic Description," in Borofsky et al., *Yanomami,* 119–125. Hames's argument, it should be noted, is vigorously challenged by other authors in the same volume, most notably Bruce Albert (161–163 and 214–217).

11. Richard Sennett, *The Craftsman* (New Haven, CT: Yale University Press, 2008), 9.

12. Bill Vitek and Wes Jackson, *The Virtues of Ignorance: Complexity, Sustainability, and the Limits of Knowledge* (Lexington: University Press of Kentucky, 2008), 5.

1. ANDEAN PRELUDE

1. Frederick Webb Hodge, "Bandelier's Researches in Peru and Bolivia," *American Anthropologist* 10 (1897): 303–311, at 308–309.

2. Christopher Sandeman, "The Northern Highway of Peru," *Geographical Journal* 105, nos. 3–4 (1945): 81–100, at 95.

3. Richard Spruce, *Notes of a Botanist on the Amazon and Andes* (London: Macmillan, 1908), 53–54.

4. François-David Hérissant, "Experiments Made on a Great Number of Living Animals, with the Poison of Lamas, and of the Ticunas, by Mons. Herissant, Doctor of Physic, and F.R.S.," *Philosophical Transactions* 47 (1751): 75–92.

5. Françoise Scazzocchio, "La conquête des Motilones du Huallaga central aux XVIIe et XVIIIe siècles," *Bulletin de l'Institut Français d'Études Andines* 10, nos. 3–5 (1981): 99–111; see also Anne-Christine Taylor, "The Western Margins of Amazonia from the Early Sixteenth to the Early Nineteenth Century," in *The Cambridge History of the Native Peoples of the Americas,* ed. Frank Salomon and Stuart B. Schwartz (Cambridge: Cambridge University Press, 1999), 188–256, at 205 and 234.

6. Antonine S. Tibesar, "The Franciscan Doctrinero versus the Franciscan Misionero in Seventeenth-Century Peru," *The Americas* 14 (1957): 115–124, at 123.

7. Francisco Izquierdo Ríos, *Pueblo y bosque: Folklore amazónico* (Lima: P. L. Villanueva, 1975), 40.

8. Weston La Barre, *The Aymara Indians of the Lake Titicaca Plateau, Bolivia* (Menasha, WI: American Anthropological Association, 1948), 15; and his "The Aymara: History and Worldview," *Journal of American Folklore* 79, no. 311 (1966): 130–144, at 133. In fairness to La Barre, it should be noted that he is not the only anthropologist to have found the Aymara to be challenging research subjects. For a debate on whether the Aymara's alleged cantankerousness is caused by

chronic hypoglycemia, see Ted C. Lewellen, "Aggression and Hypoglycemia in the Andes: Another Look at the Evidence," *Current Anthropology* 22, no. 4 (1981): 347–361. Bronislaw Malinowski's intemperate comments can be found in his *A Diary in the Strict Sense of the Term* (London: Routledge and Kegan Paul, 1967).

9. For a study of Mead and Bateson's field notes and research method in New Guinea, see Eric Kline Silverman, "Margaret Mead and Gregory Bateson in the Sepik, 1938: A Timely Polemic from a Lost Anthropological Efflorescence," *Pacific Studies* 28, nos. 3–4 (2005): 128–141.

2. Armadillo for Breakfast

1. On the complex pre- and post-Conquest history of Jivaroan populations, see especially Anne-Christine Taylor, "The Western Margins of Amazonia from the Early Sixteenth to the Early Nineteenth Century," in *The Cambridge History of the Native Peoples of the Americas,* ed. Frank Salomon and Stuart B. Schwartz (Cambridge: Cambridge University Press, 1999), 198–199, and Anne Marie Hocquenghem, *Los Guayacundos de Caxas y la sierra piurana siglos XV y XVI* (Lima: CIPCA/IFEA, 1989).

Surveys of western Amazonia often group several small societies with the more populous Shuar, Wampis, Awajún, and Achuar when classifying peoples as Jivaroan. These include the Shiwiar, Kandoshi, and Shapra, the last two sharing certain Jivaroan cultural features but a different language affiliation. The hazy historical record mentions a number of other societies, now extinct, that may have spoken a Jivaroan language in the past.

2. Taylor, "The Western Margins of Amazonia," 211. On Jesuit missions, see Piedad Peñaherrera de Costales and Alfredo Costales Samaniego, *Historia de la nación Shuar* (Quito: Editorial Abya Yala, 2006), 15–19. A table included in this work (p. 17) indicates that Awajún were the principal indigenous residents of a mission called San Ignacio de la Borrasca, visited by the administrator Diego Cabo in 1799.

3. Johann Magnin, *Breve descripción de la Provincia de Quito, en la América Meridional, y de sus missiones de Succumbíos de religiosos de*

S. Franc. O, y de Maynas de Pp. de la Comp. A de Jhs, a las orillas del gran río Marañón, hecha para el mapa que se hizo el año 1740, por Juan Magnin (Quito: Sociedad Ecuatoriana de Investigaciones Históricas y Geográficas, 1989), 473. On possible etymologies of the tribal name Aguaruna, see Simon E. Overall, "A Grammar of Aguaruna," Ph.D. dissertation, La Trobe University, 2007, 2–3.

4. Alexander von Humboldt, *Alexander von Humboldt en el Perú: Diario de viaje y otros escritos* (Lima: Banco Central de Reserva del Perú, 2002), 53; James Orton, *The Andes and the Amazon: or, Across the Continent of South America* (New York: Harper and Brothers, 1870), 171.

5. Courtenay De Kalb, "The Great Amazon: Personal Investigations on the River and Its Upper Valley," *Bulletin of the American Geographical Society* 23, no. 1 (1891): 1–46, at 37.

6. See F. W. Up de Graff, *Head Hunters of the Amazon: Seven Years of Exploration and Adventure* (New York: Garden City Publishing, 1923), 224. Up de Graff is describing "Antipas," who were probably Awajún. The ethnologist Günter Tessmann plausibly argues that Antipa is a corruption of Nantipa, the name of a powerful Awajún leader that came to be used for a subset of the Awajún. See Günter Tessmann, *Los indígenas del Perú nororiental* (Quito: Ediciones Abya-Yala, 1999 [1930]), 191. Silvio de San Bernardo's observations are from "La primera expedición en la hoya amazónica y la primera misiva al Rvmo. P. General de Pasionistas," in *Misiones pasionistas del oriente peruano* (Lima: Empresa Gráfica T. Scheuch, 1943 [1922]), 30.

7. The history of the Amazonian rubber boom and its human consequences are vividly retold in John Hemming, *Tree of Rivers: The Story of the Amazon* (New York: Thames and Hudson, 2008), 173–231. On the Awajún's involvement in the rubber trade, see José María Guallart, S.J., *Entre pongo y cordillera: Historia de la etnía aguaruna-huambisa* (Lima: Centro Amazónico de Antropología y Aplicación Práctica, 1990), 183–184.

8. Guallart, *Entre pongo y cordillera*, 139–214. See also Shane Greene, *Customizing Indigeneity: Paths to a Visionary Politics in Peru* (Stanford, CA: Stanford University Press, 2009), 104, and Enrique Brüning, *De Chiclayo a Puerto Meléndez en el Marañón* (Lima: Imprenta

y Librería de San Pedro, 1905), 110–111. On the 1914 violence, sources include multiple articles in the newspaper *La Prensa* (Lima) on January 22, March 25, April 27, May 4, and May 20, 1914. I am grateful to Fernando Santos-Granero for sharing these articles after encountering them in various Peruvian archives.

9. Martín Corera, C.P., "Mi primera expedición," in *Misiones pasionistas del oriente peruano* (Lima: Empresa Gráfica T. Scheuch, 1943 [orig. 1926]), 167, 179.

10. Martín Corera, C.P., *En el corazón de la selva* (Zaragoza, Spain: El Labaro, Padres Pasionistas, 1959), 461, author's translation. The event in question seems to have taken place in the 1930s or 1940s, although Corera is frustratingly vague about dates.

11. Leonard Clark, *The Rivers Ran East* (New York: Funk and Wagnalls, 1953).

12. José Martín Cuesta, S.J., *Entre el Condor y el Marañón: Memorias misioneras* (Salamanca: Imprenta Kadmos, 1992), 145. Other relevant missionary accounts include Mildred L. Larson and Louis Dodds, *Treasure in Clay Pots: An Amazon People on the Wheel of Change* (Palm Desert, CA: Person to Person Books, 1985); Lila Wistrand Robinson, *Eight Years in the Amazon Headwaters: My Life in Three Peruvian Tribes* (Bloomington, IN: AuthorHouse, 2005); and Guallart, *Entre pongo y cordillera*.

13. Mario Vargas Llosa, *Making Waves,* ed. and trans. John King (New York: Farrar, Straus and Giroux, 1996), 13.

14. For discussion and additional examples, see Francisco Izquierdo Ríos, *Pueblo y bosque: Folklore amazónico* (Lima: P. L. Villanueva, 1975), 179–181.

15. Claude Lévi-Strauss, *Tristes Tropiques* (New York: Criterion Books, 1961), 140.

16. For information on *Clibadium*'s significance as a fish poison, see Jorge E. Arriagada, "Ethnobotany of *Clibadium* L. (Compositae, Heliantheae) in Latin America," *Economic Botany* 49, no. 3 (1995): 328–332.

17. Rafael Karsten, *The Head-Hunters of Western Amazonas: The Life and Culture of the Jíbaro Indians of Eastern Ecuador and Peru,*

Commentationes Humanarum Litterarum, vol. 7 (Helsingfors: Societas Scientiarum Fennica, 1935), 246–247; see also Greene, *Customizing Indigeneity*, 76–78. I sometimes heard the Alto Mayo Awajún refer to the event as *igkúnia chichámu*, which translates loosely as "encounter speech." The Shuar of Ecuador apparently distinguish between the enémamu, in which two lines of men face off while holding their spears, and *aujsatin*, which more closely resembles the event described here. For details, see Steven L. Rubenstein, "On the Importance of Visions among the Amazonian Shuar," *Current Anthropology* 53, no. 1 (2012): 39–79, at 57. Alexandre Surrallés presents a comparative analysis of Amazonian greeting rituals in "Meaning, Feeling and Perception in Amazonian Welcoming Ceremonies," *Journal of the Royal Anthropological Institute* 9, no. 4 (2003), 775–791.

3. Puzzle Pieces

1. See Rafael Karsten, *The Head-Hunters of Western Amazonas: The Life and Culture of the Jíbaro Indians of Eastern Ecuador and Peru*, Commentationes Humanarum Litterarum, vol. 7 (Helsingfors: Societas Scientiarum Fennica, 1935), 62, for a description of Shuar strategies for keeping beer feasts under control.

2. This account of Awajún family structure and marriage sidesteps much complexity. Readers who wish to explore Jivaroan kinship at a deeper level should consult two essays by Anne-Christine Taylor, "The Marriage Alliance and Its Structural Variations in Jivaroan Societies," *Social Science Information* 22 (1983): 331–353, and "Jívaro Kinship: 'Simple' and 'Complex' Formulas: A Dravidian Transformation Group," in *Transformations of Kinship*, ed. Maurice Godelier et al. (Washington, DC: Smithsonian Institution Press, 1998), 187–213, as well as Charlotte Seymour-Smith, "Women Have No Affines and Men No Kin: The Politics of the Jivaroan Gender Relation," *Man* 26 (1991): 629–649. For details specific to the Awajún, see Michael F. Brown, *Una paz incierta: Comunidades aguarunas frente al impacto de la Carretera Marginal* (Lima: Centro Amazónico de Antropología y Aplicación Práctica, 1984).

3. José María Guallart, S.J., "Los Jívaros del Alto Marañón," *América Indígena* 24 (1964): 315–332, at 321.

4. JESUS VERSUS THE WARRIOR SPIRITS

1. For a provocative interpretation of spitting among Jivaroan peoples, see James S. Boster, "Blood Feud and Table Manners: A Neo-Hobbesian Approach to Jivaroan Warfare," *Antropológica* (Caracas) 99–100 (2003): 153–164.

2. In Peruvian (and now global) popular culture, *ayahuasca* refers either to several species of vines in the genus *Banisteriopsis* (most commonly *B. caapi*) or the hallucinogenic brew made with *Banisteriopsis* and other plant additives that intensify and enhance its psychotropic effects. The most common additives are *Psychotria viridis* and *Diplopteris cabrerana*, although other plant substances have occasionally been reported as admixtures to *Banisteriopsis*. The version of ayahuasca traditionally used by Awajún seeking personal visions, called *datém*, appears to be made from *Banisteriopsis* alone, whereas the ayahuasca used by shamans, typically referred to as *yáji*, is most likely a mixture of *Banisteriopsis* and *Diplopteris cabrerana*. It should be noted that during my time in the Alto Mayo datém was not prepared or used in any community in which I resided. Yáji was employed by the region's few shamans, but I never had an opportunity to observe them preparing it. For an overview of the ethnobotany of Jivaroan hallucinogens, see Bradley C. Bennett, "Hallucinogenic Plants of the Shuar and Related Indigenous Groups in Amazonian Ecuador and Peru," *Brittonia* 44, no. 4 (1992): 483–493.

5. FOUR WEDDINGS AND A FUNERAL

1. "Urucínta" is the way her Spanish name, Rosinda, was rendered by speakers of Awajún. Because I will never be able to think of her as anything other than Urucínta, I use the colloquial version here. Likewise, Wampurái's official name was Irma, which I never heard used in everyday conversation.

2. Linguists and anthropologists have published more than two thousand pages of Awajún myths, much of it in the original Awajún with interlinear translation in Spanish. Notable among these are José María Guallart, S.J., "Mitos y leyendas de los Aguarunas del Alto Marañón," *Perú Indígena* 7, nos. 16–17 (1958): 59–98; José Luis Jordana Laguna, *Mitos e historias Aguarunas y Huambisas de la selva del Alto Marañón* (Lima: Retablo de Papel, 1974); Aurelio Chumap Lucía and Manuel García-Rendueles, *"Duik múun": Universo mítico de los Aguaruna* (Lima: Centro Amazónico de Antropología y Aplicación Práctica, 1979); Timías Akuts Nugkai et al., *Historia Aguaruna* (Yarinacocha, Peru: Instituto Lingüístico de Verano, 1977), 3 vols.

3. Patrick Wilcken, *Claude Lévi-Strauss: The Poet in the Laboratory* (New York: Penguin, 2010), 287.

4. Claude Lévi-Strauss, *The Jealous Potter*, trans. Bénédicte Chorier (Chicago: University of Chicago Press, 1988), 102.

5. Versions of the story can be found in Timías Akuts Nugkai et al., *Historia Aguaruna*, 2:222–229, and Michael F. Brown, *Una paz incierta: Comunidades Aguarunas frente al impacto de la Carretera Marginal* (Lima: Centro Amazónico de Antropología y Aplicación Práctica, 1984), 241–242. For an insightful comparison of strikingly different regional variants of the Kumpanám myth and their possible significance, see Simone Garra, "El despertar de Kumpanam: Historia y mito en el marco de un conflicto socioambiental en la Amazonía," *Anthropologica* (Lima) 30 (2012): 5–28. Garra's analysis convincingly demonstrates that the story's implications for Awajún understandings of powerful beings and sacred space are far more profound than a single version of the myth may suggest.

6. I eventually collected information on five other kinds of dápu. One, for example, was linked to abdominal pains in late pregnancy. A woman afflicted by this dápu prevents another from contracting it by warming water in a bowl, spraying it over the other woman's abdomen with her mouth, and then sweeping the water away with a broom. *Wáinchi* (whirlpool) dápu, in contrast, afflicts either women or men. It occurs when someone at a party makes a joke that causes general laughter. The joke teller may suddenly be gripped by dizziness and

nausea. One remedy is for someone else who has had the condition to take a piece of smoldering wood and wave it in circles over the afflicted person's head, saying, "I cure whirlpool dápu." Another is for people to blow in the patient's mouth and on his forehead while uttering the same phrase.

6. TROUBLE IN MIND

1. Prominent among works that consider whether Carlos Castaneda perpetrated an anthropological hoax are Richard De Mille, ed., *The Don Juan Papers: Further Castaneda Controversies* (Santa Barbara, CA: Ross-Erikson, 1980), and Jay C. Fikes, *Carlos Castaneda, Academic Opportunism and the Psychedelic Sixties* (Victoria, BC: Millenia Press, 1993).

2. For comparative information about shamanism and sorcery as practiced among other Jivaroan peoples, see Michael J. Harner, *The Jívaro: People of the Sacred Waterfalls* (Berkeley: University of California Press, 1972); Steven Rubenstein, *Alejandro Tsakimp: A Shuar Healer in the Margins of History* (Lincoln: University of Nebraska Press, 2002); and Philippe Descola, *The Spears of Twilight: Life and Death in the Amazon Jungle* (New York: New Press, 1993). The work of the late Neil Whitehead was influential in nudging anthropologists toward a more complex understanding of the moral status of shamans in some Amazonian societies. See his *Dark Shamans: Kanaimà and the Poetics of Violent Death* (Durham, NC: Duke University Press, 2002) as well as the essays in Neil L. Whitehead and Robin Wright, eds., *In Darkness and Secrecy: The Anthropology of Assault Sorcery and Witchcraft in Amazonia* (Durham, NC: Duke University Press, 2004).

3. In the simplest case, the public shaman, iwishín, is contrasted with the sorcerer, *túnchi* or *wáwek*. But the term "túnchi" is often applied to public healers in everyday speech, although they may be distinguished from *uuk* or *umak túnchi*, hidden sorcerers. Exceptionally accomplished killer/healers are sometimes referred to as *tajímat túnchi* or *yápu*. Genaro mentioned a particularly dangerous type of killing shaman known as a *kúkam*, the name possibly derived from the Co-

cama, a once-powerful Amazonian people who live downriver from the Awajún.

4. In common with other aspects of Awajún knowledge, kaag or káaji can be subdivided into several distinct types based on appearance or origin. These include *júak káaji,* which is collected from a particular tree after a shaman sees it in a dream; *kúti káaji,* which is doughy in texture; *shaa káaji,* which has rings like maize kernels, and *éntsa káaji,* which has a watery appearance.

5. Influential works on the interpretation of magical acts include S. J. Tambiah, "The Magical Power of Words," *Man,* n.s. 3 (1968): 175–208, and Robin Horton and Ruth Finnegan, eds., *Modes of Thought* (London: Faber and Faber, 1973).

6. On the piripiri/ergot connection, see Timothy C. Plowman et al., "Significance of the Fungus *Balansia cyperi* Infecting Medicinal Species of *Cyperus* (Cyperaceae) from Amazonia," *Economic Botany* 44, no. 4 (1990): 452–462, and especially Glenn H. Shepard, "The Hunter in the Rye: Ergot, Sedges and Hunting Magic in the Peruvian Amazon," *Notes from the Ethnoground,* http://ethnoground.blogspot .com/2011/10/hunter-in-rye-ergot-and-hunting-magic.html, accessed December 5, 2012.

7. F. W. Up de Graff, *Head Hunters of the Amazon: Seven Years of Exploration and Adventure* (New York: Garden City Publishing, 1923), 246–247.

8. A more detailed account of another Awajún healing session can be found in Michael F. Brown, "Shamanism and Its Discontents," *Medical Anthropology Quarterly* 2 (1988): 102–120. This analysis is reinterpreted by Shane Greene in "The Shaman's Needle: Development, Shamanic Agency, and Intermedicality in Aguaruna Lands, Peru," *American Ethnologist* 25 (1998): 634–658.

9. Claude Lévi-Strauss, "The Effectiveness of Symbols," in *Structural Anthropology* (New York: Anchor, 1963), 181–201, at 198.

7. Hard Lessons

1. C. Wright Mills, *The Sociological Imagination* (New York: Oxford University Press, 1959), 10–11.

8. Civilization's Twisting Road

1. Julian H. Steward and Louis C. Faron, *Native Peoples of South America* (New York: McGraw-Hill, 1959), 8, 10.

2. José Toribio Medina, *The Discovery of the Amazon According to the Account of Friar Gaspar De Carvajal and Other Documents* (New York: American Geographical Society, 1934), 217. See also Antonio Porro, "Social Organization and Political Power in the Amazon Floodplain," in *Amazonian Indians from Prehistory to the Present: Anthropological Perspectives,* ed. Anna Curtenius Roosevelt (Tucson: University of Arizona Press, 1994); Charles C. Mann, *1491: New Revelations of the Americas before Columbus* (New York: Knopf, 2005); and Anna Curtenius Roosevelt, "The Rise and Fall of the Amazon Chiefdoms," *L'Homme* 33, nos. 126–128 (1993): 255–283. On newly discovered Amazonian earthworks, see Martti Pärssinen et al., "Pre-Columbian Geometric Earthworks in the Upper Purús: A Complex Society in Western Amazonia," *Antiquity* 83 (2009): 1084–1095. On differing densities of occupation, useful sources include Michael J. Heckenberger et al., "Village Size and Permanence in Amazonia: Two Archaeological Examples from Brazil," *Latin American Antiquity* 10, no. 4 (1999): 353–376, and Mark B. Bush et al., "Holocene Fire and Occupation in Amazonia: Records from Two Lake Districts," *Philosophical Transactions of the Royal Society B* 362 (2007): 209–218.

3. William H. Crocker and Jean G. Crocker, *The Canela: Kinship, Ritual, and Sex in an Amazonian Tribe* (Belmont, CA: Thomson-Wadsworth, 2004), 125.

4. Thomas A. Gregor, "Symbols and Rituals of Peace in Brazil's Upper Xingu," in *The Anthropology of Peace and Nonviolence,* ed. Leslie E. Sponsel and Thomas A. Gregor (Boulder, CO: Lynne Rienner, 1994), 241–258, at 246.

5. Philippe Descola, *The Spears of Twilight: Life and Death in the Amazon Jungle* (New York: New Press, 1993), 293.

6. This discussion of the early history of Jivaroan peoples benefits from Anne-Christine Taylor's magisterial survey of Western Amazonia from the sixteenth to the nineteenth centuries, "The Western

Margins of Amazonia from the Early Sixteenth to the Early Nineteenth Century," in *The Cambridge History of the Native Peoples of the Americas,* ed. Frank Salomon and Stuart B. Schwartz (Cambridge: Cambridge University Press, 1999). For a reinterpretation of evidence about the relations between the Inca and Jivaroan peoples, see especially 100–103.

7. On his 1929 visit to the Awajún of the Río Apaga, Rafael Karsten noted that the population had declined dramatically as a result of epidemics. See Karsten, *The Head-Hunters of Western Amazonas: The Life and Culture of the Jíbaro Indians of Eastern Ecuador and Peru,* Commentationes Humanarum Litterarum, vol. 7 (Helsingfors: Societas Scientiarum Fennica, 1935), 82. On slavery in indigenous Amazonia and elsewhere in the New World, see Fernando Santos-Granero, *Vital Enemies: Slavery, Predation, and the Amerindian Political Economy of Life* (Austin: University of Texas Press, 2009).

8. For a close analysis of the impact of trade on violence among the Awajún's Jivaroan neighbors, see Daniel Steel, "Trade Goods and Jívaro Warfare: The Shuar 1850–1957, and the Achuar 1940–1978," *Ethnohistory* 46, no. 4 (1999): 745–776. R. Brian Ferguson offers a historical survey of the tendency of introduced Western trade goods to foster high levels of conflict throughout the Amazon in "Blood of the Leviathan: Western Contact and Warfare in Amazonia," *American Ethnologist* 17, no. 2 (1990): 237–257.

9. The fullest articulation of the "tribal zone" theory can be found in R. Brian Ferguson and Neil L. Whitehead, eds., *War in the Tribal Zone: Expanding States and Indigenous Warfare* (Santa Fe, NM: SAR Press, 1992).

10. Courtenay De Kalb, "The Great Amazon: Personal Investigations on the River and Its Upper Valley," *Bulletin of the American Geographical Society* 23, no. 1 (1891): 1–46, at 39; Günter Tessmann, *Los indígenas del Perú nororiental* (Quito: Ediciones Abya-Yala, 1999 [orig. 1930]), 202. A useful source on Awajún resistance is Henning Siverts, "Jívaro Headhunters in a Headless Time," in *Western Expansion and Indigenous Peoples: The Heritage of Las Casas,* ed. Elías Sevilla-Casas (The Hague: Mouton, 1977), 193–202. On the broader

question of cultures of resistance and the importance of zones of refuge, a key source is James C. Scott, *The Art of Not Being Governed: An Anarchist History of Upland Southeast Asia* (New Haven, CT: Yale University Press, 2009).

11. For description and analysis of Jivaroan tsántsa rituals, see Descola, *The Spears of Twilight*, 271–278, and Steven Rubenstein, "A Head for Adventure," in *Tarzan Was an Ecotourist . . . and Other Tales in the Anthropology of Adventure,* ed. Luis A. Vivanco and Robert J. Gordon (New York: Berghahn Books, 2006), 235–254, at 237–243. On the broader problem of revenge and its cultural roots, see Stephen Beckerman and Paul Valentine, eds., *Revenge in the Cultures of Lowland South America* (Gainesville: University Press of Florida, 2008).

12. Steven Pinker, *The Better Angels of Our Nature: Why Violence Has Declined* (New York: Viking, 2011), 49, Figure 2-2. Similar evidence is presented in Jared Diamond, *The World until Yesterday: What Can We Learn from Traditional Societies?* (New York: Viking, 2003), 139–141.

13. Pinker, *The Better Angels of Our Nature,* 266. The reference to the developed world's exportation of war to distant places is John Gray, "Delusions of Peace," *Prospect* (London), September 21, 2011, www.prospectmagazine.co.uk/2011/09/john-gray-steven-pinker-violence-review, accessed July 6, 2012. Among the first of what is likely to be a wave of close examinations of Pinker's empirical data on prehistoric and tribal violence is R. Brian Ferguson, "Pinker's List: Exaggerating Prehistoric War Mortality," in *War, Peace, and Human Nature: The Convergence of Evolutionary and Cultural Views,* ed. Douglas P. Fry (Oxford: Oxford University Press, 2013), 112–131. Ferguson (116) argues that Pinker's book draws on "cherry-picked cases with high casualties, clearly unrepresentative of prehistory in general."

14. See especially Paul Farmer, "On Suffering and Structural Violence: A View from Below," *Daedalus* 125, no. 1 (1996): 261–282.

15. Norbert Elias, "The Social Constraint towards Self-Constraint," *On Civilization, Power, and Knowledge: Selected Writings,* ed. Stephen Mennell and Johan Goudsblom (Chicago: University of Chicago Press, 1998 [orig. 1939]), 58.

16. On the history of Peruvian oil production in the Amazon, see Matt Finer and Martí Orta-Martínez, "A Second Hydrocarbon Boom Threatens the Peruvian Amazon: Trends, Projections, and Policy Implications," *Environmental Research Letters* 5 (2010), doi:10.1088/1748-9326/5/1/014012.

17. While expressing admiration for the educational efforts and self-sacrifice of the priests and nuns at the Catholic mission in Santa María de Nieva, Mario Vargas Llosa declares that their aggressive efforts to educate indigenous girls often led to children being brought to the school involuntarily and later handed off to educated Peruvians to work as servants. "That with the best intentions in the world, and at a cost of limitless sacrifice, they could cause so much damage is a lesson that I have never forgotten." See Mario Vargas Llosa, *Making Waves,* ed. and trans. John King (New York: Farrar, Straus and Giroux, 1996), 14.

18. SIL's role in creating new forms of leadership among the Awajún is considered in Deborah J. Yashar, *Contesting Citizenship in Latin America: The Rise of Indigenous Movements and the Postliberal Challenge* (New York: Cambridge University Press, 2005), 259, and especially in Shane Greene, *Customizing Indigeneity: Paths to a Visionary Politics in Peru* (Stanford, CA: Stanford University Press, 2009), 112–127. On how this looked from the perspective of SIL International, see Mildred L. Larson and Louis Dodds, *Treasure in Clay Pots: An Amazon People on the Wheel of Change* (Palm Desert, CA: Person to Person Books, 1985). Data on the number of Peruvians who self-identify as Protestant are from www.state.gov/j/drl/rls/irf/2006/71471.htm. The estimated percentage of Awajún who are practicing evangelicals, which dates to the 1980s, is from Robert J. Priest, "'I Discovered My Sin!': Aguaruna Evangelical Conversion Narratives," in *The Anthropology of Religious Conversion,* ed. Andrew Buckster and Stephen Glazier (Lanham, MD: Rowman and Littlefield, 2003), 95.

19. See James S. Boster, James Yost, and Catherine Peeke, "Rage, Revenge, and Religion: Honest Signaling of Aggression and Nonaggression in the Waorani Coalitional Violence," *Ethos* 31, no. 4 (2004): 471–494. Another account of the impact of missionaries on violence among the Waorani people of Ecuador is Clayton A. Robarchek and

Carole J. Robarchek, "The Aucas, the Cannibals, and the Missionaries: From Warfare to Peacefulness among the Waorani," in *A Natural History of Peace,* ed. Thomas A. Gregor (Nashville, TN: Vanderbilt University Press, 1996), 189–212.

20. On the interpretation of witchcraft and sorcery as an act of translation, I am indebted to Kathleen Lowrey, "Witchcraft as Metaculture in the Bolivian Chaco," *Journal de la Société des Américanistes* 93, no. 2 (2007): 121–152. A handful of ethnographic accounts raise the possibility that there is more literal truth to sorcery beliefs than most anthropologists accept. These works include Paul Stoller and Cheryl Olkes, *In Sorcery's Shadow: A Memoir of Apprenticeship among the Songhay of Niger* (Chicago: University of Chicago Press, 1987), and Harry G. West, *Ethnographic Sorcery* (Chicago: University of Chicago Press, 2007).

21. E. E. Evans-Pritchard, *Witchcraft, Oracles, and Magic among the Azande,* abridged ed. (Oxford: Clarendon Press, 1976), 18, 24. Following Zande practice, Evans-Pritchard distinguishes witches from sorcerers. Witches inherit their malign power in the form of a mystical essence and sometimes harm others without realizing it. Sorcerers, in contrast, intentionally use ritual knowledge to cause harm. This distinction becomes blurred in other cultural settings. Although the Awajún case more closely resembles sorcery than witchcraft in Zande terms, the interpretation of Tiwijám's sorcery substance as something introduced without his knowledge, described in Chapter 7, reveals the ambiguity of such distinctions.

22. Neil L. Whitehead, *Dark Shamans: Kanaimà and the Poetics of Violent Death* (Durham, NC: Duke University Press, 2002), 204.

23. Monica Hunter Wilson, "Witch Beliefs and Social Structure," *American Journal of Sociology* 56, no. 4 (1951): 307–313, at 313. For additional background on functionalist theories of magic, see John G. Kennedy, "Psychological and Social Explanations of Witchcraft," *Man* 2 (1967): 216–225.

24. On Awajún suicide, sources include Astrid A. Bant, "Parentesco, matrimonio e intereses de género en una sociedad Amazónica: El caso aguaruna," *Amazonía Peruana* 12, no. 24 (1994): 77–103, and her "La política de suicidio: El caso de las mujeres aguaruna en la Ama-

zonía peruana," in *Relaciones de género en la Amazonía Peruana,* ed. María Heise et al. (Lima: Centro Amazónico de Antropología y Aplicación Práctica, 1999), 119–144; Michael F. Brown, "Power, Gender, and the Social Meaning of Aguaruna Suicide," *Man* 21 (1986): 311–328; Norma Fuller, *Relaciones de género en la sociedad Awajún* (Lima: CARE Peru, 2009); Willy Guevara, *El suicidio feminino Aguaruna,* 2006, http://bvs.per.paho.org/SCT/SCT2006-005/SCT2006005 .pdf, accessed December 10, 2012; Henning Siverts, "Broken Hearts and Pots: Suicide and Patterns of Signification Among the Aguaruna Jívaro of Alto Marañón, Peru," *Livstegn* 4, no. 2 (1987): 211–248, and Irma Tuesta Cerrón et al., "Perú: Oportunidad para los niños y el suicidio continuado de jóvenes de la nación awajún en el noroeste peruano," in *Suicidio adolescente en pueblos indígenas: Tres estudios de caso* (Lima: Unicef, 2012), 26–110. The last study, the most comprehensive assessment of Awajún suicide yet published, arrived too late in the preparation of this book for its conclusions to be fully integrated into the analysis. Suicide among the Awajún was remarked upon as early as 1905 by the explorer Enrique Brüning and a few decades later by Rafael Karsten. See Enrique Brüning, *De Chiclayo a Puerto Meléndez en el Marañón* (Lima: Imprenta y Librería de San Pedro, 1905), 72, and Karsten, *The Head-Hunters of Western Amazonas,* 223.

News of the Awajún's high suicide rate has percolated into Peru's popular press. In 1986, for instance, the Lima newspaper *Expreso* carried a story on Awajún female suicide under the headline "Aguaruna Women Die from Love," with the subhead "Each Month an Average of Two Women Kill Themselves." The article blamed the suicides on the "deplorable" circumstances of Awajún wives and the frequent adultery of their husbands (Vicky Terán, "Las Aguarunas se mueren de amor," *Expreso,* August 13, 1986, 10).

25. On imitation and other social variables associated with suicide rates, see Matt Wray et al., "The Sociology of Suicide," *Annual Review of Sociology* 37 (2011): 505–528.

26. Additional information on Genaro's murder is found in Greene, *Customizing Indigeneity,* 218 n. 2.

27. The Awajún-Herzog affair is documented in Michael F. Brown, "Art of Darkness," *The Progressive* 46, no. 8 (1982): 20–21, and Greene,

Customizing Indigeneity, 183–184. The murder, apparently by Awajún, of four tourists in 1989 is briefly described in "Peru Indians Reportedly Kill Film Crew," *San Francisco Chronicle,* October 30, 1989, A16. On the rise of belief in predatory gringos in Amazonia, see Fernando Santos-Granero and Frederica Barclay, "Bundles, Stampers, and Flying Gringos: Native Perceptions of Capitalist Violence in Peruvian Amazonia," *Journal of Latin American and Caribbean Anthropology* 16 (2010): 143–167.

28. This brief description of the 2002 killings at Flor de la Frontera is based on multiple newspaper accounts as well as Shane Greene and Mamais Juep Greene, "Settlers Clash with Aguaruna in Peru's Amazon," *Cultural Survival Quarterly* (2002): 71–72, and Greene, *Customizing Indigeneity,* 151–154. There is frustrating inconsistency in published claims about the number of deaths at Flor de la Frontera, although most recent reports set the number at sixteen.

29. Alan Garcia, "Dog in the Manger," *Peruvian Times,* October 30, 2007, www.peruviantimes.com/30/president-alan-garcias-policy-doctrinethe-dog-in-the-manger-syndrome/2860, accessed July 15, 2013. Garcia's essay was originally published in Spanish in the newspaper *El Comercio* on October 28, 2007.

30. Finer and Orta-Martínez, "A Second Hydrocarbon Boom Threatens the Peruvian Amazon."

31. The boom in hydrocarbon prospecting in the Peruvian Amazon is documented in ibid. An important study of the efforts of the government to allow gold-mining firms into formerly protected lands in Awajún country is *Peru: A Chronicle of Deception: Attempts to Transfer the Awajún Border Territory in the Cordillera del Condor to the Mining Industry,* Organization for the Development of the Border Communities of the Cenepa (ODECOFROC), 2010. For general background to events leading to the wave of Amazonian protest between 2007 and 2009, useful recent analyses include Gerardo Renique, "Against the Law of the Jungle: Peru's Amazonian Uprising," *NACLA Report on the Americas* 42, no. 1 (2009): 5, and Margarita Benavides, "Industrias extractivas, protesta indígena y consulta en la Amazonía peruana," *Anthropologica* (Lima) 28, supl. 1 (2010): 263–287.

32. Nearly every detail of the Baguazo remains contested, and information on the number of dead and wounded differs from source to source, even years after the event. In the interest of conciseness, I have limited this description to the barest of outlines. Sources of information include the official report of a government special commission assigned the task of analyzing the conflict, *Informe final de la Comisión Especial para Investigar y Analizar los Sucesos de Bagua* (Lima, 2009); a minority report issued by two members of the special commission, Jesús Manacés Valverder and Carmen Gómez Calleja, *Informe en minoría de la Comisión Especial para Investigar y Analizar los Sucesos de Bagua* (Lima, 2010); a report by Amnesty International, *Peru: Bagua, Six Months On* (London: Amnesty International Publications, 2009); and journalists' accounts, including Arno Kopecky, "A Proxy War in Peru," *Foreign Policy,* May 19, 2010, www.foreign policy.com/articles/2010/05/19/a_proxy_war_in_peru, accessed February 10, 2013.

33. As of this writing (October 2013), criminal investigations of the purported leaders of the Baguazo protests, as well as scores of other indigenous participants, are continuing in Bagua and Lima. On October 4, 2013, Peruvian newspapers reported that an Awajún leader who played a key role in the Bagua protests, Pedro Tiwi Jempets, had died of complications from a spearing sustained during the 2009 confrontation. Credible witnesses to the Baguazo insist that Tiwi was wounded while trying to convince other protesters not to execute the policemen held captive at Pumping Station No. 6. For reasons known only to the government, however, he was subject to a standing arrest warrant that forced him into hiding and prevented him from receiving medical attention during the four years prior to his death.

34. The search for norms of intercultural justice and procedures by which peaceful legal solutions can be achieved in Awajún communities were themes voiced in interviews with Felipe Shimbucat Taish, Fermín Tiwi Paati, and others conducted in May 2012. See also M. Torres Wong, "Codificación de normas indígenas en una comunidad awajún de Datem del Marañón: Estrategias de defensa territorial y redefinición de identidades," 2010, www.ibcperu.org/doc/isis/12642.pdf, accessed

January 22, 2013, and Laureano Saldaña Ikan, "Experiencias de justicia del pueblo awajún," *III Congreso Internacional Sobre Justicia Intercultural* (Huaraz, Peru: Poder Justicial del Perú, 2012), 141–143.

35. Beth A. Conklin, "Body Paint, Feathers, and VCRs: Aesthetics and Authenticity in Amazonian Activism," *American Ethnologist* 24 (1997): 711–737, at 712.

36. Greene, *Customizing Indigeneity,* especially 17–20.

9. Boundary Condition

1. One Awajún community in the Alto Mayo, San Rafael, does not currently belong to FERIAAM. It is a member of a different organization called ORDISAM (Regional Organization for Indigenous Development in San Martín).

2. Information on the 2006 killings can be found in the *Décimo informe annual de la Defensoría del Pueblo,* 2007, 236–238, www.de fensoria.gob.pe, accessed August 31, 2012. Most regional and national news outlets carried stories on the 2010 murders in Morroyacu. A typical example is "Tres nativos awajún y tres colonos asesinados en pueblo de San Martín," *La Republica,* August 11, 2010, www.larepublica.pe, accessed May 5, 2012. For general background on violence between the Awajún and colonists in the Alto Mayo, see Kenneth E. Garcés Trelles and V. Javier Echevarría Mejía, "Entre propietarios y migrantes: Los encuentros y desencuentros entre colonos y Aguarunas en el Alto Mayo," *Jangwa Pana, Revista de Antropología* (Universidad de Magdalena, Santa Marta, Colombia) 8 (2009): 53–75.

3. Document distributed by the Comisión de Renovación de la Administración Comunal, Bajo Naranjillo, dated May 24, 2012, in author's possession.

4. A detailed analysis of the leasing pattern of the Alto Mayo Awajún in the late 1990s and early 2000s can be found in Shane Greene, *Customizing Indigeneity: Paths to a Visionary Politics in Peru* (Stanford, CA: Stanford University Press, 2009), 149–164.

5. David Treuer, *Rez Life: An Indian's Journey through Reservation Life* (New York: Atlantic Monthly Press, 2012), 247. On the link between the privatization of land in Native North America and else-

where, see Stuart Banner, *How the Indians Lost Their Land: Law and Power on the Frontier* (Cambridge, MA: Harvard University Press, 2005), 287.

6. The sub-ápu of Alto Naranjillo, Abel Chumapi, informed me that in the Alto Mayo, at least, the Awajún no longer use the term "ápu," a word from the Quechua language. It has been replaced by the Awajún term *pámuk* (wise person, leader). A sub-ápu is now called *waisjam* (deputy).

7. Useful sources on the Israelitas include Harald O. Skar, "Quest for a New Covenant: The Israelita Movement in Peru," in *Natives and Neighbors in South America: Anthropological Essays*, ed. Harald O. Skar and Frank Salomon, Etnologiska Studier vol. 38 (Göteborg: Götesborgs Etnografiska Museum, 1987), 233–266; and Arturo E. de la Torre López, "El paraíso escondido: El proceso de colonización del oriente peruano por los 'Israelitas Del Nuevo Pacto,' " in *Orbis incognitus: Avisos y legajos del Nuevo Mundo*, XII Congreso Internacional de la AEA, ed. Fernando Navarro Antolín (Huelva, Spain: Universidad de Huelva, 2009), 661–678.

8. Peru's shaman killings are described in Dan Collyns, "Peru Shaman Murders Investigated," *The Guardian* (U.K.), October 6, 2011. The growth of shamanic tourism in Peru is assessed by Evgenia Fotiou in "Encounters with Sorcery: An Ethnographer's Account," *Anthropology and Humanism* 35, no. 2 (2010): 192–203.

9. Robert J. Priest, "Worship in the Amazon: The Case of the Aguaruna Evangelical Church," in *Christian Worship Worldwide: Expanding Horizons, Deepening Practices*, ed. Charles E. Farhadian (Grand Rapids, MI: William B. Eerdmans, 2007), 131–155, at 133–134. On the question of conversion to Protestantism in Latin America, a seminal work is David M. Stoll's *Is Latin America Turning Protestant?* (Berkeley: University of California Press, 1990). Stoll makes a compelling case that Protestant conversion has become an important, self-perpetuating element of many indigenous societies even if, as in parts of Central America, it has sometimes been aligned with the policies of right-wing governments.

10. On inequality in the Alto Mayo, see Greene, *Customizing Indigeneity*, 155–164. Similar social inequality and its effects have been

documented among the Ecuadorian Shuar by Steven Rubenstein in *Alejandro Tsakimp: A Shuar Healer in the Margins of History* (Lincoln: University of Nebraska Press, 2002). The impact of unequal wealth in Oklahoma Indian Territory is assessed in Alexandra Harmon, *Rich Indians: Native People and the Problem of Wealth in American History* (Chapel Hill: University of North Carolina Press, 2010), 142–170.

11. Information on an Awajún community called Sasa in the Upper Río Utiquinía, not far from the Brazilian border, was provided by Richard Chase Smith (personal communication).

12. Allegations that Nayap's 2011 election involved voter fraud in Awajún communities surfaced again in early 2013. At the time of this writing, October 2013, the case is still under review by various judicial bodies.

13. Law 29785, formally entitled Law of the Right of Prior Consultation for Indigenous or Native Peoples Recognized in Convention 169 of the International Labor Organization (ILO); the pertinent regulations were issued as Supreme Decree 001-2012-MC in 2012.

14. Matthew Clark, "Latin America's Surprise Rising Economic Star: Peru," *Christian Science Monitor,* January 5, 2010, accessed 16 August 2012.

15. Similar comments on the key role of Christian missions in indigenous self-assertion can be found in Deborah J. Yashar, *Contesting Citizenship in Latin America: The Rise of Indigenous Movements and the Postliberal Challenge* (New York: Cambridge University Press, 2005), 258–259.

16. Sources on the number of Awajún communities currently recognized by the state differ substantially. A 2007 report prepared by the government identifies 281 communities, 222 of which are formally recognized; only 195 are known to be titled. See Instituto Nacional de Estadística e Informática, *II censo de comunidades indígenas de la Amazonía peruana 2007* (Lima, 2008).

17. Versions of the Bíkut myth can be found in Michael F. Brown, "From the Hero's Bones: Three Aguaruna Hallucinogens and Their Uses," in *The Nature and Status of Ethnobotany,* ed. Richard I. Ford (Ann Arbor: Museum of Anthropology, University of Michigan, 1978),

118–136; and Aurelio Chumap Lucía and Manuel García-Rendueles, *"Duik múun . . .": Universo mítico de los Aguaruna* (Lima: Centro Amazónico de Antropología y Aplicación Práctica, 1979), 297–311. On recent Awajún notions of Bíkut's significance, see especially Greene, *Customizing Indigeneity*, 92–95, and Julián Maanchi Taish, "Pedagogía ancestral Awajún: La elaboración de textiles y su enseñanza en las comunidades de Nuevo Israel y Nuevo Jerusalén," M.A. thesis, Universidad Mayor de San Simón, Cochabamba, Bolivia, 2001, 95 n. 29.

18. The statement about Bíkut comes from Resolución Indígena No. 0001-2009, issued by FERIAAM on December 16, 2009, in author's possession. The role of visionary power in contemporary Awajún politics is assessed in considerable detail in Greene, *Customizing Indigeneity*, 71–95.

19. T. J. Jackson Lears, "The Trigger of History: Capitalism, Modernity, and the Politics of Place," *Hedgehog Review*, Spring 2012, 81–91. Lears borrows the term "off-modern" from the literary scholar Svetlana Boym.

20. On the status of Awajún women, see especially Astrid A. Bant, "La política de suicidio: El caso de las mujeres aguaruna en la amazonía peruana," in *Relaciones de género en la Amazonía peruana*, ed. María Heise et al. (Lima: Centro Amazónico de Antropología y Aplicación Práctica, 1999), and Norma Fuller Osores, *Relaciones de género en la sociedad awajún* (Lima: CARE Peru, 2009).

21. Rafael Karsten, *The Head-Hunters of Western Amazonas: The Life and Culture of the Jíbaro Indians of Eastern Ecuador and Peru*, Commentationes Humanarum Litterarum, vol. 7 (Helsingfors: Societas Scientiarum Fennica, 1935), 20.

10. Looking Back

1. A recent Amazonian study that illustrates the new realities of ethnographic work is Michael Cepek's *A Future for Amazonia: Randy Borman and Cofán Environmental Politics* (Austin: University of Texas Press, 2012).

2. This story receives some confirmation in independently collected oral histories apparently dating to an earthquake in 1928. See

Robert J. Priest, "'I Discovered My Sin!': Aguaruna Evangelical Conversion Narratives," in *The Anthropology of Religious Conversion*, ed. Andrew Buckster and Stephen Glazier (Lanham, MD: Rowman and Littlefield, 2003), 95–108, at 101.

3. See, for example, Linda Tuhiwai Smith, *Decolonizing Methodologies: Research and Indigenous Peoples* (London: Zed Books, 1999).

4. An example of denunciatory ethnography focused on the Awajún is Luisa Abad González, *Resistencia india organizada: El caso del Perú* (Quito: Ediciones Abya-Yala, 2006).

5. For an extended discussion of these issues, see Kay B. Warren, "Perils and Promises of Engaged Anthropology: Historical Transitions and Ethnographic Dilemmas," in *Engaged Observer: Anthropology, Advocacy, and Activism*, ed. Victoria Sanford and Asale Angel-Ajani (New Brunswick, NJ: Rutgers University Press, 2006).

6. Bronislaw Malinowski, *Argonauts of the Western Pacific* (Prospect Heights, IL: Waveland Press, 1984 [orig. 1922]), 8.

7. Sophisticated versions of this question are taken up by Jean Jackson in a much-admired essay, "Is There a Way to Talk about Making Culture Without Making Enemies?" *Dialectical Anthropology* 14, no. 2 (1989): 127–144.

8. The metaphor of ethnography as conversation is developed by Paul Sullivan in *Unfinished Conversations: Mayas and Foreigners between Two Wars* (Berkeley: University of California Press, 1989).

9. Matthew B. Crawford, *Shop Class as Soulcraft: An Inquiry into the Value of Work* (New York: Penguin, 2009), 65.

10. Gregory Bateson, *Steps to an Ecology of Mind* (Chicago: University of Chicago Press, 1972), 315.

Sources on the Awajún and Related Societies

Jivaroan peoples have figured prominently in the chronicles of Amazonian explorers, missionaries, and government officials for centuries. A disproportionate number of these documents focus on the now long-abandoned practice of preparing tsántsa, the smoked, shrunken heads of war victims. More systematic and reliable studies of Jivaroan social life began to emerge in the mid-twentieth century. The works below are offered for readers who wish to know more about the Awajún and other Jivaroan peoples, including the Shuar (Jívaro proper), Achuar (sometimes referred to as Achuara or Achual), and Wampis (Huambisa).

I have included only a handful of Spanish-language sources, of which there are hundreds. Spanish-speaking readers may wish to consult the comprehensive but dated bibliography by Imelda Vega Centeno, Daniel Rodríguez, and Blanca Cerpa, *Bibliografía aguaruna-huambiza*, Documento 8 (Lima: Centro de Investigación y Promoción Amazónica, 1986). Other useful sources include the series Mundo Shuar, published in Ecuador, and multiple titles of the Ecuadorian publisher Editorial Abya Yala (www.abyayala.org).

DESCRIPTIONS OF JIVAROAN SOCIETIES BY EXPLORERS, MISSIONARIES, AND SPIRITUAL SEEKERS

Bitsch, Jørgen. 1958. *Across the River of Death: True Adventure in the Green Hell of the Amazon*. London: Scientific Book Press.

Clark, Leonard. 1953. *The Rivers Ran East*. New York: Funk and Wagnalls.

Dickerman, Ethel King. 1967. *The Call of the Aguaruna.* Kansas City, MO: Nazarene Publishing House.

Drown, Frank, and Marie Drown. 1962. *Mission to the Head-Hunters.* London: Hodder and Stoughton.

Flornoy, Bertrand. 1954. *Jívaro: Among the Head-Shrinkers of the Amazon.* New York: Library Publishers.

Guallart Martínez, José María, S.J. 1990. *Entre pongo y cordillera: Historia de la etnía aguaruna-huambisa.* Lima: Centro Amazónico de Antropología y Aplicación Práctica.

Larson, Mildred L., and Louis Dodds. 1985. *Treasure in Clay Pots: An Amazon People on the Wheel of Change.* Palm Desert, CA: Person to Person Books.

Perkins, John, and Shakaim Mariano Shakai Ijisam Chumpi. 2001. *Spirit of the Shuar: Wisdom from the Last Unconquered People of the Amazon.* Rochester, VT: Destiny Books.

Up de Graff, F. W. 1923. *Head Hunters of the Amazon: Seven Years of Exploration and Adventure.* New York: Garden City Publishing Co.

SELECTED ENGLISH-LANGUAGE SOURCES ON THE AWAJÚN

Berlin, Brent. 1976. "The Concept of Rank in Ethnobiological Classification: Some Evidence from Aguaruna Folk Botany." *American Ethnologist* 3: 381–399.

Berlin, Brent, and E. A. Berlin. 1977. *Ethnobiology, Subsistence, and Nutrition in a Tropical Forest Society: The Aguaruna Jívaro.* Studies in Aguaruna Jívaro Ethnobiology, no. 1. Berkeley: University of California Language-Behavior Research Laboratory.

Berlin, Elois Ann, and Edward K. Markell. 1977. "An Assessment of the Nutritional and Health Status of an Aguaruna Jívaro Community, Amazonas, Peru." *Ecology of Food and Nutrition* 6: 69–81.

Boster, James S. 1983. "A Comparison of the Diversity of Jivaroan Gardens with That of the Tropical Forest." *Human Ecology* 11, no. 1: 47–68.

———. 1986. "Exchange of Varieties and Information between Aguaruna Manioc Cultivators." *American Anthropologist* 88, no. 2: 428–436.

———. 2003. "Blood Feud and Table Manners: A Neo-Hobbesian Approach to Jivaroan Warfare." *Antropológica* (Caracas) 99–100: 153–164.

Brown, Michael F. 1978. "From the Hero's Bones: Three Aguaruna Hallucinogens and Their Uses." In *The Nature and Status of Ethnobotany*, edited by Richard I. Ford, 118–136. Ann Arbor: Museum of Anthropology, University of Michigan.

———. 1984. "The Role of Words in Aguaruna Hunting Magic." *American Ethnologist* 11, no. 3: 545–558.

———. 1986. "Power, Gender, and the Social Meaning of Aguaruna Suicide." *Man* (London) 21, no. 2: 311–328.

———. 1986. *Tsewa's Gift: Magic and Meaning in an Amazonian Society*. Washington, DC: Smithsonian Institution Press.

———. 1988. "Shamanism and Its Discontents." *Medical Anthropology* 2, no. 2: 102–120.

———. 1989. "Dark Side of the Shaman." *Natural History* 98: 8–10.

———. 1992. "Ropes of Sand: Order and Imagery in Aguaruna Dreams." In *Dreaming: Anthropological and Psychological Interpretations*, edited by Barbara Tedlock, 154–170. Santa Fe, NM: SAR Press.

Brown, Michael F., and Margaret L. Van Bolt. 1980. "Aguaruna Jívaro Gardening Magic in the Alto Río Mayo, Peru." *Ethnology* 19, no. 2: 169–190.

Field Museum of Natural History. 2012. *Perú: Cerros de Kampankis*. Rapid Biological and Social Inventories, No. 24. Chicago, IL: Field Museum.

Greene, Shane. 1998. "The Shaman's Needle: Development, Shamanic Agency and Intermedicality in Aguaruna Lands, Peru." *American Ethnologist* 25, no. 4: 634–658.

———. 2004. "Indigenous People Incorporated? Culture as Politics, Culture as Property in Pharmaceutical Bioprospecting." *Current Anthropology* 45, no. 2: 211–237.

———. 2008. "Tiwi's Creek: Indigenous Movements for, against, and across the Contested Peruvian Border." *Latin American and Caribbean Ethnic Studies* 3, no. 3: 227–252.

————. 2009. *Customizing Indigeneity: Paths to a Visionary Politics in Peru*. Stanford, CA: Stanford University Press.

Jernigan, Kevin A. 2008. "The Importance of Chemosensory Clues in Aguaruna Tree Classification and Identification." *Journal of Ethnobiology and Ethnomedicine* 4, doi:10.1186/1746-4269-4-12.

————. 2009. "Barking up the Same Tree: A Comparison of Ethnomedicine and Canine Ethnoveterinary Medicine among the Aguaruna." *Journal of Ethnobiology and Ethnomedicine* 5, doi:10.1186/1746-4269-5-33.

Jernigan, Kevin A., and Nico Dauphiné. 2008. "Aguaruna Knowledge of Bird Foraging Ecology: A Comparison with Scientific Data." *Ethnobotany Research and Applications* 6: 93–106.

Priest, Robert J. 2003. "'I Discovered My Sin!': Aguaruna Evangelical Conversion Narratives." In *The Anthropology of Religious Conversion*, edited by Andrew Buckster and Stephen Glazier, 95–108. Lanham, MD: Rowman and Littlefield.

————. 2006. "'Experience-Near Theologizing' in Diverse Human Contexts." In *Globalizing Theology: Belief and Practice in an Era of World Christianity*, edited by Craig Ott and Harold A. Netland, 180–195. Grand Rapids, MI: Baker Academic.

Santos-Granero, Fernando, and Frederica Barclay. 2010. "Bundles, Stampers, and Flying Gringos: Native Perceptions of Capitalist Violence in Peruvian Amazonia." *Journal of Latin American and Caribbean Anthropology* 16, no. 1: 143–167.

Siverts, Henning. 1972. *Tribal Survival in the Alto Marañón: The Aguaruna Case*. IWGIA Document no. 10. Copenhagen: IWGIA.

————. 1987. "Broken Hearts and Pots: Suicide and Patterns of Signification among the Aguaruna Jívaro of Alto Marañón, Peru." *Livstegn* 4, no. 2: 211–248.

Works, Martha A. 1985. "Development and Change in the Traditional Landscape of the Mayo Aguaruna." *Journal of Cultural Geography* 6, no. 1: 1–18.

————. 1987. "Aguaruna Agriculture in Eastern Peru." *Geographical Review* 77, no. 3: 343–358.

BOOK-LENGTH STUDIES OF OTHER JIVAROAN SOCIETIES

Descola, Philippe. 1993. *The Spears of Twilight: Life and Death in the Amazon Jungle.* New York: New Press.

———. 1994. *In the Society of Nature: A Native Ecology in Amazonia.* Cambridge, UK: Cambridge University Press.

Harner, Michael J. 1972. *The Jívaro: People of the Sacred Waterfalls.* Berkeley: University of California Press.

Hendricks, Janet Wall. 1993. *To Drink of Death: The Narrative of a Shuar Warrior.* Tucson: University of Arizona Press.

Karsten, Rafael. 1935. *The Head-Hunters of Western Amazonas: The Life and Culture of the Jíbaro Indians of Eastern Ecuador and Peru.* Commentationes Humanarum Litterarum, vol. 7. Helsingfors: Societas Scientiarum Fennica.

Perruchon, Marie. 2003. *I Am Tsunki: Gender and Shamanism among the Shuar of Western Amazonia.* Uppsala: Uppsala University Press.

Rubenstein, Steven. 2002. *Alejandro Tsakimp: A Shuar Healer in the Margins of History.* Lincoln: University of Nebraska Press.

Stirling, Matthew W. 1938. *Historical and Ethnographic Material on the Jívaro Indians.* Bulletin No. 117. Washington, DC: Bureau of American Ethnology, Smithsonian Institution.

Acknowledgments

Upriver draws on work conducted over nearly four decades. The debts accrued over such a long period are substantial, and I cannot do them justice here. Of the many people who influenced my early work in Peru, three stand out. My graduate school patrón, Richard I. Ford, provided me and his other students with steadfast support while encouraging us to refine our own points of view. In Peru, Luis M. Uriarte served as an inspiring model of the passionately engaged Amazonian fieldworker. During my first long stay with the Awajún, Margaret L. Van Bolt shared some of the experiences described here. Despite the passage of time, my admiration for her insight and fortitude remains undiminished. Financial support for my earliest Alto Mayo fieldwork was provided by the Henry L. and Grace Doherty Charitable Foundation, the Centro Amazónico de Antropología y Aplicación Práctica, and the Wenner-Gren Foundation for Anthropological Research, to which organizations I extend heartfelt thanks.

On my 2012 trip to Peru, I benefited from the financial support of Williams College and the logistical help of Manuel Cornejo, Lincoln Rojas, and Jaime Regan of the Centro Amazónico de Antropología y Aplicación Práctica, an organization with which I have had a long and cordial association. Conversations with anthropologists currently working in Peru—some old friends, some new—brought me up to date on current realities. They include Alejandro Camino, Jean-Pierre Chaumeil, Oscar Espinosa de Rivero, Norma Fuller Osores, Joshua Homan, and Richard Chase Smith.

A number of scholars provided specific information or clarified complicated issues as this project moved forward, including Frederica Barclay, Eduardo Fernández, R. Brian Ferguson, Shane Greene, Kevin Jernigan, Fernando Santos-Granero, Glenn Shepard, and Carla Soria Arrasco. The book's maps drew on the GIS expertise of Sharron Macklin at Williams College, land-titling data generously provided by the Instituto del Bien Común, Lima, and the design skill of Philip Schwartzberg of Meridian Mapping in Minneapolis.

I'm grateful for close readings of all or part of the book by Beth Conklin, Robert F. Dalzell Jr., David B. Edwards, Eduardo Fernández, Antonia Foias, Shane Greene, Thomas Gregor, Robert Jackall, Peter Just, Casey Kittrell, Kenda Mutongi, James L. Nolan Jr., Olga Shevchenko, and Orin Starn. During my term as director of the Oakley Center for the Humanities and Social Sciences, individual chapters profited from the critical attention of several cohorts of resident fellows—most notably senior fellow Francis C. Oakley, president emeritus of Williams College, frequent conversations with whom were one of the job's greatest pleasures.

Joyce Seltzer, senior executive editor at Harvard University Press, has served as judge, taskmaster, and advocate for three of my books. Working with her has been one of my professional life's most rewarding apprenticeships. I am thankful, too, for the help of Brian J. Distelberg, her able assistant.

Scores of Awajún contributed to this book through a willingness to share their lives with a stranger. Many also provided me with food and shelter. The years have taken their toll, and few of the men and women I knew best are alive today. Of those still living, Adolfo Juep Nampin stands out for the constancy of his friendship and the clarity of his vision.

A work that chronicles family bonds in a distant place cannot close without acknowledging the author's own family. My mother, Marilyn M. Brown, and my late father, Alan F. Brown, offered unflagging support for a son pursuing a strange vocation. Today I am similarly sustained by Sylvia Kennick Brown and Emily Cheng Li Brown, both of whom should, through the stories in this book, finally learn what I was up to during some of the years before life brought us together in the shadow of Mount Greylock.

Index